FrameMaker® 5.5.6 For Dummies®

Cheat Sheet

These commands work across all platforms, except where noted. For platform-specific shortcuts, see your FrameMaker documentation.

Commands separated by spaces indicate that you press each key in sequence. Commands that are connected by plus signs indicate that you press the hyphenated keys at the same time. For example, Esc j c means press and release the Esc key, then press and release the j key, then press and release the c key. Ctrl+8 means to press the Ctrl key and the 8 key at the same time.

Basic File Commands

New file	Mac: **Esc f n**
Open file	**Esc f o**
Save	**Esc f s**
Save all open files	**Shift+Save All Open Files** in the File menu
Close file	**Esc f c**
Close all open files	**Shift+Close All Open Files** in the File menu
Print	**Esc f p**
Quit	Mac: **Esc f q**
Import file	**Esc f i f**
Import formats	**Esc f i o**

Editing Commands

Copy	**Esc e c**
Cut	**Esc e x**
Paste	**Esc e p**
Find/Change	**Esc e f**
Transpose characters	PC: **Ctrl+F9**
	UNIX/Mac: **Ctrl+T**
Undo	**Esc e u**
Thesaurus	**Esc e t**
Spelling	**Esc e s**
Select all in flow	**Esc e a**
Select next character	**Shift**+Right Arrow
Select previous character	**Shift**+Left Arrow

P9-CSW-215

For Dummies®: Bestselling Book Series for Beginners

FrameMaker® 5.5.6 For Dummies®

Cheat Sheet

View/Navigation Commands

Refresh screen display	**Ctrl+l** (lowercase L)
Borders (show/hide)	**Esc v b**
Rulers (show/hide)	**Esc v r**
Text symbols (show/hide)	**Esc v t**
Go to	Click the page number area in the status bar
Go to body pages	**Esc v Shift+b**
Go to first page	**Shift**+click Page Up icon in status bar
Go to last page	**Shift**+click Page Down icon
Go to master pages	**Esc v Shift+m**
Go to reference pages	**Esc v Shift+r**
Zoom to 100%	**Esc z z**

Text Formatting Commands

Apply character format	PC/UNIX: **F8** Mac: **Ctrl+8** or **Command+**
Display Character Designer	**Esc o c d** or select from context menu (all) PC/UNIX: **Ctrl**+click tag in character catalog Mac: **Option**+click
Apply paragraph format	PC/UNIX: **F9** and type the first few letters Mac: **Command**+space bar and type the first few letters
Display Paragraph Designer	**Esc o p d** PC/UNIX: **Ctrl**+click tag in paragraph catalog Mac: **Option**+click

Table Commands

Table Designer	**Esc t d**
Insert tab in table	**Esc Tab**
Resize table column(s)	**Esc t z**
Select table	PC/UNIX: **Ctrl**+triple-click Mac: **Option**+triple-click

Refer to Appendix A for a more detailed list and to FrameMaker's *Quick Reference* booklet for an exhaustive list of keyboard shortcuts.

For Dummies®: Bestselling Book Series for Beginners

 ™

BESTSELLING BOOK SERIES

References for the Rest of Us! ®

1/99

FrameMaker® 5.5.6

FOR

DUMMIES®

by Sarah O'Keefe

Foreword by Dr. John Warnock, CEO,

Adobe Systems, Inc.

IDG
BOOKS
WORLDWIDE

IDG Books Worldwide, Inc.
An International Data Group Company

Foster City, CA ◆ Chicago, IL ◆ Indianapolis, IN ◆ New York, NY

FrameMaker® 5.5.6 For Dummies®

Published by
IDG Books Worldwide, Inc.
An International Data Group Company
919 E. Hillsdale Blvd.
Suite 400
Foster City, CA 94404
www.idgbooks.com (IDG Books Worldwide Web site)
www.dummies.com (Dummies Press Web site)

Library of Congress Catalog Card No.: 99-66417

ISBN: 0-7645-0637-4

Printed in the United States of America

10 9 8 7 6 5 4 3 2

1O/SW/QW/QQ/IN

Distributed in the United States by IDG Books Worldwide, Inc.

Distributed by CDG Books Canada Inc. for Canada; by Transworld Publishers Limited in the United Kingdom; by IDG Norge Books for Norway; by IDG Sweden Books for Sweden; by IDG Books Australia Publishing Corporation Pty. Ltd. for Australia and New Zealand; by TransQuest Publishers Pte Ltd. for Singapore, Malaysia, Thailand, Indonesia, and Hong Kong; by Gotop Information Inc. for Taiwan; by ICG Muse, Inc. for Japan; by Intersoft for South Africa; by Eyrolles for France; by International Thomson Publishing for Germany, Austria and Switzerland; by Distribuidora Cuspide for Argentina; by LR International for Brazil; by Galileo Libros for Chile; by Ediciones ZETA S.C.R. Ltda. for Peru; by WS Computer Publishing Corporation, Inc., for the Philippines; by Contemporanea de Ediciones for Venezuela; by Express Computer Distributors for the Caribbean and West Indies; by Micronesia Media Distributor, Inc. for Micronesia; by Chips Computadoras S.A. de C.V. for Mexico; by Editorial Norma de Panama S.A. for Panama; by American Bookshops for Finland.

For general information on IDG Books Worldwide's books in the U.S., please call our Consumer Customer Service department at 800-762-2974. For reseller information, including discounts and premium sales, please call our Reseller Customer Service department at 800-434-3422.

For information on where to purchase IDG Books Worldwide's books outside the U.S., please contact our International Sales department at 317-596-5530 or fax 317-572-4002.

For consumer information on foreign language translations, please contact our Customer Service department at 1-800-434-3422, fax 317-572-4002, or e-mail rights@idgbooks.com.

For information on licensing foreign or domestic rights, please phone +1-650-653-7098.

For sales inquiries and special prices for bulk quantities, please contact our Order Services department at 800-434-3422 or write to the address above.

For information on using IDG Books Worldwide's books in the classroom or for ordering examination copies, please contact our Educational Sales department at 800-434-2086 or fax 317-572-4005.

For press review copies, author interviews, or other publicity information, please contact our Public Relations department at 650-653-7000 or fax 650-653-7500.

For authorization to photocopy items for corporate, personal, or educational use, please contact Copyright Clearance Center, 222 Rosewood Drive, Danvers, MA 01923, or fax 978-750-4470.

 is a registered trademark under exclusive license to IDG Books Worldwide, Inc. from International Data Group, Inc.

About the Author

Sarah O'Keefe is founder and president of Scriptorium Publishing Services, Inc. (www.scriptorium.com). Her company provides technical documentation services to high-tech companies, including everything from start-ups to Fortune 100 companies. Ms. O'Keefe is an Adobe Certified Expert in FrameMaker and certified WebWorks Publisher trainer. Her background includes technical writing, technical editing, production editing, and extensive online help development with various help authoring tools. Ms. O'Keefe currently works as a consultant to assist companies in implementing single-sourcing systems and other publishing solutions. You can reach her at fmbooks@scriptorium.com.

ABOUT IDG BOOKS WORLDWIDE

Welcome to the world of IDG Books Worldwide.

IDG Books Worldwide, Inc., is a subsidiary of International Data Group, the world's largest publisher of computer-related information and the leading global provider of information services on information technology. IDG was founded more than 30 years ago by Patrick J. McGovern and now employs more than 9,000 people worldwide. IDG publishes more than 290 computer publications in over 75 countries. More than 90 million people read one or more IDG publications each month.

Launched in 1990, IDG Books Worldwide is today the #1 publisher of best-selling computer books in the United States. We are proud to have received eight awards from the Computer Press Association in recognition of editorial excellence and three from Computer Currents' First Annual Readers' Choice Awards. Our best-selling *...For Dummies®* series has more than 50 million copies in print with translations in 31 languages. IDG Books Worldwide, through a joint venture with IDG's Hi-Tech Beijing, became the first U.S. publisher to publish a computer book in the People's Republic of China. In record time, IDG Books Worldwide has become the first choice for millions of readers around the world who want to learn how to better manage their businesses.

Our mission is simple: Every one of our books is designed to bring extra value and skill-building instructions to the reader. Our books are written by experts who understand and care about our readers. The knowledge base of our editorial staff comes from years of experience in publishing, education, and journalism — experience we use to produce books to carry us into the new millennium. In short, we care about books, so we attract the best people. We devote special attention to details such as audience, interior design, use of icons, and illustrations. And because we use an efficient process of authoring, editing, and desktop publishing our books electronically, we can spend more time ensuring superior content and less time on the technicalities of making books.

You can count on our commitment to deliver high-quality books at competitive prices on topics you want to read about. At IDG Books Worldwide, we continue in the IDG tradition of delivering quality for more than 30 years. You'll find no better book on a subject than one from IDG Books Worldwide.

IDG BOOKS WORLDWIDE

John Kilcullen
Chairman and CEO
IDG Books Worldwide, Inc.

VIII WINNER
Eighth Annual Computer Press Awards ≥1992

IX WINNER
Ninth Annual Computer Press Awards ≥1993

X WINNER
Tenth Annual Computer Press Awards ≥1994

XI WINNER
Eleventh Annual Computer Press Awards ≥1995

IDG is the world's leading IT media, research and exposition company. Founded in 1964, IDG had 1997 revenues of $2.05 billion and has more than 9,000 employees worldwide. IDG offers the widest range of media options that reach IT buyers in 75 countries representing 95% of worldwide IT spending. IDG's diverse product and services portfolio spans six key areas including print publishing, online publishing, expositions and conferences, market research, education and training, and global marketing services. More than 90 million people read one or more of IDG's 290 magazines and newspapers, including IDG's leading global brands — Computerworld, PC World, Network World, Macworld and the Channel World family of publications. IDG Books Worldwide is one of the fastest-growing computer book publishers in the world, with more than 700 titles in 36 languages. The "...For Dummies®" series alone has more than 50 million copies in print. IDG offers online users the largest network of technology-specific Web sites around the world through IDG.net (http://www.idg.net), which comprises more than 225 targeted Web sites in 55 countries worldwide. International Data Corporation (IDC) is the world's largest provider of information technology data, analysis and consulting, with research centers in over 41 countries and more than 400 research analysts worldwide. IDG World Expo is a leading producer of more than 168 globally branded conferences and expositions in 35 countries including E3 (Electronic Entertainment Expo), Macworld Expo, ComNet, Windows World Expo, ICE (Internet Commerce Expo), Agenda, DEMO, and Spotlight. IDG's training subsidiary, ExecuTrain, is the world's largest computer training company, with more than 230 locations worldwide and 785 training courses. IDG Marketing Services helps industry-leading IT companies build international brand recognition by developing global integrated marketing programs via IDG's print, online and exposition products worldwide. Further information about the company can be found at www.idg.com.   1/26/00

Dedication

For Mark.

Author's Acknowledgments

Many people worked behind the scenes to help make this book happen. I'd like to acknowledge David Fugate of Waterside Productions for his agently assistance; John Hedtke for excellent proposal advice; Erich Champion and Sheila Loring for their help with screen shots; Karen Brown for some last-minute ghostwriting; Alexia Prendergast for an excellent technical review and encouragement along the way; Alan Pringle for unofficial but always excellent developmental editing; Bruce Bicknell, Michael Bourke, Lorraine Elder, and Mark Penman for their help in refining my FrameMaker knowledge way back when; my long-time cohorts on the framers list; and all the people at Scriptorium Publishing who picked up the slack while I disappeared into the writing dungeon, especially Pam Castro.

And let's not forget the talented people at IDG Books: Kathy Yankton, Colleen Esterline, E. Shawn Aylsworth, Constance Carlisle, Mary Corder, Beth Parlon, and Dick Evans of Infodex.

Publisher's Acknowledgments

We're proud of this book; please register your comments through our IDG Books Worldwide Online Registration Form located at http://my2cents.dummies.com.

Some of the people who helped bring this book to market include the following:

Acquisitions, Editorial, and Media Development

Project Editor: Colleen Williams Esterline

Acquisitions Editor: Kathy Yankton

Technical Editor: Alexia Prendergast

Media Development Editor: Megan Decraene

Associate Permissions Editor: Carmen Krikorian

Media Development Coordinator: Megan Roney

Media Development Manager: Heather Heath Dismore

Editorial Assistant: Beth Parlon

Production

Project Coordinator: E. Shawn Aylsworth

Layout and Graphics: Amy M. Adrian, Kate Jenkins, Jill Piscitelli, Doug Rollison, Jacque Schneider, Janet Seib, Michael A. Sullivan, Brian Torwelle, Maggie Ubertini, Dan Whetstine

Proofreaders: Laura Albert, Vickie Broyles, John Greenough, Marianne Santy, Rebecca Senninger, Toni Settle

Indexer: Infodex Indexing Services, Inc.

Special Help
Sanders Groups, Constance Carlisle, Suzanne Thomas

General and Administrative

IDG Books Worldwide, Inc.: John Kilcullen, CEO

IDG Books Technology Publishing Group: Richard Swadley, Senior Vice President and Publisher; Walter R. Bruce III, Vice President and Publisher; Joseph Wikert, Vice President and Publisher; Mary Bednarek, Vice President and Director, Product Development; Andy Cummings, Publishing Director, General User Group; Mary C. Corder, Editorial Director; Barry Pruett, Publishing Director

IDG Books Consumer Publishing Group: Roland Elgey, Senior Vice President and Publisher; Kathleen A. Welton, Vice President and Publisher; Kevin Thornton, Acquisitions Manager; Kristin A. Cocks, Editorial Director

IDG Books Internet Publishing Group: Brenda McLaughlin, Senior Vice President and Publisher; Sofia Marchant, Online Marketing Manager

IDG Books Production for Branded Press: Debbie Stailey, Director of Production; Cindy L. Phipps, Manager of Project Coordination, Production Proofreading, and Indexing; Tony Augsburger, Manager of Prepress, Reprints, and Systems; Laura Carpenter, Production Control Manager; Shelley Lea, Supervisor of Graphics and Design; Debbie J. Gates, Production Systems Specialist; Robert Springer, Supervisor of Proofreading; Trudy Coler, Page Layout Manager; Troy Barnes, Page Layout Supervisor, Kathie Schutte, Senior Page Layout Supervisor; Michael Sullivan, Production Supervisor

Packaging and Book Design: Patty Page, Manager, Promotions Marketing

◆

The publisher would like to give special thanks to Patrick J. McGovern, without whom this book would not have been possible.

◆

Contents at a Glance

Cartoons at a Glance

By Rich Tennant

page 43

"Great goulash, Stan. That reminds me, are you still creating your own table of contents?"

page 227

"WELL, SHOOT! THIS EGGPLANT CHART IS JUST AS CONFUSING AS THE BUTTERNUT SQUASH CHART AND THE GOURD CHART. CAN'T YOU JUST MAKE A PIE CHART LIKE EVERYONE ELSE?"

page 261

page 299

"You know kids— you can't buy them just ANY page layout program anymore."

page 5

"It says,' Seth- Please see us about your idea to wrap newsletter text around company logo. Production.'"

page 113

Fax: 978-546-7747
E-mail: richtennant@the5thwave.com
World Wide Web: www.the5thwave.com

Table of Contents

Foreword

● ●

*M*any people think of FrameMaker as a program only used by professional publishers of text books, technical manuals, or other long
complex documents. Although it's true that FrameMaker has established
itself as *the* tool for difficult, long documents, using FrameMaker makes the
construction and maintenance of any systematic documentation easier than
other products on the market. The output also looks much better. Since I use
FrameMaker every day and appreciate its power and scope, I'm delighted
that *FrameMaker 5.5.6 For Dummies* is now available so that other people can
be exposed to the magic inside this remarkable tool.

Adobe FrameMaker users are a passionate bunch. They believe in our product, and that affection shines through in this book. Sarah O'Keefe is a
long-time FrameMaker user, and she's provided an information-packed book
that will make FrameMaker work for you. I especially enjoyed the "from the
trenches" approach of this book.

We have made an evaluation version of FrameMaker available on the CD to
help new users learn and understand the software.

Welcome to the FrameMaker community, and to the power it gives you.

Dr. John Warnock
CEO, Adobe Systems

Introduction

● ●

*W*elcome to *FrameMaker 5.5.6 For Dummies!*

If you never thought you'd pick up a Dummies book, you're in good company. I never thought I'd write one. But when IDG Books offered me the opportunity to write a FrameMaker book for beginners, I couldn't resist. I have even forgiven them (mostly) for making me write this book without using FrameMaker. (I tried, really. I explained how much faster and easier it would be to write and produce this book in FrameMaker. They explained how they would pay me — if I followed their process, which involved writing text in a product that shall remain nameless — I'll say only that it starts with *W*, ends with *rd*.)

About This Book

FrameMaker For Dummies is your introduction to the wonderful world of using Adobe's FrameMaker software. FrameMaker is a well-known, industry-standard tool — if you're in the business of producing long, technical documents, such as software manuals, technical books (like this one), theses, and dissertations.

As you may already know, learning FrameMaker is not easy. The software includes a ton of features, and the vast majority make no sense whatsoever at first glance. In this book, I'll explain how to harness those features and make them work for you.

Why You Need This Book

Normally, learning FrameMaker is a long, painful, and difficult process. But with this book, you can make that process much easier. I've been there. After using FrameMaker for seven years, I've made lots and lots of mistakes. I'd like to spare you the pain of repeating them, so this book is full of the tips and tricks that I've accumulated while working as a technical editor, technical writer, and (especially) production editor.

If you're familiar with desktop publishing and FrameMaker's interface, you can probably skip Part I. If you're new to publishing, check out Part I for FrameMaker basics.

Part II discusses how to insert and manage text, tables, and graphics. In Parts III and IV, you'll find information about FrameMaker's more interesting and unique features (books in Part IV). Part V provides some tips and tricks, and the appendixes in Part VI include some keyboard shortcuts and other information.

How to Use This Book

FrameMaker For Dummies is a little different from the other FrameMaker books. Sure, it's a reference, but not just any reference. You'll find steps broken down so that you can follow along, so you can use this as a learning tool. Read it from cover to cover if you'd like. If you want to learn certain aspects of FrameMaker, you can just look through the table of contents or index, find the topic you're interested in, flip to that page, and get your answer.

How This Book Is Organized

This book is divided into several parts:

Part I: Figuring Out FrameMaker

In this part, I'll get you started and show you the word-processing features.

Part II: Supplying Text, Tables, and Graphics

In Part II, you'll see how to set up your FrameMaker files with content, including text, tables, and pictures. You'll be introduced to paragraph tags and character tags, which will come in handy throughout the book.

Part III: Making FrameMaker Do the Heavy Lifting

In Part III, you get to the good stuff. Various FrameMaker features help you organize and maintain your documents with minimal manual labor. And after all, reducing your workload is what it's all about. . . . Check out the chapters on creating page layouts, automating cross-references, using variables, working with colors and modular text, printing and publishing online, and so on.

Part IV: Working with Books

Part IV takes a look at how to create and maintain book files (a list of related files) and how to set up and format tables of contents, indexes, and other files that are created by scanning the contents of the book (FrameMaker calls these *generated* files).

Part V: The Part of Tens

Part V contains some tips and tricks to get you going. It includes some help on creating templates, some information about FrameMaker building blocks, lots of autonumbering examples, and more.

Part VI: Appendixes

In Part VI, you'll encounter information about keyboard shortcuts, a list of the information in the CD, and more.

A Note About Screen Shots

If you flip through this book, you'll notice that the screen shots are taken from Windows, Macintosh, and UNIX versions of FrameMaker. Because the product is almost identical across platforms, I have included screen shots from all three versions. Where there are platform differences, I have noted them. But I think you'll find it interesting to look at the different platforms and compare them to what appears on your screen. Adobe has done an excellent job of making the platforms consistent. As a result, once you learn FrameMaker on one platform, you'll be able to use it on any platform!

Conventions Used in This Book

I have a few conventions you should know about before you get started. To begin with, when you see a word (or words) in bold, you should type it in. For example, type **My dog likes to chase squirrels**. If text appears on-screen, it's noted as such in this book: My dog is too slow to catch even snails.

Icons Used in This Book

Tips give you ideas on how to save your precious time and effort.

When you see this, definitely pay attention and heed its warnings. You'll save yourself lots of painful heartache!

You can skip over these sections if you're not interested in understanding the nitty-gritty of FrameMaker. But if you do read these sections, consider yourself a little more advanced in the know-how of FrameMaker ways.

The Platform Differences icon points out places where FrameMaker is a little different between PC, Mac, and UNIX platforms.

Where to Go From Here

If you're creating complex technical documents, FrameMaker is your ticket to job sanity. It automates the hard stuff so that you can focus on creating really useful documents. So dive in — start reading from the beginning or pick a topic and explore — and get ready to learn FrameMaker!

Part I
Figuring Out FrameMaker

In this part . . .

Before scaling the big mountain, it might be wise to start training on the molehill. In this part, you'll take a look at the basics: opening, saving, and closing files; the FrameMaker interface; what type of work FrameMaker is most suited for; and basic word processing.

Chapter 1

FrameMaker: The Long Document's Best Friend

In This Chapter

▶ Deciding whether FrameMaker is for you

▶ Working with its word-processing capabilities

▶ Introducing features that make FrameMaker special

▶ Understanding templates

● ●

*I*f you want to create a great oil painting, you probably would not use a piano. Okay, in today's modern art you just might, but bear with me here. The point is that you need to choose the right tool for the right job.

FrameMaker Is for You If . . .

FrameMaker is a powerful, complex piece of document processing software that is for you if your documents

- ✔ Are long
- ✔ Need structure
- ✔ Need consistency
- ✔ Use cross-references
- ✔ Have tables of contents
- ✔ Have indexes
- ✔ Have running headers and footers
- ✔ Are delivered in multiple formats (print and online)
- ✔ Have lots of graphics
- ✔ Are revised often

Basically, FrameMaker is for you if you create long documents, such as books, technical manuals, and dissertations. FrameMaker includes many features that help you create documents that are consistent from chapter to chapter. For example, you can set up FrameMaker to grab the title of the current chapter and put that in the header automatically. You only have to touch the header once — to tell FrameMaker what to include there. After that, the chapter title in the header is updated every time you start a new chapter.

FrameMaker is probably *not* for you if your documents

- ✔ Are highly designed with little consistency from page to page
- ✔ Do not need structure or consistency

For these cases, you should probably choose a visual page layout tool, such as PageMaker or QuarkXPress (or perhaps Adobe's new InDesign).

FrameMaker has a reputation for being difficult to learn. This is partly because it's packed with powerful features. This book gets you started with the easier, more familiar stuff, such as word-processing features, and then gently launches you into more advanced information. The old 80/20 rule applies: 80 percent is easy to learn and includes the basics, like general word processing. The other 20 percent is where you find the real power, and you can learn that as you go.

Word Processing in FrameMaker

FrameMaker offers the basic word-processing features that you expect (see Chapters 2 and 3 for details). You may find, though, that FrameMaker is a bit more Spartan than some word processors. It does not, for example, support drag-and-drop editing. To me, it's a small price to pay for the power that FrameMaker offers in other areas.

FrameMaker on Multiple Platforms

As you flip through this book, you'll see that I've included screen shots from Windows, Macintosh, and UNIX environments. FrameMaker works almost identically across platforms, so all the knowledge you acquire on the Windows version can be transferred immediately to the UNIX or Macintosh version (or the other way around).

Furthermore, the data files in FrameMaker transfer seamlessly from one platform to another. You may have an occasional font problem or a graphic that works on one platform but not another, but the FrameMaker content is not a problem.

Special Features in FrameMaker

FrameMaker includes lots of powerful features that help automate book production: cross-references, indexes, book paginations, tables of contents, variables, cross-reference, and more. Each of these items has its own chapter (except for books, which has a whole part!). Just jump in with the features that you need most!

Template Tantrum

FrameMaker can help you create a set of documents that is completely consistent — the documents use the same numbering style, same type of headers and footers, same formatting for the text, same lines and spacing in the tables, and more.

You accomplish all of this using FrameMaker's formatting catalogs. Each major item in FrameMaker, such as paragraphs, characters, tables, and cross-references, has a list of formats. You can easily transfer formats from one document to another. This is a simple statement, but it means that you can set up the appearance of your pages in one document and then transfer that appearance to a completely different document.

These formatting catalogs are the basic feature that separates FrameMaker from other publishing tools. Most word processors nowadays have formats defined for paragraphs (often called style sheets), but FrameMaker uses formatting catalogs for lots of things, including the following items:

- Paragraphs
- Characters
- Tables
- Master pages
- Content of headers and footers
- Formatting for tables of contents and indexes
- Cross-references

These extensive formatting catalogs, which "live" in each document, can be copied from one document to another. More importantly, you can overwrite the definitions in one file with definitions from another file (provided that the style names are the same). This makes it possible to maintain your formatting catalogs in a template file and periodically import the template into your documents to keep them consistent.

Unlike some other desktop publishing packages and word processors, FrameMaker files don't have an external template file attached to the FrameMaker file. Instead, a complete copy of the formatting information is maintained in each file. You don't have to worry about keeping track of a separate template file to maintain the formatting in your files.

Any file can be used as a template, but to simplify maintenance (and prevent rogue formats from sneaking in), it's probably a good idea to create an official template file and make some rules about who's allowed to update it. Better yet, lock it up in a safe place where only the designated template owner has access to the file.

Chapter 2

Firing Up FrameMaker

● ●

In This Chapter

▶ Starting FrameMaker

▶ Creating a new document

▶ Opening existing documents

▶ Converting from other formats

▶ Understanding basic (word-processor) training

▶ Getting around

▶ Saving what you've got

▶ Printing

▶ Closing your document

▶ Quitting for the day

● ●

*I*n this chapter, you'll find out how to get going with FrameMaker. I explain how to start FrameMaker, move around in your documents, save, print, and shut down.

Enough talk. Time for action.

Starting FrameMaker

To start FrameMaker, you need to locate the folder where you installed it, and double-click the FrameMaker icon. The exact process depends on which platform you're using, so check the instructions for your operating system.

Windows

Go to the Start menu, and select Programs➪Adobe➪FrameMaker 5.5➪ Adobe FrameMaker 5.5 to start FrameMaker.

This works only if you installed FrameMaker in its default location. If you installed it elsewhere, you need to change the instructions above to match your setup.

Mac

On a Macintosh, the location of your FrameMaker application depends on how you installed it. Usually, it's on the primary hard drive, in a FrameMaker 5.5 folder. For example, on my machine, I have a hard drive icon called Applications. To run FrameMaker, I open the Applications icon, then open FrameMaker 5.5, then double-click the FrameMaker 5.5 PowerPC icon.

On your system, the FrameMaker 5.5 folder may be in a slightly different location. If you have trouble finding it, go to the Finder and select File⇨Find to display the Find dialog box. In the Find dialog box, type in **FrameMaker** and then click Find.

If you want to open FrameMaker more quickly, locate the FrameMaker application icon and create an alias (select File⇨Make Alias). Drag the alias onto your desktop. Next time you launch FrameMaker, you can just double-click the alias. (You can tell the difference between an alias and the real thing because the alias uses italic text.)

UNIX

The location of your FrameMaker application depends on how you installed it. Locate the FrameMaker application folder and double-click the FrameMaker icon. You can also type **maker** at the command line.

The very first time you start FrameMaker, you'll see an introduction to FrameMaker. You'll find some useful information in there, so take a few minutes to read through it. When you start FrameMaker after that first time, you don't see any documents. FrameMaker doesn't give you a blank document when you start. Instead, it launches and just sits there, staring at you. You can open a document or create a new one, but until then, you're basically dead in the water.

On the UNIX platform, you have a small set of FrameMaker buttons (see Figure 2-1). You can use these buttons instead of the equivalent File menu command. The Info button gives you information about whether you have a license available.

Figure 2-1:
On the UNIX version, these buttons provide a sort of launch pad.

Creating a New Document

To create a new document, select File⇨New. This displays the New dialog box (see Figure 2-2). If you want something plain, choose the Portrait or Landscape button. (Portrait creates a new 8.5-inch wide by 11-inch tall document; Landscape creates a new 11-inch wide by 8.5-inch tall document.)

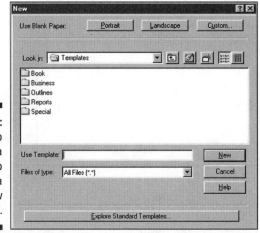

Figure 2-2:
You have to select a template to create a new document.

At this point, you can either open a copy of a document (which means you use the selected document as a template), use one of the templates supplied with FrameMaker, or create a blank document. The next three sections describe how these choices work.

Copy from your neighbor

FrameMaker doesn't have a special format for template files. Instead, you can use any FrameMaker document as a template. Locate the file you want to use in the directory navigation box. Select it and then click Open. FrameMaker creates a copy of the file and opens it as a new, untitled document.

This new document includes all the contents of the original document along with all the formatting tags.

Use a standard template

If you want to use one of FrameMaker's templates as a starting point for your document, click the Explore Standard Templates button. This displays a window with a list of all the standard templates (see Figure 2-3). Click a template name on the left to see a summary of the template's features and a preview on the right.

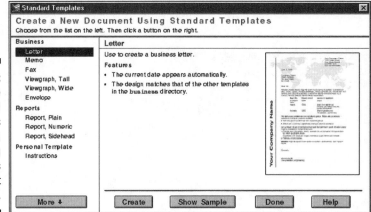

Figure 2-3: The standard templates offer a starting point for lots of different documents.

To view a full-sized sample of a template, click Show Sample. (Close the document to return to the template list.) When you have decided on the template you want, make sure it's selected in the template list and then click Create.

Start from scratch

To start with a blank document, click the Portrait or Landscape button.

Even if you create a blank document, you'll start with some default styles. FrameMaker includes these to give you some basic formatting options.

Gimme more templates!

If you need a template that's not included with the product, you may want to try one of these resources:

✔ **Adobe FrameMaker Template Series:** Adobe has produced additional templates for FrameMaker. Here's an excerpt from the description of these templates: "The templates range from technical manuals to cookbooks to Web sites. You also get over 30 custom table formats, multi-purpose borders, plus special features such as guidelines and tables of contents." Check them out at `www.adobe.com/ prodindex/framemaker/tempseries/ main.html`.

✔ **FrameUsers Web site:** This resource site for FrameMaker users includes a few templates. It can be found at `www.frameusers.com`.

✔ **Corporate or academic resources:** Many universities provide FrameMaker templates

for academic papers, including theses and dissertations. Check with your computer resources department to see whether anything's available. If you work in a large corporation, check with other FrameMaker users to see whether they have already created the template you need.

✔ **Professional template designers:** If you want to create a template customized for your particular requirements and you're willing to spend some money, consider hiring a FrameMaker expert and professional template designer. Several companies (including mine) offer this service. A custom template design project can be expensive, but you get quick turnaround, a template customized for your requirements, and typically some training on how to use the template.

Opening Existing Documents

To open existing documents (both FrameMaker and non-FrameMaker files), follow these two steps:

1. **Select File⇨Open to display the Open dialog box (see Figure 2-4).**

2. **Use the directory navigation box to locate the file you want, select it, and then click Open (or just double-click the file).**

FrameMaker opens the file.

Figure 2-4:
The Open
dialog box
lets you
open more
than just
FrameMaker
files. You
can convert
other file
formats by
opening
them here.

Converting from Other Formats

You can import content from many other word-processing formats into
FrameMaker. In many cases, you can open the file directly; FrameMaker identifies the file type and uses the appropriate import filter. For example, if you
try to open a rich text format (RTF) file on the Windows platform,
FrameMaker identifies the RTF format and asks you to confirm that it should
use the RTF filter (see Figure 2-5).

Figure 2-5:
Once you
confirm that
you really
want to
process an
RTF file,
FrameMaker
converts the
file.

FrameMaker doesn't always prompt you to confirm the file type. In some
cases, it just converts and opens the file.

Because the filters are different for each platform, you may see a confirmation prompt (like the one shown in Figure 2-4) for some platforms but not for
others. Some formats can be opened on one platform but not others. In general, the Macintosh version contains the most versatile set of filters with the

best conversion results. The UNIX version contains the smallest number of filters; the Windows version is somewhere in between.

On the Macintosh, the Claris XTND translators are also available. This is a set of filters made by Claris that can be used inside FrameMaker (and other applications). If the FrameMaker filter doesn't give you the result you want, try specifying the filter you want to use in the Format drop-down list. This filter selection is not available on any other platform.

Interleaf

If you want to convert Interleaf files, you first need to save the Interleaf file to Interleaf ASCII format. (This is a text version of the Interleaf format.) Then, import the Interleaf ASCII file.

On the UNIX version, you need to run the Interleaf ASCII format (IAF) file through the iaf2mif filter, which is in your FrameMaker filters directory. This is done from the UNIX command line, not through the FrameMaker interface. For more details, refer to the online manual *Using Filter* (go to Help⇨Online Manuals).

PageMaker and QuarkXPress

FrameMaker doesn't offer a direct import filter from PageMaker or QuarkXPress format (nor do they, in turn, offer a FrameMaker export filter). If you need to extract information from PageMaker or QuarkXPress, your best choice is to save it to RTF format and then import the RTF files into FrameMaker. You'll lose your graphics and much of your formatting, but the text is preserved.

Ventura Publisher

The Windows version of FrameMaker includes a filter for Ventura Publisher files. Just open the Ventura Publisher file in FrameMaker.

The Mac and UNIX versions don't include a Ventura Publisher filter.

Microsoft Word

FrameMaker 5.5.6 includes a filter for Word 97 filters. Earlier versions of FrameMaker (including version 5.5.3) don't include the Word 97 filter. If you need to import Word files, I strongly recommend that you upgrade to version

5.5.6 (available from Adobe for $25 or less if upgrading from version 5.5.*x*). If you're working with an earlier version and cannot upgrade to version 5.5.6, save your Word files to RTF format (choose File⇨Save As in Microsoft Word) and then import the RTF file.

If you're using a newer version of Word, like Word 2000, you may need to save your file to RTF or to an earlier version of Word before you import the file into FrameMaker.

When you import a Word file, the Word style sheets are converted to FrameMaker paragraph tags. Word headers and footers are moved to FrameMaker master pages.

But after that, things get a little uglier. Word tables become FrameMaker tables, but all of the formatting in the Word table is imported as customization (not as part of the table format). Some of the graphics from the Word file are converted, but often they are unacceptably fuzzy. The best solution to that problem is to get the original graphic file and import the graphic directly into FrameMaker.

WordPerfect

The FrameMaker WordPerfect filter converts WordPerfect version 5 for Windows or version 3 for Macintosh format files. On the Mac, you may also have Claris XTND filters for more recent versions. If possible, save your WordPerfect file to one of the formats supported by FrameMaker and then import the file.

Additional conversion filters

If you need to convert from a file type not listed here, first try opening the file in FrameMaker. The filters are different for each platform, so if possible, try the file on different platforms. If that doesn't work, a number of third-party conversion filters are available — some shareware, some freeware, and some commercial. One of them, Filtrix, is included on the CD that comes with this book. Visit www.frameusers.com for a list of other filters.

Understanding Word Processing

When you create a new, blank document (choose File⇨New and select the Portrait button), FrameMaker presents you with a boring blank document.

Your document has a dotted line around the edge (if you don't see the dotted line, select View⇨Borders). This dotted line is the border of the text area. You can put text inside this area. (In effect, the dotted line shows you where the margins are on the page.) At the top left inside the text area, you see a squiggly symbol. This is the *end-of-flow symbol*. It indicates that the content of the document ends here. If you click the end-of-flow symbol and type in some text, the end-of-flow symbol moves to the end of the next text. (If you don't see the end-of-flow symbol, select View⇨Text Symbols.)

If you have more than one flow in your document, you can have multiple end-of-flow symbols, but we're going to ignore this for now. If you can't wait to find out more, see Chapter 8. You'll also see end-of-flow symbols in table cells (see Chapter 7).

To insert text, just type it in. You can also copy and paste from other applications. (On the Windows platform, make sure that you select Edit⇨Paste Special⇨Text; otherwise, you'll get a link to the text by default.)

To create separate paragraphs, press Return (or Enter). Notice that a paragraph symbol is inserted to indicate the end of the paragraph (see Figure 2-6).

When you insert a Tab character, FrameMaker inserts a symbol that looks a little like a chubby closing parenthesis. If your tab doesn't appear to be working, don't panic! By default, FrameMaker paragraphs do not have any preset tab stops. Your tab character won't accomplish anything until you create tab stop settings for the paragraph (see Chapter 4 for details).

Eventually, you'll create markers in your document. Markers are used to store nonprinting text, and they are important for indexing, cross-references, and conditional text, all of which I'll discuss in detail later on (in Chapters 19, 9, and 16, respectively). Figure 2-6 shows an example of a marker.

Getting Around

It's time to settle into your new application and take a look at some basic navigation features. If you look at the bottom of your window in the middle, you'll see the status bar, which tells you the current page, the total number of pages, and whether the file needs to be saved (see Figure 2-7). If an asterisk appears after the page information, the file needs to be saved.

Border of text area   Marker   Tab   End-of-flow symbol

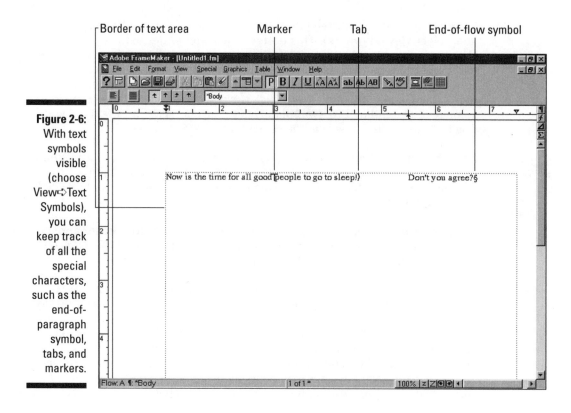

Figure 2-6:
With text symbols visible (choose View➪Text Symbols), you can keep track of all the special characters, such as the end-of-paragraph symbol, tabs, and markers.

Figure 2-7:
The status bar offers useful information about the page count. An asterisk indicates that the file has changed since you last saved it.

Current page number   Page Up button

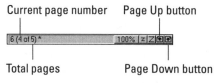

Total pages   Page Down button

As you work in FrameMaker, you'll discover that files are almost always marked as "dirty" (the asterisk appears in the status bar to indicate that the file needs to be saved). Even immediately after opening the file, you may notice the asterisk. This occurs because FrameMaker checks and updates certain items in your files (such as the cross-references), and often those updates cause the asterisk to appear. If this bothers you, you can prevent this by turning off automatic updates (select Edit⇨Update References, then select Suppress Automatic Updates from the Commands drop-down list). However, now you must remember to update your cross-references.

Moving from page to page

FrameMaker gives you lots of ways to get around. In the status bar, click the Page Up and Page Down buttons (refer to Figure 2-7) to go to the previous or next page in the document. Hold down the Shift key and click Page Up to go to the first page in the document. Similarly, hold down the Shift key and click Page Down to go to the last page in the document.

Click the page count information in the status bar to display the Go to Page dialog box (see Figure 2-8).

Figure 2-8: Click the Page Count Information section of the status bar to display the Go to Page dialog box.

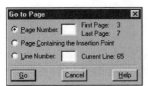

From this dialog box, you can jump to any page in the document.

You can also use the Page Up and Page Down keys on your keyboard. On the Windows and UNIX platforms, these move you to the top of the previous or next page. On the Macintosh, you move one screenful.

You also have a set of scroll bars on the right and bottom of the window, which you can use to get around in the document.

Changing the page magnification

You can view your page at different magnification (or zoom) levels. The status bar offers several ways to change the zoom setting (see Figure 2-9).

Figure 2-9:
Click the
Zoom In or
Zoom Out to
change
zoom by one
level, or dis-
play the
Zoom menu
to jump to
any zoom
setting.

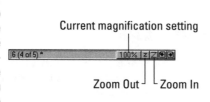

Current magnification setting

Zoom Out ⌐ Zoom In

✔ Click the small z (Zoom Out) to reduce the magnification one level. Click the large Z (Zoom In) to increase the magnification one level.

You can find the Zoom In and Zoom Out buttons on the bottom of the window.

✔ You can also click the Current Magnification setting to display a pop-up menu.

Select a zoom setting to change to that setting or one of the other settings (Fit Page to Window, for example) to adjust the zoom level to match your window.

The Zoom pop-up menu also lets you change the available zoom settings. You can never have more than ten zoom percentages, but you can specify what settings are available. Click Set on the Zoom pop-up menu to display the Zoom Menu Options dialog box (see Figure 2-10).

To change the zoom settings, replace the numbers in the fields with the numbers you want. You don't have to type them in order; FrameMaker sorts them for you to make sure they go from smallest to largest.

Setting preferences and views

To set your FrameMaker preferences, select File⇨Preferences to display the Preferences dialog box (see Figure 2-11).

Figure 2-10:
If you don't
like Frame-
Maker's
zoom
settings, you
can change
them in the
Zoom Menu
Options
dialog box.

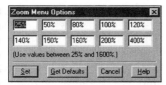

Figure 2-11:
Your options
include
automatic
saving and
several set-
tings related
to cross-
platform
compatibil-
ity.

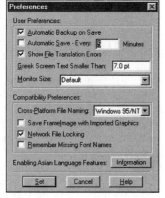

Table 2-1 lists the available preferences.

Table 2-1	Preference Options in FrameMaker
Option	*Description*
Automatic Backup on Save	If checked, this creates a backup file when you save a document. I recommend this option, especially if you're working on an unstable system. Unfortunately, the backup files clutter the document directory and there's no way to store them elsewhere.

(continued)

Table 2-1 *(continued)*

Option	Description
Automatic Save	If checked, this saves the file every 15 minutes (or whatever number you specify). The autosave files are deleted when you save the document normally. If your system crashes, the autosave file is not deleted. When you reopen the file that you were working on when the system crashed, you're asked whether you want to open the autosaved version of the file (if one exists). The autosave version is usually more up-to-date than the regular version. I recommend this option.
Greek Text Smaller Than	Select this and you won't see text smaller than the specified point size. This can improve display speed. Smaller text is *greeked,* that is, shown as a gray line.
Monitor Size (Windows only)	Tells FrameMaker the size of the monitor that you are using.
Cross-Platform File Naming	This helps you keep file names compatible with the specified platform. For example, if you choose Windows 3.1, and then attempt to save a file with a name that contains space or is more than eight characters with a three-character extension (8.3), FrameMaker reminds you that the specified file name would not work on a Windows 3.1 platform. You can still ignore the warning and save the non-compatible file name.
Saving FrameImage with Imported Graphics	If checked, a FrameImage is created for each graphic that you copy into the document. The FrameImage displays (and prints) on all platforms, so if the imported graphic doesn't work on a particular platform, the FrameImage is used instead. For example, Windows bitmap (BMP) format is displayed as a gray box on the Macintosh version of FrameMaker unless you check this option *before* you import the graphic on the Windows platform.

Option	Description
Remember Missing Font Names	If checked, fonts are substituted only temporarily if you open a file on a system that doesn't have all the fonts required for that document. When you move the document to a system that has all the right fonts, the original fonts are restored. If not checked, the missing fonts are permanently replaced with fonts available on the system.
Show File Translation Errors	If checked, a FrameMaker console is displayed that lists any errors that occur while opening or filtering a file.
Interface (Mac only)	Choose US English or UK English. If you're using an international version of FrameMaker, your choices may be different.
Network File Locking (Windows only)	If checked, it prevents you from opening a file that's already being used by someone else. (For Macintosh and UNIX versions, this is handled by the operating system.)

Saving What You've Got

Your motto should be, "Save early and often." When you're ready to save, just select File⇨Save. The first time you save the document, you'll be prompted to name it and specify the directory where you want to put it. After that, when you select File⇨Save nothing obvious happens, but the asterisk disappears from your status bar and the file is saved. (Also, the Save option on the File menu is grayed out if you just saved and haven't made any additional changes.)

The default extension for FrameMaker files is .fm on the Windows platform.

Printing

To print, select File⇨Print to display the Print dialog box (see Figure 2-12).

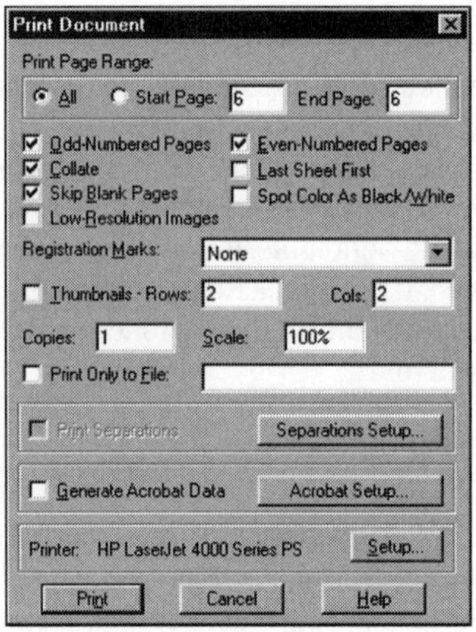

Figure 2-12:
Make your
decisions on
how you
want the
page to
appear in
the Print
dialog box.

In addition to the FrameMaker printing options, you'll have options that vary
based on your printer (and your operating system).

Table 2-2	FrameMaker Printing Options
Option	*Description*
Pages (or Page Range): All or Start Page and End Page	Select the All radio button to print every page in your document. Type in a starting page number and ending page number to print only a particular section of the document.
Odd-Numbered Pages	If checked, the odd pages are printed. (Printing only even and then only odd pages lets you duplex without a duplex printer.)
Even-Numbered Pages	If checked, the even pages are printed. Normally, you select both Odd and Even pages. (You must select at least one of the two, or nothing will print!)
Last Sheet First	If checked, the document is printed starting from the last page instead of the first page.
Spot Color as Black/White	If checked, spot colors are printed in solid black (or pure white). If not checked, spot colors are printed in color on a color printer and in shades of gray on a black and white printer. (Printing in solid black is faster than printing shades of gray.)
Collate	If checked, multiple copies are collated; that is, the entire first copy of the document is printed, followed by the entire second copy, and so on. If Collate is not checked, then all page 1 copies are printed, followed by all page 2 copies, and so on.

Option	*Description*
Skip Blank Pages	If checked, pages that do not contain any information are skipped. (Background items such as headers and footers count as content; the page must be completely blank.)
Low-Resolution Images (Windows and UNIX)	If checked, graphics are printed in low-resolution instead of high resolution. This option is useful if you want to print a quick draft and don't need beautiful graphics.
Registration Marks	You can print Western or Tombo (Japanese) registration marks (or None). Usually selected only if you are creating final files for your commercial printer. Registration marks are also called crop marks; they provide guidelines around the edge of your document where the printer will cut the document. Tombo registration marks are used only for Japanese documents.
Thumbnails	If checked, you must specify how many FrameMaker pages you want to print on a single page (for example two rows and two columns would be four thumbnails per page). FrameMaker will size the pages so that the number you specify fit onto a single page.
Copies	Specifies how many copies of the document you want to print. The default is 1.
Scale	Specifies the size of the printed document. The default is 100%.
Print Only to File	If checked, you specify a file name for the output file. Lets you print a PostScript file. See Chapter 14 for details.
Print Separations	If checked, you must specify how you want to set up your color separations using the Separations Setup dialog box. Used only when you are sending files to a commercial printer. (And even then only if you are printing a color document.)
Separations Setup	Lets you specify how you want to print the different colors in your document onto separate pages (required for commercial color printing). For details, see Chapter 14.

(continued)

Table 2-2 *(continued)*	
Option	*Description*
Generate Acrobat Data	If checked, you can include additional information in the print file that is used when you convert to PDF (Adobe Acrobat format). See Chapter 14 for details.
Acrobat Setup	Lets you set up your Acrobat options. See Chapter 14 for details.
Setup (Windows only)	Lets you change the printer setup.

Closing Your Document

To close your document, first make sure that you save your file, then select File⇨Close (or the Close box, which is located in the upper-right corner in a UNIX or Windows environment or in the upper-left corner in a Macintosh environment). If you haven't saved, FrameMaker reminds you to save your file before closing it.

Closing your document doesn't exit FrameMaker.

Quitting for the Day

To shut down FrameMaker, make sure that you save your file, and then select File⇨Quit (or Exit). If you have not saved, FrameMaker reminds you to save your file before quitting.

Chapter 3

Word Processing: The FrameMaker Way

*F*rameMaker includes the basic features that you would expect in any word processor. Chapter 2 talks about how to type in text, so now take a look at some of the other word-processing features available in FrameMaker.

Check Your Spelling

FrameMaker includes a spell-checking feature. To begin checking your work, select Edit⇨Spelling Checker, which displays the Spelling Checker dialog box (see Figure 3-1).

Select the Start Checking button to begin spell-checking. As FrameMaker finds possible problems, they are displayed at the top of the dialog box. The recommended correction is shown in the Correction field, with additional suggestions underneath. If you approve of the correction, click Correct; otherwise, select one of the other correction choices or type the correction directly into the Correction field, and then select Correct. FrameMaker automatically moves on to the next questionable item.

Figure 3-1:
You can
check the
current
page or the
entire
document.

If you want FrameMaker to make this correction every time, click the Automatic Correction check box before you click the Correct button. FrameMaker will memorize this correction and perform it automatically during each subsequent check of this document.

Setting up Spelling Checker options

The Spelling Checker provides many different options. To access them, display the Spelling Checker dialog box (to do so, select Edit➪Spelling Checker) and then click Options. This displays the Spelling Checker Options dialog box (see Figure 3-2).

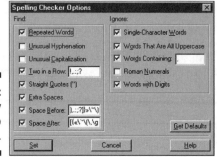

Figure 3-2:
So many
choices, so
little time . . .

Easter egg: FrameMaker's way of just having fun

An *Easter egg* is hacker's slang for a function embedded in a program that isn't supposed to be there, such as an inside joke or list of people who worked on a product. FrameMaker has one, too: See what happens when you type *Interleaf,* FrameMaker's competitor, into your document and then check spelling.

Table 3-1 explains the options.

Table 3-1	Spelling Checker Options
Option	*Description*
Find: Repeated Words	Finds two identical words in a row (like "the the").
Find: Unusual Hyphenation	Finds words with unusual hyphenation. By default, this option is off, which means that FrameMaker checks the word before a hyphen and the word after a hyphen, but not the compound word.
Find: Unusual Capitalization	Finds words with unusual capitalization, like "SoftWare."
Find: Two in a Row	Finds two in a row of the specified symbols.
Find: Straight Quotes	Finds straight quotes (") and replaces them with curly quotes (" "). But you should know that FrameMaker does not find single straight quotes; only double straight quotes. To fix single straight quotes, you'll need to use the Find/Change feature instead of the spell-checker.
Find: Extra Spaces	Finds two spaces in a row.
Find: Space Before	Finds spaces before the specified symbols.
Find: Space After	Finds spaces after the specified symbols.
Ignore: Single-Character Words	Ignores any words that are a single character (Project X).
Ignore: Words That Are All Uppercase	Ignores words that are in all capital letters (VERY IMPORTNT).
Ignore: Words Containing	Ignores words that contain the specified symbols (by default, this includes a period, so www.scriptorium.com would not be spell-checked).
Ignore: Roman Numerals	Ignores Roman numerals (LIX, viii).
Ignore: Words with Digits	Ignores words that contain digits (Site1).
Get Defaults	Restores the default spell-checking options.

Space(s): The final frontier

Writers, editors, typesetters, and other publishing professionals have this ongoing debate about how many spaces should go after the end of a sentence — one or two spaces.

I won't volunteer my personal opinion, but I will say this: In FrameMaker, it is much easier to maintain a document with one space after the period instead of two because

✔ The Spelling Checker, by default, flags two spaces in a row. You can turn off this option to avoid correcting the two spaces after a period, but if you do so, the Spelling Checker won't catch double spaces anywhere in the document.

✔ FrameMaker's Smart Space option (described later in this chapter), when selected, prevents you from typing two spaces in a row.

If you're a die-hard double-spacer, you may not care that FrameMaker makes it easier for single spaces. If you're fairly neutral, go with one space, at least in this product, and save yourself some trouble.

Understanding the FrameMaker dictionaries

When you're working in a document, the Spelling Checker actually looks at four different dictionaries. They are

✔ **Main dictionary:** This dictionary contains all the words you'd expect in a standard dictionary.

✔ **Site dictionary:** Your company's system administrator maintains the site dictionary. The site dictionary contains words that are company-specific, so it might include product names, the company name, and terms that are used throughout your company (but aren't standard usage elsewhere).

✔ **Personal dictionary:** The personal dictionary contains words that you have added to FrameMaker (when you click Learn in the Spelling Checker dialog box, the specific word is added to your personal dictionary).

✔ **Document dictionary:** Each document contains a list of words that are allowed in that particular document. Whenever you click Allow in Document in the Spelling Checker dialog box, the document dictionary adds the specified word.

Checking hyphenation points for a word

You can use the Spelling Checker to verify the hyphenation points for a word. Type the word in the Correction field, and then click Show Hyphenation. The hyphenation is displayed in the Correction field (see Figure 3-3).

Figure 3-3:
FrameMaker
shows
you the
hyphenation
points
stored for
this word.

To change the hyphenation points, add the hyphens where you want them and delete the hyphens as appropriate. Then click Learn to store the new hyphenation in FrameMaker's dictionaries.

I have never been able to get custom hyphenation to work properly. I can usually add hyphens, but I've had trouble deleting them. I suspect that a word with hyphenation requires at least one hyphen, but I don't have any evidence for this.

What's Another Word for Thesaurus?

FrameMaker includes a thesaurus to help you polish your prose to a precise, pristine preparation.

To use the thesaurus, select a word in your document for which you want to find synonyms. Then select Edit⇨Thesaurus to display the Thesaurus dialog box (see Figure 3-4).

If you find a word in the list that looks promising but isn't quite right, click it to display its thesaurus entry. (This works only for words that are displayed in bold.) You can use the Page Up/Page Down buttons on the Thesaurus dialog box to go through the various entries.

To replace your original word with a new choice, first click the new word and then click the Replace button. The new word is inserted into your document and replaces the selected word.

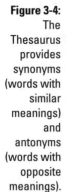

Figure 3-4:
The
Thesaurus
provides
synonyms
(words with
similar
meanings)
and
antonyms
(words with
opposite
meanings).

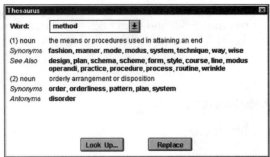

Instead of selecting a word and displaying information about it, you can also look up words. To do so, display the Thesaurus dialog box (select Edit⇨Thesaurus), and then click the Look Up button at the bottom of the dialog box to display the Thesaurus Look Up dialog box. Type in a word, then click Look Up to display the entry for that word.

Education: The Path to Smart Spaces

FrameMaker's Smart Spaces feature prevents you from typing two spaces in a row. To turn it on, select Format⇨Document⇨Text Options to display the Text Options dialog box (see Figure 3-5).

Figure 3-5:
You can set
up smart
quotes and
smart
spaces
here.

Check the Smart Spaces check box and then click Apply.

Street-Smart Quotes

Smart quotes mean that FrameMaker automatically creates curly quotes ("") when you type in quotation marks. To turn on smart quotes, select Format⇨Document⇨Text Options to display the Text Options dialog box (shown in Figure 3-5). Check the Smart Quotes check box and click Apply.

Turning on Smart Quotes doesn't replace the existing straight quotes in your document with curly quotes. You need to use the Spelling Checker to do that. In the Spelling Checker options, make sure that you have Find Straight Quotes checked.

Automating Pagination

You can manage pagination for individual files, but this makes sense only if you *don't* plan to set up a book file. (Chapters 17-19 discuss book files.) You can, for example, set up a file to start on page 5 instead of page 1 (the default). This is useful when you have front matter (like title pages) that are not included in your FrameMaker files.

Here are the steps to set pagination for a file:

1. **Open that file and select Format⇨Document⇨Number to display the Numbering Properties dialog box.**

   Figure 3-6 shows the Numbering Properties dialog box.

Figure 3-6:
You can set your document to start on page iii instead of the default, page 1.

2. **In the 1st Page # field, type the page number that you want to start with.**

3. **In the Page # Style field, select the pagination type. Numeric starts with 1, 2, 3; roman with i, ii, iii; alphabetic with a, b, c, and so on.**

4. **If you want this file to restart paragraph numbering, check the corresponding check box.**

   Restarting paragraph numbering resets all the autonumbers in the chapter to start with 0. This normally matters only if this file is part of a book, see Chapter 17 for more information.

5. **Select an option in the Before Saving & Printing drop-down list.**

   FrameMaker can manage your pagination to make sure that your total page count is always odd or even. You can also delete any blank pages at the end of the document when you save or print.

   If the document is going to be printed double-sided (on the front and back of each page), you need to make the total page even. For each sheet of paper you need two pages (1+2, 3+4, 5+6), and so the total number of pages should be even.

   If you have applied a custom master page to a page at the end of the document, that page is not deleted, even if it is blank. To delete such a page, select Special⇨Delete Pages. (For details about master pages, see Chapter 8.)

6. **Click Set to close the Numbering Properties dialog box and save your settings.**

Your Mission: Search and Replace

FrameMaker's Find/Change utility offers lots of different choices — you can do much more than just search for text. But let's start with the basics.

Searching and replacing text

By default, you search for text and replace it with other text. For example, you could search for *dog* and replace it with *cat*. To do so:

1. **Select Edit⇨Find/Change to display the Find/Change dialog box (see Figure 3-7).**

   The default is to find text. Leave this default.

2. **Leave the default and type** dog **in the field at the top.**

   The default for the Change option is To Text.

3. **Again, leave the default and type** cat **in the field at the bottom.**

Figure 3-7:
It looks
simple, but
this dialog
box includes
lots of
powerful
features.

4. **Click Find to locate the first instance of dog. If you want to replace it, click Change.**

   You can also click Change & Find to make the change here and locate the next match.

   If you're feeling gutsy, click Change All In Document or Change All in Selection to perform a global search and replace.

When you search for text, text in variables, master pages, and cross-references is *not* searched.

Searching and replacing other items

You can search for many different items from the Find/Change dialog box. Figure 3-8 shows some of the choices. Not all of these options require that you include text in the Find field, but otherwise, the process is the same as what's described in the "Searching and replacing text" section above.

Figure 3-8:
Find/Change
is not just
for text any-
more . . .

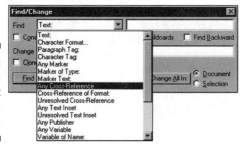

Replacing with a character format

Instead of replacing the word *dog* with *cat,* you could replace it with a character format. This doesn't actually change the text, but it lets you change all occurrences of dog from regular text to, say, bold blue text in one step. To do this, follow these steps:

1. **Select Edit⇨Find/Change to display the Find/Change dialog box (refer to Figure 3-7).**

2. **Select Text as your Find option and type dog in the field at the top.**

3. **Select To Character Format as your Change option. This displays the Change to Character Format dialog box (see Figure 3-9).**

Figure 3-9:
These
character
settings will
be applied
every time
you select
Change.

4. **Set up the character format that you want and click Set. This returns you to the Find/Change dialog box.**

5. **Use the Find, Change, Change & Find, and Change All buttons as appropriate to apply the new character formatting to the *dog* text.**

This technique applies overrides to your text. It would be better to apply a character tag with the formatting that you want. To do this, you need to use the technique described in the next section.

Replacing from the clipboard

Like most word processors and other applications, FrameMaker has a clipboard. You can copy information onto the clipboard (by selecting Edit⇨Copy) and retrieve it by pasting (select Edit⇨Paste). You can also use information stored on the clipboard when you are doing a search and replace operation. In the Find/Change dialog box, the Change drop-down list offers an option called By Pasting. This retrieves the information on the clipboard and uses it as the replacement information.

By Pasting is handy in lots of ways. Imagine, for example, that you want to replace a fairly short piece of text (like "address block") with a somewhat lengthy chunk of text, like:

PO Box 12761
Research Triangle Park, NC 27709

You could try to type this information into the Change field, but it might be easier just to type it into your document somewhere, and then copy it to the clipboard (select Edit⇨Copy) and set the Change option to By Pasting.

Changing paragraph formats

The Replace By Pasting option is also useful for several special operations. Take a look at the Copy Special submenu on the Edit menu.

You can, for example, copy a paragraph tag to the clipboard and then search for a particular paragraph tag (in the Find drop-down list, select Paragraph Tag and type the name of the paragraph tag into the Find field). Then, you replace it with the paragraph tag stored on the clipboard. This is a convenient way to do a global replace of one paragraph tag with another.

Changing character formats

The same technique as described for paragraph formats works for character formats. Just locate some text in your document that uses the character tag you want, then select Edit⇨Copy Special⇨Character Format to copy the character tag to the clipboard. Then, find the character tag you want to replace and change by pasting.

Changing conditional text settings

If you have complicated conditional text settings in your document, you may want to copy those settings from one place to another. You can store conditional text settings on the clipboard using Edit⇨Copy Special⇨Conditional Text Settings and use it in the Find/Change dialog box with the Change By Pasting option.

Changing table column widths

You can use the Copy Special command to copy the column width of a single column or of several columns. Later, you can paste the column widths onto another set of columns in a different table. This gives you a quick and efficient way to make every table in a document consistent. For example, imagine that you have a series of three-column tables in the document, and you want to make sure that they all use the same column width settings. (You can't remember if you changed them while editing the document.) So, you go to the first table and set up all the column widths exactly right (for details on how to do this, see Chapter 7). Then, you select Edit⇨Copy Special⇨Table Column Widths to store the widths on the clipboard. Now, go to the Find/Change dialog box (by selecting Edit⇨Find/Change). In the Find drop-down list, select Any Table. In the Change drop-down list, select By Pasting. Click Change All in Document and every table in the document will have the same column widths.

Barring Any Changes . . .

Change bars let you keep track of where you (or someone else) makes changes to a document. Once you turn on the change bars, editing the document causes a bar to appear in the margin.

Turning on change bars

To turn on the change bars, follow these steps:

1. **Select Format⇨Document⇨Change Bars to display the Change Bar Properties dialog box (see Figure 3-10).**

Figure 3-10: You can adjust the location, color, and thickness of your change bars here.

2. **Change the change bar options in this dialog box, or leave the defaults.**
3. **Check the Automatic Change Bars check box.**
4. **Click Set.**

Once you turn on change bars, the bars keep appearing in your document until you turn them off.

Clearing change bars

To clear change bars, display the Change Bar Properties dialog box (select Format⇨Document⇨Change Bars), check the Clear All Change Bars check box, and click Set.

This clears the change bars, but doesn't turn them on or off. You have to do that separately.

Turning off change bars

To turn off change bars, display the Change Bar Properties dialog box (select Format⇨Document⇨Change Bars), uncheck the Automatic Change Bars check box, and click Set.

Any change bars that are in your document are *not* removed when you turn off change bars.

Something Old, Something New

As you're working along in a new document, you may need to compare the new information to an older version of the document. The Compare Document feature lets you do just that. You create a composite document that shows where text was inserted and deleted, along with a summary document that provides document statistics. (You can also skip the composite document and create just the summary.) To compare documents, follow these steps:

1. **Open the new document and the old document.**

   Make sure that the new document is the active document. That is, your cursor should be blinking in the new document.

2. **From the newer document, select File⇨Utilities⇨Compare Documents.**

   This displays the Compare Documents dialog box (see Figure 3-11).

   You cannot change the newer document selection here (it's always the active document). If the wrong document is selected, cancel the compare and make the new document the active document before you return to this dialog box.

3. **In the Older Document drop-down list, select the older document. Only currently open documents are available in this list.**

Figure 3-11:
Comparing
documents
creates a
composite
document
with inser-
tions and
deletions.

4. **Select Summary and Composite Documents (the default) to create a summary document that lists changes and document statistics along with a composite document that shows insertions and deletions. Select Summary Document Only to create just the list with the statistics.**

5. **Click Compare to create the comparison documents you requested.**

For large documents, the comparison process could take some time. And I don't recommend comparing two documents that don't have anything in common. That could freeze your machine.

Part II
Supplying Text, Tables, and Graphics

The 5th Wave   By Rich Tennant

In this part . . .

Once you have content, you'll want to mangle, er, manage it. For text, you have the Paragraph and Character Designers, which let you create tags (or styles) for your content. For tables, you have — ta-da! — the Table Designer. I'll also talk about how to create graphics, both by importing them and by creating them directly inside FrameMaker.

Chapter 4

Formatting Paragraphs with Paragraph Tags

I f you've worked with other desktop publishing applications or with Word, you're probably familiar with style sheets. If, until now, you have managed to avoid the concept of a style sheet, you obviously have too much fun in your life. Time for that to stop. A *style sheet,* for those of you who previously had a life, is a collection of formatting instructions. For example, the style sheet for your body text might say, "make the text Times New Roman, 12 points, with a left indent of 2 inches, and leave 2 points of space above and below the paragraph." Instead of formatting each paragraph individually, you assign the "body text" style, which automatically applies all the formatting that is saved as part of the style. This is a huge time-saver.

FrameMaker's *paragraph tags* are style sheets for your paragraph formatting. FrameMaker doesn't actually use the term *style sheet.* FrameMaker's paragraph tags are like style sheets. They let you store all the different properties for a paragraph, and you can set up different properties for different paragraph types.

This chapter introduces you to FrameMaker's paragraph tags, which are much spiffier (yes, that is a technical term) than style sheets in other applications. You'll find out how to create and modify paragraph tags, and I'll include some goodies about how to set numbering and other automatic formatting for your paragraphs.

Understanding Paragraph Tags and the Paragraph Catalog

In FrameMaker, style sheets are available for lots of different items, including paragraphs. They're usually called tags, and when you apply them, you *tag* an item. So, for your paragraphs, you have paragraph tags and you can apply a style to a paragraph by tagging it.

The reason that the styles are called tags is because deep inside FrameMaker, formatting information is actually stored in a tagged format. When you apply a paragraph tag, FrameMaker inserts the "use paragraph tag X" command at the beginning of the paragraph and "end paragraph tag X" at the end of the paragraph. It looks as though you're selecting and applying, but you're really inserting tags. If you're familiar with some of the tagged markup languages, like troff, GML/Bookmaster, LaTeX, or even HTML, the tagging thing will make sense to you. (If the previous sentence looks like a collection of random letters, consider yourself lucky.)

Paragraph tags give you complete control over every aspect of a paragraph that you might want (and probably a few that never even occurred to you before). Of course, you can store font information in a paragraph tag, but that's not all. Your paragraph attributes include the space above and below the paragraph, tab settings, the next paragraph tag used, whether hyphenation is active or not, the way the paragraph behaves inside a table, and much more. The ability to apply all these attributes in a single step saves time, and it also makes it much easier to make your document consistent.

Applying Paragraph Tags Using the Paragraph Catalog

The paragraph catalog lists the paragraph tags defined in your document. (Even brand-new documents include a few default tags that FrameMaker inserts for you.) To display the paragraph catalog, click the ¶ button at the top right of the FrameMaker window. To apply one of the paragraph tags to a particular paragraph, make sure that your cursor is in that paragraph (you *don't* have to select the paragraph), and then click the tag in the paragraph catalog (see Figure 4-1).

Aaack! My paragraph catalog is completely empty

If you run across a document whose paragraph catalog is completely empty, don't panic. You'll need to import some tags from another document. Visit Chapter 13 for detailed instructions, but here's the quick version: Open the document from which you want to steal tags, go back to the empty document, select File⇨Import⇨Format, select the other document, and click Import.

Figure 4-1:
The paragraph catalog lists the paragraph tags in your document. Just click one to apply it to the selected paragraph.

Every paragraph in a FrameMaker document has a paragraph tag.

The current paragraph tag is displayed in the bottom left of the status bar (see Figure 4-2). You can select the entire paragraph or just put your cursor in the paragraph without selecting to see the tag name in the status bar.

Figure 4-2:
Check the
bottom left
of the status
bar for your
current
paragraph
tag.

| Flow: A ¶: step 1 | 72 (4 of 10) * | 120% ▾ z Z ⊞ ⊡ ◀ ▦ | ▶ ▨ |

Creating a Paragraph Tag

Approximately 20 seconds after discovering the paragraph tags, you'll probably decide that you hate the default formatting of the tags. You're not alone. To mangle Orson Welles's words, "No passion in the world is greater than the passion to alter someone else's template."

FrameMaker gives you all the tools you need to create and modify paragraph tags in the Paragraph Designer (Format⇨Paragraph⇨Paragraph Designer). It has six pages of properties where you set your paragraph's attributes.

To create a new paragraph tag, it's usually most efficient to start with an existing tag that's similar to what you need. (That way, you can keep all the attributes that are identical and change only a few. If you create a new tag from scratch, you have to go through and define *everything*.) I also recommend that you preview what's happening as you work on the paragraph tag.

Here's how to do it:

1. **Display the Paragraph Designer (Ctrl+M or Command+M).**

2. **From the tags drop-down list, select the tag that's closest to what you need.**

3. **In the Tag field, type a name for the new tag.**

4. **Click Apply. This displays the New Format dialog box.**

5. **Click Create (make sure both check boxes are checked).**

6. **Now, modify the Basic properties to get the settings you want. (Check out the next few sections for a blow-by-blow description of each properties sheet.) When you are finished, click Update All.**

7. **Select the next set of properties you want to modify, either by clicking the tab (Windows only) or by selecting it from the Properties drop-down list. Modify the properties to get the settings you want. When you are finished, click Update All. Repeat this until you're done with all the tabs, then close the Paragraph Designer.**

Basic properties

In the Basic properties, you set the indents, line spacing, tabs, alignment, and next paragraph tag. Figure 4-3 shows the Basic properties.

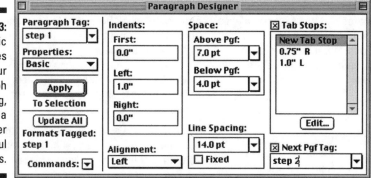

Figure 4-3: The Basic properties control your paragraph spacing, tabs, and a few other useful options.

When to use Update All versus Apply

When you're modifying a paragraph tag, make sure that you use the Update All button — *except when you create the paragraph tag the first time.* Update All applies your changes to the following items:

✔ The paragraph tag definition

✔ All paragraphs that use this paragraph tag

So, using Update All ensures that your document uses a single tag definition consistently. (But when you create the tag, you click Apply, because otherwise you will change the definition of the tag that you're using as a starting point. Probably not the effect you're looking for.)

By contrast, clicking the Apply to Selection button applies your changes only to the currently selected paragraph, and not to the paragraph tag definition or the other paragraphs that use the selected tag. This means that clicking Apply creates a *formatting override* — a paragraph whose appearance does not match the paragraph tag definition stored in your document's paragraph catalog. (But again, clicking Apply after you rename the tag is important, because it creates the new tag.)

You can tell whether a paragraph has an override by looking in the status bar. Click in the paragraph, and then check the bottom left of the status bar. If the paragraph is "clean," the status bar looks like this:

Paragraph tag

Flow: A ¶: heading 2   76 (8 of 10) *   120% z z ⊕ ⊕ ◀

(continued)

(continued)

If the paragraph is "dirty"; that is, if that paragraph's settings don't match the paragraph tag definition, an asterisk appears in front of the paragraph tag in the status bar:

| Flow: A ¶: *heading 2 | 76 (8 of 10) * | 120% ⌐z⌐z⌐⊕⌐⊕◄▥ | ► |

The asterisk indicates that this paragraph uses a custom override. Tsk, tsk. (The override is that the left indent is different than the default setting. You can't see any difference, but FrameMaker knows . . . .)

To remove an override from a paragraph, just reapply the appropriate paragraph tag.

If you apply a character tag to an entire paragraph, the paragraph indicates an override. FrameMaker interprets applying a character tag to a whole paragraph as a paragraph override. To remove this type of override, you will need to select the entire paragraph (triple-click in the paragraph), click Default Para Font in the character catalog, and then click the paragraph tag in the paragraph catalog. (Clicking Default Para Font doesn't do anything visible, but it strips the character-level overrides. Then, you reapply the paragraph tag to strip the paragraph-level overrides.)

If you need to remove overrides from the entire document and not just a single paragraph, select File⇔Import⇔Formats. Make sure that the current document is selected, and check the remove manual overrides buttons at the bottom of the window. Then click Import.

Import Formats

Import from Document: Current ▼

Import and Update:

⊠ Paragraph Formats	⊠ Reference Pages
⊠ Character Formats	⊠ Variable Definitions
⊠ Page Layouts	⊠ Cross-Reference Formats
⊠ Table Formats	⊠ Conditional Text Settings
⊠ Color Definitions	⊠ Math Definitions
⊠ Document Properties	

While Updating, Remove:

⊠ Manual Page Breaks   ⊠ Other Format/Layout Overrides

[Import]   (Cancel)   (Help)
(No Undo)

On all platforms, you can switch from one property sheet to another by selecting from the Properties drop-down list. However, in the Windows version, you also have a set of tabs across the top of the Paragraph Designer. Switching tabs is the same as changing properties from the drop-down list.

The items on the left side of the window are common to each one of the property sheets. Table 4-1 describes them.

Table 4-1	Common Items in the Paragraph Designer
Item	*Description*
Paragraph Tag	Shows the paragraph tag for the selected paragraph.
Properties	Lists the six property sheets. Identical to the tabs found in the Windows version.
Apply button	Applies changes made on the current sheet to the selected paragraph only. Creates a formatting override. (Formatting overrides are bad; avoid the Apply button in most circumstances.)
Update All	Applies changes made on the current sheet to every paragraph in the document that uses that paragraph tag. Also updates the paragraph's tag definition.
Commands⇨New Format	Creates a new paragraph tag with the same settings as the current tag. (Remember, creating a new tag from a similar existing tag is usually more efficient.)
Commands⇨Global Update Options	Lets you apply the current settings to another tag. For example, you can globally change all "Normal" tags to use "Body."
Commands⇨Delete Format	Displays a window where you can delete paragraph tags.
Commands⇨Set Window to As Is	Sets every attribute in the sheet to As Is. More commonly used in the Character Designer than in the Paragraph Designer.
Commands⇨Reset Window from Selection	Changes the attribute settings to match the selected text. This is useful when you have a paragraph full of overrides and you've decided to create a new paragraph tag with those settings.

Table 4-2 describes the paragraph settings you can configure in the Basic properties.

Table 4-2   Basics Properties in the Paragraph Designer

Item	Description
Indents⇨First, Left, Right	First: Sets the left indent for the first line of text. Left: Sets the left indent for all but the first line of text. Right: Sets the right indent for every line in the paragraph. All indent settings are measured from where the text column begins. If you change the Pagination Format setting, your indent's starting point also changes. (See Chapter 8 for details.)
Alignment	Sets the alignment of the paragraph: left, center, right, or justified.
Space⇨Above Paragraph and Below Paragraph	Sets the amount of space before and after the paragraph. The larger spacing value always prevails. So, if you have a paragraph that has its Space After set to 3 points and the next paragraph has its Space Before set to 12 points, the paragraphs would have 12 points of space between them.
Line Spacing	Sets the amount of space between each line in a paragraph. It's automatically set to a default value when you change the font size in the Default Font properties, but you can change that value. By default, line spacing is relative to the tallest item on the line. Check the Fixed box to force the line spacing to stay constant even when you have larger text on the line.
Tab Stops	Lists the tab stops defined in this paragraph. By default, paragraphs have no tabs defined. This means that inserting a tab doesn't shift the text over. To make the tab work, you have to create a tab stop. (By the way, if you uncheck the Tab Stops check box, all your tab settings are ignored.)
Tab Stops⇨Edit	Displays the Edit Tab Stop dialog box, where you create tabs. Tab measurements start from the left edge of the text column, not from the edge of the document.
Next Paragraph Tag	Check to set a default paragraph tag for the next paragraph. Often used for headings, so set the default after a heading to Body.

Default Font properties

The Default Font properties are where you set the font attributes for the paragraph. These include font, font size, text color, italics, underlines, the paragraph's language, and more.

Table 4-3 explains the settings you can customize in the Default Font properties.

Table 4-3   The Default Font Properties in the Paragraph Designer

Item	Description
Family	Sets the font face. For example, your choices here might include Arial, Times, Garamond, and Zapf Dingbats.
Size	Sets the font size.
Angle	Sets the angle of the font, such as Italic or Oblique. Choices available depend on the selected font.
Weight	Sets the weight of the font, such as Light, Medium, Bold, or Black. Choices available depend on the selected font.
Variation	Sets a font variation, which could be Alternate, Condensed, Compressed, Extended, or others. Choices available depend on the selected font.
Color	Sets the text color. The colors available are those defined in the color catalog (see Chapter 11 for more on defining colors).
Spread	Sets the amount of spacing between characters. The default is 0%, which is normal spacing. (In some other applications, this is called *tracking*.)
Stretch	Changes the width of the character shapes by stretching them horizontally. The default is 100%, which is no stretch. Setting this attribute to less than 100% condenses the characters, setting it to more than 100% stretches the characters.
Language	Determines which dictionary FrameMaker uses to hyphenate and spell-check the paragraph. *Note:* In FrameMaker 5, this attribute was in the Advanced properties. It was moved to the Default Font properties in version 5.5.

If you use different languages in your document, you can set up different paragraph tags for the different languages. If you have the dictionaries for the various languages you use, you could then spell-check the document, and FrameMaker would use the proper dictionaries for each paragraph.

If you set the Language to None, the paragraph is not spell-checked. This can be very useful for paragraphs that contain programming code, 16th-century English poetry, or any other material that the spell-checker cannot handle. Setting the Language to None is also a reasonable solution if you have material in a language for which you lack the corresponding dictionary.

Pagination properties

The Pagination properties (see Figure 4-4 and Table 4-4) control where a paragraph appears on the page. You can force a paragraph to begin at the top of a page or column (these are different in a two-column document), and you can also control how the side head area is used and widow/orphan protection.

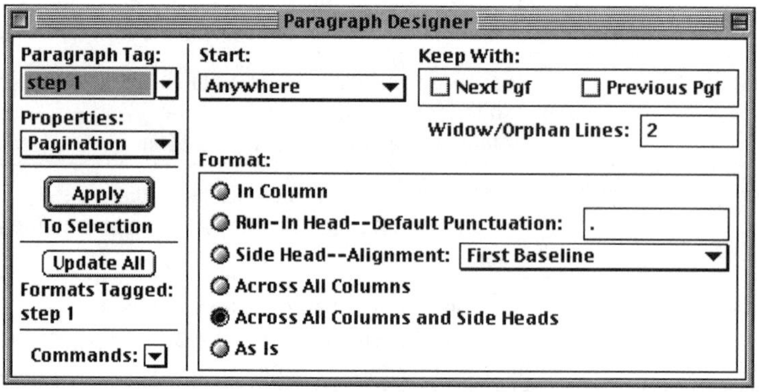

Figure 4-4: The Pagination properties let you set position for your paragraph.

Table 4-4   The Pagination Properties in the Paragraph Designer

Item	Description
Start	Controls where the paragraph can begin. You can set up a paragraph to start at the top of a page, at the top of a left or right page, at the top of a column, or anywhere else your heart desires.
Keep With	If checked, the paragraph is "glued" to the preceding or following paragraph. It's useful especially for headings, which should probably always stay with the following paragraph to prevent awkward page breaks.

Item	Description
Widow/Orphan Lines	A setting of 2 means that a paragraph cannot break with one line at the top or bottom of a page. Instead, at least two lines are always kept together.
Format	The Format radio button lets you specify your paragraph's location relative to the text column.
Format⇨In Column	Sets the paragraph to appear inside the text column.
Format⇨Run-In Head	Sets the paragraph to appear on the same line as the following paragraph. (See Figure 4-5.)
Format⇨Side Head	Sets the paragraph to appear only in the side head area. See Chapter 8 for information about setting up side heads.
Format⇨Across All Columns	Sets the paragraph to run across all columns in the main text area, but not in the side head area.
Format⇨Across All Columns and Side Heads	Sets the paragraph to run across all columns in the main text area and in the side head area.

Figure 4-5:
Here's an
example of
a run-in
head.

 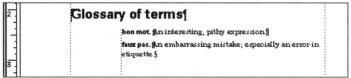

Numbering properties

The Numbering properties (see Figure 4-6) are a powerful and (sob) misunderstood feature. You can set up step numbering with autonumbers, but in addition to that, you can do so much more! For example, you can set up a paragraph tag that automatically inserts a bullet at the beginning of your paragraph, or you can automatically insert the word *NOTE:* followed by a tab. Chapter 22 provides lots of examples of how to use autonumbers.

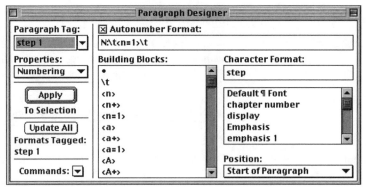

Table 4-5 describes the options in the Numbering properties.

Table 4-5   The Numbering Properties in the Paragraph Designer

Item	*Description*
Autonumber Format	Specifies the autonumbering code. The code is used only if the Autonumber Format check box is checked. See "Understanding the autonumbering codes" for information about the building blocks you can use and Chapter 22 for some detailed examples.
Building Blocks list	Provides a list of building blocks that you can click to add them to the autonumbering format. See Chapter 22 for lots of examples and a quick reference of all the available building blocks.
Character Format	Specifies the character tag used to display the autonumber. If you want the autonumber to match the rest of the paragraph, specify Default Para Font.
Position	Determines whether the autonumber is displayed at the beginning or the end of the paragraph.

Advanced properties

The Advanced properties (see Figure 4-7) aren't really advanced at all! (Autonumbering is much more complex.) It's my personal theory that the people developing FrameMaker ran out of catchy labels, so they decided to lump everything that was left over into "advanced." The Advanced properties let you set hyphenation and word spacing and set up paragraphs to always include a particular graphic above or below the paragraph.

Figure 4-7:
Advanced
properties
include
hyphenation
settings,
word
spacing,
and
graphics
above or
below the
paragraph.

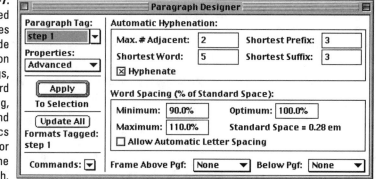

Table 4-6 lists the Advanced properties.

Table 4-6   The Advanced Properties in the Paragraph Designer

Item	Description
Automatic Hyphenation	If the Hyphenate box is checked, paragraphs that use this tag are hyphenated. FrameMaker uses the hyphenation rules for the language specified in the Default Font properties, along with the global settings, here.
Automatic Hyphenation⇨ Max. # Adjacent	Sets the maximum number of consecutive lines that can be hyphenated.
Automatic Hyphenation⇨ Shortest Word	Specifies the minimum number of letters required before hyphenation is allowed.
Automatic Hyphenation⇨ Shortest Prefix	Specifies the minimum number of letters required before a hyphen.
Automatic Hyphenation⇨ Shortest Suffix	Specifies the minimum number of letters required after a hyphen.
Automatic Hyphenation⇨ Hyphenate	If checked, FrameMaker uses hyphenation in those paragraphs.
Word Spacing	These settings control how much FrameMaker can change the spaces between words to fill lines. These values are measured as a percentage of the standard space for that font and size. The standard space is calculated by FrameMaker and is shown under the Optimum value.

(continued)

Table 4-6 *(continued)*

Item	Description
Word Spacing⇨Minimum	Sets the smallest space allowed between words, as a percentage of the standard space.
Word Spacing⇨Maximum	Sets the largest space allowed between words, as a percentage of the standard space.
Word Spacing⇨Optimum	Sets the ideal spacing between words, as a percentage of the standard space.
Word Spacing⇨ Allow Automatic Letter Spacing	If checked, allows FrameMaker to adjust spaces between characters if word spacing isn't within the allowed values on a particular line. If not checked, some lines may not fall within the minimum and maximum ranges (often because a word cannot be hyphenated).
Frame Above Pgf	Lets you specify a graphic (stored on the reference pages) to be displayed above this paragraph. Used for graphics that are repeated each time a particular paragraph tag occurs. See Chapter 15 for details about reference page graphics.
Frame Below Pgf	Similar to Frame Above Pgf, but puts the graphic below the paragraph.

Table Cell properties

The items in the Table Cell properties (see Figure 4-8) are relevant only if your paragraph happens to be in a table. For paragraphs in regular text, these roperties are completely ignored. In a table, Table Cell properties let you set the vertical alignment (top, bottom, or middle) of the text in a cell and also control the margins from the text to the edge of the table cell. The Table Cell properties work in tandem with the settings in the Table Designer (see Chapter 7). You can add to the settings in the Table Designer or override them. Table 4-7 presents the options in the Paragraph Designer.

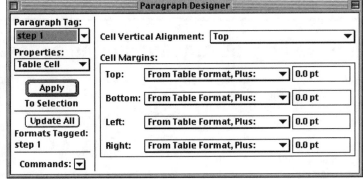

Figure 4-8:
The
Table Cell
properties
provide
control over
alignment
and margins
in a table.

Table 4-7	Table Cell Properties in the Paragraph Designer
Item	**Description**
Cell Vertical Alignment	Controls the alignment of the paragraph within a cell. A Middle alignment would always center the paragraph vertically.
Cell Margins	In the Table Designer, you can set default cell margins. The settings here override the default margins in the Table Designer for specific paragraph tags. (See Chapter 7 for more on the Table Designer.)
Cell Margins⇨Top, Bottom, Left, Right	Sets the cell margin for the specified side.
	The From Table Format, Plus setting increases the default cell margin from the Table Designer by the specified amount.
	The Custom setting ignores the setting in the Table Designer and specifies a different value here.

Modifying an Existing Paragraph Tag

To modify an existing paragraph tag, first display the Paragraph Designer. Then, select the tag that you want to change in the Tag field. Make the changes you want in the Basic tab and click Update All. Make sure that your tag is still selected in the tags field (reselect it if it isn't), move to the Default Font tab, and make your changes there. Repeat this process for each tab.

Understanding the autonumbering codes

When you're creating autonumbers, you have several building blocks available. Refer to Chapter 22 for lots of examples on how to implement them. But here are the components that you can use:

- ✔ **Text:** You can include regular text in the autonumbering definition. Just type in the text, such as *NOTE:*

- ✔ **A:, B:, C: (series label)** The series label is not printed on your page. It identifies the autonumbering sequence that you're working on as part of a grouping with other series. For example, if your autonumbering definition is B:<n+>, every paragraph tag that uses the series label B: is considered part of the same autonumbering series.

- ✔ **\b or •:** Inserts a bullet in your definition. \b is used on PC and UNIX; • is used on the Mac.

- ✔ **\t:** Inserts a tab into your definition.

  Remember: Don't forget to define a tab stop for the tab or it won't work.

- ✔ **<n>, <n+>, <n=1>:** Inserts an Arabic number (1, 2, 3).

  <n> prints the current value of the counter.

  <n+> increases the counter by 1 and prints that number.

  <n=1> resets the counter to 1 and prints a 1.

- ✔ **<a>, <a+>, <a=1>:** Inserts a lowercase letter (a, b, c).

  <a> prints the current value of the counter.

  <a+> increases the counter by one letter and prints that letter.

  <a=1> resets the counter to a and prints an *a*.

- ✔ **<A>, <A+>, <A=1>:** Same as the <a> sequence, but prints uppercase letters.

- ✔ **<r>, <r+>, <r=1>:** Inserts a lowercase Roman numeral (i, ii, iii).

  <r> prints the current value of the counter.

  <r+> increases the counter by one and prints that number.

  <r=1> resets the counter to 1 and prints *i*.

- ✔ **<R>:** Same as the <r> sequence, but prints uppercase Roman numerals.

- ✔ **< >:** Suppresses display of the counter, but doesn't change the value of the counter.

The empty counter with a space in it is used in complex numbering sequences. Check out Chapter 22 for some examples.

To insert a building block in your autonumbering definition, you can select it from the building blocks list, but typing it in is usually faster.

Deleting Paragraph Tags

When you delete a paragraph tag from your document, you delete it from the paragraph catalog. But this doesn't strip the paragraph tag from the text that you applied it to. (For information on deleting paragraph tags from the entire text, see Chapter 3.)

To delete a paragraph tag from the paragraph catalog, follow these steps:

1. **Display the paragraph catalog (press the ¶ button in the upper-right corner of the window).**

2. **Click the Delete button at the bottom of the window.**

   This displays the Delete Formats from Catalog dialog box.

3. **Select the format that you want to delete and then click the Delete button.**

4. **Repeat this for all the tags you want to delete, and then click Done.**

You cannot undo (Edit⇨Undo) paragraph tag deletion. But if you cancel before clicking Done, no tags are deleted.

Chapter 5

Formatting Inside Paragraphs with Character Tags

• •

In This Chapter

▶ Seeing the difference between paragraph tags and character tags

▶ Understanding the Character Designer

▶ Creating character tags

▶ Sighting character tags

• •

*I*f you just finished Chapter 4, you're probably wondering, "What's left? What more could you possibly say about text?" It's time to introduce you to character tags.

FrameMaker's character tags let you apply formatting to a single word or just a few characters. Unlike paragraph tags, whose properties are always applied to the *entire* paragraph, character tags apply only to selected text. For example, you can use a character tag to italicize a single word within a paragraph. But character tags also let you group more complicated formatting into a single tag. You can, for example, create a character tag that makes text blue, underlined, and small caps. Now this is useful! Instead of having to change the text color, then underline the text, and then apply small caps, you can use a character tag to do the heavy lifting all at once.

Applying Character Tags Using the Character Catalog

ƒ The default FrameMaker template includes the Emphasis character tag, which italicizes text for you. To apply it to some text, select the text, then display the character catalog (press the *f* button in the top right of the FrameMaker window), and click Emphasis. Figure 5-1 shows a character catalog.

Figure 5-1:
The character catalog lists all of the character tags that are currently defined in your document.

So, obviously, to remove Emphasis, you just click it again, right? Nope. That would be intuitive, and FrameMaker is not often intuitive. To remove Emphasis, or any other character tag, make sure the text is selected again, and then click Default Para Font in the character catalog.

The evils of the B, I, and U buttons

The character tags let you italicize a word in a paragraph for emphasis. But why would you make the effort to define a character style and use it for italics, when FrameMaker's QuickAccess bar provides a button for italics? The B, I, and U buttons apply untagged formatting to your files, and untagged formatting is difficult to manage. There are several reasons to use tags:

✔ Your character catalog can be imported into other documents. If you have many writers working on documents that all use the same template, you can define a character format named "book name" that everyone can use for the names of books. Nobody has to go look in the style guide to figure out how to do the formatting — they simply apply the character tag.

✔ The formats in your character catalog are available to various other template components, including cross-reference formats (see Chapter 9), variables (see Chapter 10), and reference pages (see Chapter 15). In many cases, this is the only way to set up character-level formatting in those components.

✔ If you want to make a global change to your character formats, for example, changing from italics to boldface for a specific usage, it's much easier to change a character tag and apply it to various documents than it is to search all the documents for the manual formatting.

Incidentally, the buttons on the QuickAccess bar that let you increase or decrease the font size cause the same override problem.

If you're wondering whether you applied a character tag or not, check the status bar. In the bottom left, it tells you both the current paragraph tag and the current character tag.

Creating a New Character Tag

The Character Designer (select Format➪Character➪Character Designer or Ctrl+D or Command+D) is where you create and modify your character tags. See Figure 5-2.

Character Designer		
Character Tag:	Family: As Is	☐ Underline
Subscript	Size:	☐ Overline
	Angle: As Is	
Apply	Weight: As Is	☐ Strikethrough
To Selection	Variation: As Is	☐ Change Bar
Update All	Color: As Is	☐ Subscript
Formats Tagged:	Spread:	
Subscript	Stretch:	☐ Small Caps
Commands:	Language: As Is	☐ Pair Kern

Figure 5-2:
The
Character
Designer.

Compare the Character Designer to the Paragraph Designer. The Character Designer is basically identical to the Paragraph Designer's Default Font tab. See Chapter 4 for an example.

To create a new character tag, follow these steps:

1. **(Optional) Select some text on which you can "test" your new character tag.**

2. **Display the Character Designer (select Format➪Characters➪ Character Designer).**

3. **Click the Commands drop-down arrow, and select Set Window to As Is from the pop-up menu (see Figure 5-3).**

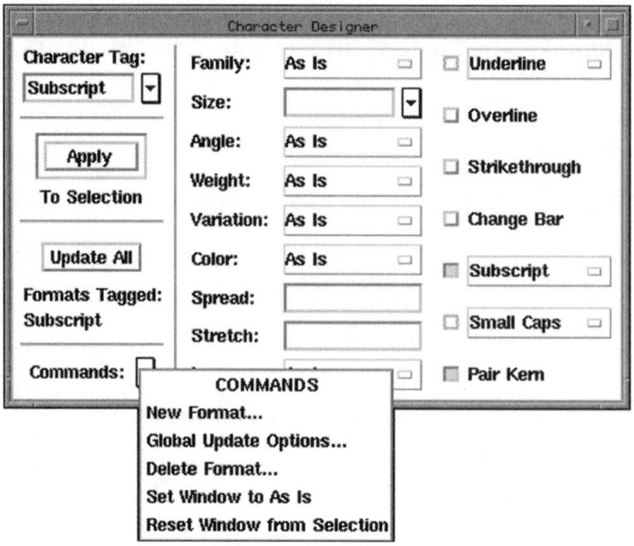

Figure 5-3:
The
Character
Designer
with the
Commands
drop-down
menu
displayed.

4. **Click the Commands drop-down arrow again and select New Format. This displays the New Format dialog box (see Figure 5-4).**

5. **Type a name for the new character tag in the Tag field.**

   Make sure that Store in Catalog is checked (to create the character tag definition in the character catalog). If you want to try out the character tag on selected text, check Apply to Selection. If you didn't select any text in Step 1, don't check Apply to Selection (it won't have any effect).

6. **Click Create.**

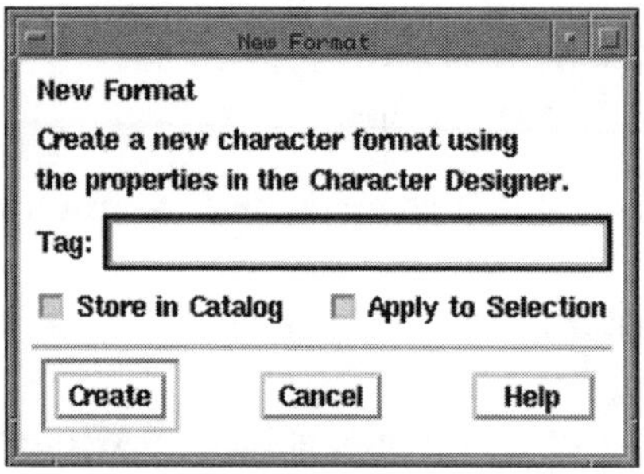

Figure 5-4:
The New
Format
dialog box.

The new character tag now appears in the character catalog. At this point, all your As Is settings disappear. Instead, you see the settings of the currently selected text.

7. **Don't panic; just select your new character tag name in the character tag drop-down list.**

   For some reason, when you first display a tag in the Character Designer, the Character Designer displays the settings of the selected text instead of the settings of the selected character tag. It's annoying, but there you have it.

8. **You're ready to actually do something with your new character tag. Change only those settings that you really need.**

   For example, to create a character tag that underlines text, change the Underline check box from As Is to checked (see the sidebar, "What's checked and what's not").

9. **After making all your changes, select the Update All button.**

The Importance of As Is

Take a look at how the Bold character tag is defined in Figure 5-5. This character tag doesn't work when it's used on a heading. Because the font (Family) and font size are specified, this character tag doesn't just apply boldface; it changes the font and the font size, too!

Specifying the language for a character tag

In FrameMaker 5.5, you can specify the language in a character tag. In previous versions, you could specify the language in a paragraph tag, but not in a character tag. The language setting controls which dictionary (for example, English, German, or Russian) is used to spell-check the text. Dictionaries are important because they are used for spell-checking and to set hyphenation. So, providing character-level language control means that you can mix different languages in a single paragraph and still use hyphenation and spell-checking. If the paragraph tag is labeled English, FrameMaker uses the English dictionary for the paragraph. But perhaps you used some clever French phrases like *bon mot* and *en masse*. If you tag these with a character tag that has the language set to French, FrameMaker uses the French dictionary to hyphenate and spell-check those words.

To make this work, you need to install the dictionary file for every language you're using. Several dictionaries are included on your FrameMaker CD but are not installed by default.

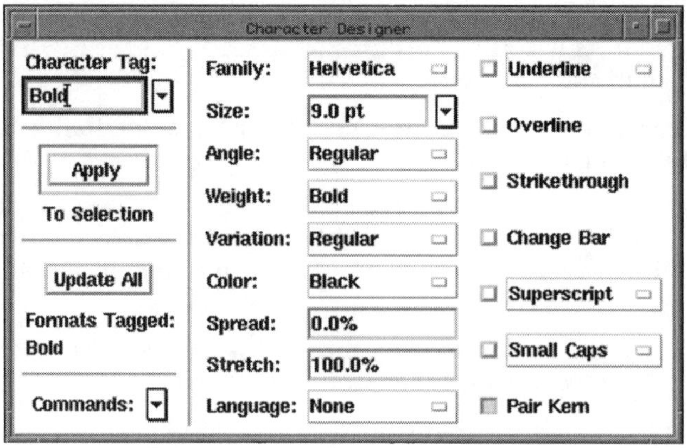

Figure 5-5:
Using As Is
prevents
problems
like this one.

As you can see in Figure 5-5, the character tag works fine when the paragraph's font is the same as what's specified in the Character Designer but looks a little odd when the paragraph's font is different. (Of course, if this is the effect you're looking for, everything's fine.)

But in Figure 5-6, on the other hand, only the weight (Bold) is specified. Every other setting is As Is. This gives you a character tag that only changes the weight of the type. The As Is settings for the other properties preserve the underlying formatting from the paragraph tag.

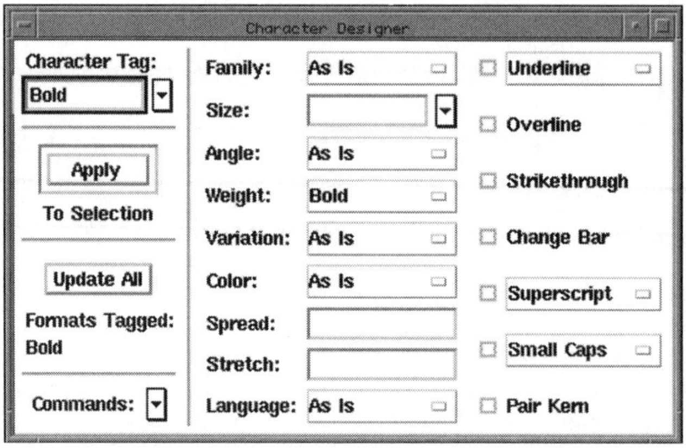

Figure 5-6:
Use As Is to
prevent odd
formatting
problems.
This
character
tag will
apply bold
(and only
bold)
formatting.

What's checked and what's not

In most applications, a check box is either checked (on) or not checked (off). But in FrameMaker, some check boxes have *three* settings: checked, not checked, and As Is (sort of checked?). To make matters worse, these check boxes look quite different on the different platforms:

	Mac	UNIX	Windows
Checked	☒	☐	☑
Unchecked	☐	☐	☐
As Is	⊟	☐	☑

Modifying Existing Character Tags

This process is similar to creating a new character tag, but again, you have to make sure that you get the proper settings displayed in the Character Designer before you proceed:

1. **Display the Character Designer (select Format⇨Characters⇨ Character Designer).**

2. **In the Character Tag drop-down list, select the character tag you want to modify. Do this even if the character tag name already appears in the tag field.**

   You have to reselect the character tag because when you first display the Character Designer, it shows your character tag name, *but not its settings*. Instead, you're going to see the settings of the selected text in your document (if you have any selected).

3. **Modify the character tag settings.**

   Select any of the checkboxes or drop-down lists to change the information.

4. **Click Update All.**

   Your new character tag is ready to go!

Deleting Character Tags

When you delete a character tag from your document, you delete it from the character catalog. But this does not strip the character tag from the text that you applied it to. (For information on deleting character tags from the entire text, see Chapter 3.)

To delete a character tag from the character catalog, display the character catalog (press the *f* button in the upper-right corner of the window) and click the Delete button at the bottom of the window. This displays the Delete Formats from Catalog dialog box. Select the format that you want to delete and then click the Delete button. Repeat this for all the tags you want to delete, then click Done.

You cannot undo (Edit⇨Undo) character tag deletion.

They show up in the strangest places...

Character tags are not just used to format your regular text. Your list of character formats shows up in the most unusual places.

✔ **Autonumbering:** When you set up a paragraph autonumber, you can either use the default paragraph format for the autonumber or a character format. This gives you a lot of formatting options.

✔ **Variables:** Your character tags are also available when you're defining variables. I discuss this in excruciating detail in Chapter 10. By embedding a character tag in the variable definition, you can change the appearance of the variable to be different from the surrounding text.

✔ **Cross-references:** In cross-reference formats, you'll see a phenomenon similar to that in variables. If you simply can't wait to find out more about cross-references, check out Chapter 9.

✔ **Reference pages for generated files:** You'll also see character tags on your *reference pages* (which provide formatting instructions for generated files, such as your table of contents). For all the details, see Chapter 18.

✔ **Index markers:** Character tags will make an appearance in your index markers. Here, Adobe adds insult to injury. Not only do you have to use the infamous <italics> to get the character tag in there, the marker dialog box doesn't even provide you with a way to select from the character catalog. You have to know the name of the tag you want and type it in yourself with angle brackets. There's no validation, so if you type <Italics> instead of <italics>, and your character tag is named *italics,* the result will be no italics. Aaaargh. For the gruesome details, see Chapter 19.

Chapter 6

Inserting Graphics — Anchored Frames Aweigh

In This Chapter

▶ Creating an anchored frame

▶ Importing information

▶ Understanding the drawing tools

▶ Understanding the Graphics menu commands

*P*erhaps you lie awake at night wondering why FrameMaker is called *Frame*Maker. If you do, please seek professional help — or just read this chapter.

In FrameMaker, both text and graphics reside inside containers, which are called *frames*. For example, the text area on your page where you type is called a *text frame* (or text column). Graphics are usually placed inside an *anchored frame*.

Why anchored? It's not a nautical term. When you create a frame for a graphic, you glue (or anchor) that frame to a particular paragraph. This lets you control where the frame (and its contents) are positioned. When the paragraph that contains the anchor moves, the anchored frame also moves. This means that your graphics always move with the text that you anchored them to. (You can also anchor graphics inside a table cell.)

Creating an Anchored Frame

To create an anchored frame, first click in your text where you want the frame to be anchored. Then select Special⇨Anchored Frame. In the Anchored Frame dialog box (see Figure 6-1), select the options you want and then click Create.

Figure 6-1:
The
Anchored
Frame
dialog box.

The first step is to give the anchored frame a height and width.

You can anchor an anchored frame in several different locations. Table 6-1 describes them all.

Table 6-1	Anchoring Positions
Position	*Description*
Below Current Line	Positions the frame on the next line of text. The frame displaces other content.
	Alignment: Sets the horizontal alignment of the frame. You cannot change the vertical alignment.
	Cropped: If checked, the text frame will crop the anchored frame. That is, if the anchored frame is larger than the text frame, any content in the anchored frame that falls outside the text frame is hidden. (If your frame is five inches wide and your graphic is six inches wide, you'll lose an inch of the graphic.)
	Floating: If checked, the frame doesn't have to appear in the same column as the anchor; it can "float" to the next available space (usually at the top of the following page). If not checked, the anchor and the frame are always in the same column. Be careful with floating graphics — they can float to a position far away from their captions!
At Top of Column	Positions the frame at the top of the column that the anchor is in. The frame displaces other content, which flows to the next page.

Position	Description
At Bottom of Column	Positions the frame at the bottom of the column that the anchor is in. The frame displaces other content.
At Insertion Point	Positions the frame inline with the text. The frame displaces other content in the line with the anchor. If your paragraph tags are set to Fixed line spacing (Basic properties), then the frame will overlap content on other lines. If the line spacing is not fixed, then the frame will cause the paragraph's line spacing to increase to accommodate the frame. **Distance above Baseline:** Sets the vertical alignment. A positive distance above baseline moves the frame up the page, a negative setting moves it down.
Outside Column	Positions the frame outside the main text column (could be inside the text frame if you have a side head column). The frame doesn't displace other content; you can move it on top of the text column. **Side:** Sets the alignment of the frame. **Distance above Baseline:** Sets the vertical alignment. A positive distance above baseline moves the frame up the page, a negative setting moves it down. **Distance from Text Frame:** Sets the horizontal position. A positive value creates a gap between the text frame and the anchored frame; a negative value makes the anchored frame overlap the text frame.
Outside Text Frame	Positions the frame outside the text frame. The frame doesn't displace other content; you can move it on top of the text column.
Run into Paragraph	The frame is aligned with the top line in the current paragraph. The rest of the paragraph runs around the frame. **Gap:** Sets the margin between the anchored frame and the text that is run around it.

Once you've figured out where you want to put the table, you need to select an alignment option for it. Table 6-2 describes the various alignment options.

Table 6-2	Alignment options
Alignment	*Description*
Left	Aligns the frame with the left edge of the text frame.
Center	Aligns the frame in the center of the text frame.
Right	Aligns the frame with the right edge of the text frame.
Side Closer to Binding	Aligns the frame with the inside edge of the book (on the right side for even pages, on the left side for odd pages). As the frame is moved from page to page, it changes sides. Available only for double-sided documents.
Side Farther from Binding	Aligns the frame with the outside edge of the book (on the left side for even pages, on the right side for odd pages). As the frame is moved from page to page, it changes sides. Available only for double-sided documents.
Ride Closer to Page Edge	Aligns the frame on the side closer to the edge of the page.
Side Farther from Page Edge	Aligns the frame on the side farther from the edge of the page.

Once you've created your anchored frame, you'll probably want to put it to use. You can use FrameMaker's drawing tools to create a graphic, or you can import an existing graphic into your file.

Importing Information — It's Import-ant!

FrameMaker supports many different graphics formats. The exact list varies by platform; for example, Sun raster images are supported in the UNIX version, PICT images in the Macintosh version, and BMP images in the Windows version. But in addition to the platform-specific formats, a few, such as EPS, are supported on every platform.

To import a graphic into your anchored frame, follow these steps:

1. **Select the anchored frame.**

2. **Select File➪Import➪File to display the Import File dialog box (see Figure 6-2).**

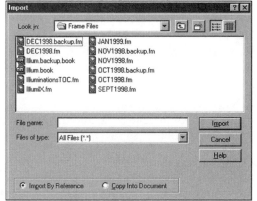

Figure 6-2: The Import File dialog box.

3. **Select the file that you want.**

   Now, you need to make an important decision: Do you import by reference or copy the graphic into the document?

4. **The bottom of the Import File dialog box has two radio buttons; you need to choose one or the other.**

   If you're at a loss, the following two sections will help you determine which button to choose.

Import by reference

When you import by reference, you insert a pointer to the location of the graphic on your system into your FrameMaker file. You don't actually copy the graphic into your FrameMaker document.

Importing by reference has some advantages:

✔ If you update the original graphic, the reference graphic in your FrameMaker file is updated automatically.

✔ Because your FrameMaker files contain only a link to the graphic, your FrameMaker files stay very small. You can import a very large number of graphics by reference without affecting the performance of your FrameMaker files.

> ✔ Because you can see the file path from within the FrameMaker file (select the graphic, then select Graphics➪Object Properties and look at the bottom of the dialog box), maintenance is made easier. You can verify the source file, and then make changes to the file.

But importing a referenced graphic also has some disadvantages:

> ✔ In addition to keeping track of your FrameMaker file, you have to make sure that you keep track of all the referenced graphics. If a graphic is moved, the link to it is broken.
>
> ✔ If you need to transfer your files to another location, you have to make sure that you copy both the FrameMaker file and the imported graphics.

Copy into document

When you copy a graphic into the FrameMaker document, you insert the entire graphic into your FrameMaker file.

Importing by copy has some advantages:

> ✔ All of your graphics are contained in a single file, so you can just ship that one file, which contains all the information you need.
>
> ✔ Because the graphic is copied in, you don't have to worry about losing the external graphic file.

But importing copied graphic also has some disadvantages:

> ✔ If you update the original graphic, you must reimport the graphic to get the update into your FrameMaker file; there is no link to the original graphic.
>
> ✔ Every time you import a graphic and copy it into your FrameMaker file, you increase the file size of your FrameMaker file. If you import many graphics into a FrameMaker file, your file can become unmanageably large. In some cases, the file may become corrupted, and you can lose your graphics.
>
> ✔ If you use the same graphic in several different places in a FrameMaker file, importing by copy will place several copies of that graphic into your FrameMaker file. Importing by reference will insert several pointers to a single external graphic, which is much more efficient. (It takes up less space and, more important, if you update the original graphic, all the places where that graphic is referenced are updated automatically. If you copied it in, you have to update each one manually.)

Which should you choose? That's up to you. If you have very few graphics that are not updated very often, importing by copy is probably fine. If you have a large number of graphics, and you are willing to spend the time to organize a graphic storage system, then importing by reference is probably a better approach.

Understanding the Drawing Tools

Once you create an anchored frame, you can use the drawing tools to draw graphics inside the frame.

FrameMaker offers a fairly standard array of drawing tools. If you plan to create an illustrator's masterpiece, I strongly recommend that you use a dedicated illustration program (such as Adobe's own Illustrator or Macromedia FreeHand) and import the file into FrameMaker. The tools included in FrameMaker are adequate for simple stuff, but they are not going to make any technical illustrator happy.

To access the drawing tools, you need to display the Graphics tools, shown in Figure 6-3. To display the Graphics tools, select Graphics⇨Tools or click the triangle icon in the top-right corner under the paragraph catalog and character catalog icons.

Here, then, is a summary of the tools available.

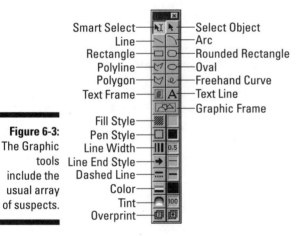

Figure 6-3: The Graphic tools include the usual array of suspects.

Smart Select

The Smart Select pointer is your default pointer. If you place it over text, you can click inside the text and edit the text. If you place it over an object (like an anchored frame), you can select that item. If you want to select a text frame with the Smart Select pointer, hold down the Ctrl (PC), Option (Mac), or Meta (UNIX) key and click.

Line

Line lets you draw lines. Click the Line icon, then click where you want to start the line and click again where you want to end it. If you want to constrain the line to 45-degree increments, hold down the Shift key when you click the end point.

Rectangle

The Rectangle lets you draw rectangles. Click the Rectangle icon, then click and drag to create the rectangle. To create a square, hold down the Shift key while you click and drag.

Polyline

Polyline lets you draw a line with multiple segments. Click the Polyline icon, then click to begin the line and click at each corner point. Double-click to finish the line.

When you first create the polyline, you can move the corner points — until you deselect the polyline. After deselecting the polyline, reselecting it selects the polyline as an object. See Figure 6-4 for an example of each. In object selection mode, you can move and distort the line, but you can't move the corner points individually. If you want to adjust the corner points, select Graphics⇨Reshape.

Figure 6-4:
Polyline in "creation" mode and polyline after being deselected and reselected.

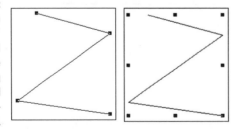

Polygon

You can create a polygon. Click the Polygon icon, and then click to begin the shape and click at each corner point. Double-click to finish the polygon.

The restrictions on corner point movement noted in the Polyline section also apply to polygons.

Text Frame

Text Frame lets you create a new text frame, which is a container for text. Click the Text Frame icon, and then click and drag to create the text frame. When you release the mouse, a dialog box prompts you to specify additional information about the text frame. Depending on whether you're creating a text frame on a body page or a master page, you will see a different dialog box (see Figures 6-5 and 6-6).

Figure 6-5:
Create New Text Frame dialog box (shown when you add a text frame on a body page).

Figure 6-6:
Add New Text Frame dialog box (shown when you add a text frame on a master page).

Table 6-3 gives you the scoop on New Text Frame options.

Table 6-3	New Text Frame Options
Option	*Description*
(Master page only) Text Frame Type⇨Background Text or Template for Body Page Text	Select Background Text to create a text frame for items that you want to put on the master page (such as headers and footers). Select Template for Body Page Text to create a placeholder for information that you want to insert on the body pages that use this master page. You must also select a flow tag; the default is A, which is probably what you'll need.
Columns⇨Number	Specify the number of columns you want in this new text frame.
Columns⇨Gap	Specify the distance between the columns in the text frame. If you only have one column, the gap is irrelevant.

Graphic Frame

Graphic Frame allows you create a graphic (unanchored) frame. Click the Graphic Frame icon, and then click and drag to create the frame. Once you've created it, you can drag it to move it around the page.

Graphic frames are most useful for information you want to put on your master pages (where you don't need an anchored frame).

Arc

The Arc tool lets you create an arc segment. Click the Arc icon, and then click and drag to create the arc. Hold down the Shift key to create an arc that is a circle segment.

Rounded Rectangle

To create a rectangle with rounded corners, use the Rounded Rectangle tool. Click the Rounded Rectangle icon, and then click and drag to create the rectangle. Hold down the Shift key to create a rounded square.

Once you have created the rounded rectangle, you can adjust the roundness of the corners. Click the rectangle, and then select Graphics⏷Object Properties. In the Object Properties dialog box (shown in Figure 6-7), you can change the Corner Radius setting to adjust the rounding. Make the corner radius value larger to make the corners rounder; make it smaller to make the corners sharper.

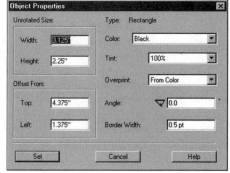

Figure 6-7:
The Object
Properties
dialog box
for a
rounded
rectangle.

Oval

To create an oval, try the Oval tool. Click the Oval icon, and then click and drag to create the oval. You can hold down the Shift key to create a circle.

Freehand Curve

The Freehand Curve tool allows you create a squiggly line by dragging the cursor across the screen. Click the Freehand Curve icon, and then click and drag to create the line.

Text Line

You can insert a text line using the Text Line tool. Click the Text Line icon, click to start the text line, and type the text for the text line.

Once you create a text line, you can stretch and compress the text by dragging the selection handles.

You can apply character formats in a text line, but you cannot use paragraph tags in a text line.

If you plan to convert your FrameMaker files to HTML, use text frames instead of text lines, even for your smallest callouts and other text items. Text lines do not always convert properly.

Fill Style, Pen Style, Line Width, Line End Style, Dashed Line Pattern, Color, Tint, and Overprint

For each of these items, the left side of the palette provides a pop-up menu where you can select the setting you want and modify the default settings. The right side shows the current (or default) setting.

To change the settings for any object, first select that object, and then select the setting you want from the pop-up menu.

The colors available in the Colors pop-up menu are only those colors in your color catalog. For information about creating additional colors, see Chapter 11.

Understanding the Graphics Menu Commands

Once you've created various graphic objects with the drawing tools, you can use the Graphics menu to move them around and line them up.

Group/Ungroup

The Group command lets you group several objects into a single object. To group objects, first select them (Shift-click on all the objects you want) and then select Graphics⇨Group.

The Ungroup command separates grouped objects into their components.

Once you have grouped various objects, they are treated like a single object, which means you can select them in a single click and move them around easily.

Bring to Front/Send to Back

The Bring to Front command moves the selected object in front of other objects on the page.

The Send to Back command moves the selected object behind other objects on the page.

Align

The Align command aligns the selected objects. The object selected last is used as the "reference" object. That is, everything is aligned based on the last item that's selected. Selecting Graphics⇨Align displays the Align dialog box (see Figure 6-8).

Figure 6-8:
The Align
dialog box.

The Align dialog box (see Figure 6-8) can be confusing. The Top/Bottom align section lines up the selected objects on a horizontal axis (see Figure 6-9).

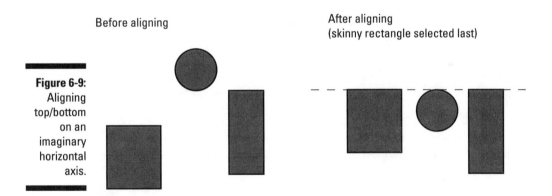

Figure 6-9:
Aligning
top/bottom
on an
imaginary
horizontal
axis.

The Left/Right section aligns the selected objects on a vertical axis (see Figure 6-10).

Distribute

You can set a consistent amount of space between several objects by using the Distribute command. To distribute objects, first select all the objects you want to distribute. Then, select Graphics⇨Distribute to display the Distribute dialog box (see Figure 6-11).

Before aligning

After aligning
(circle selected last)

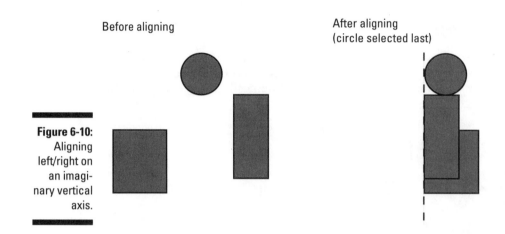

Figure 6-10:
Aligning
left/right on
an imagi-
nary vertical
axis.

Figure 6-11:
The
Distribute
dialog box.

The Vertical Spacing section lets you distribute the objects on a vertical axis (see Figure 6-12).

Before distributing

After distributing

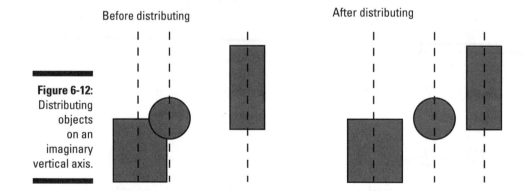

Figure 6-12:
Distributing
objects
on an
imaginary
vertical axis.

The Horizontal Spacing section lets you distribute the objects on a horizontal axis (see Figure 6-13).

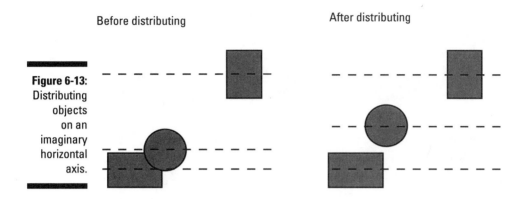

Figure 6-13: Distributing objects on an imaginary horizontal axis.

Reshape

Reshape lets you move the segment points instead of working on the object as a unit. In English, that means that you can change the shape of the object. Normally, when you select an object, you just get four selection points at the four corner and you can use these to stretch the selected object or move it around. But if you want to change the shape of the line, you need to be able to move each point individually, and Reshape lets you do just that. Figure 6-14 shows how the selection changes.

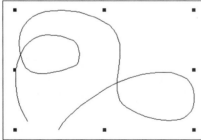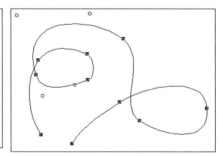

Figure 6-14: A selected object before and after the Reshape command.

Smooth/Unsmooth

Smooth/Unsmooth allows you change points to curves and vice versa.

Flip Up/Down, Flip Left/Right

Flip mirrors the selected object on a horizontal axis (up/down) or vertical axis (left/right). See Figure 6-15 for an example of what this does.

Flip Up/Down

Flip Left/Right

Figure 6-15:
Flipping
objects.

Rotate

You can rotate the selected object by using the Rotate command. You specify
the degree of rotation and the direction (clockwise or counterclockwise) in
the Rotate Selected Objects dialog box (see Figure 6-16).

Figure 6-16:
The Rotate
Selected
Objects
dialog box.

Certain items, such as text in a table, can be rotated only in 90-degree increments. If you select one of those items, then instead of the Rotate dialog box
shown in Figure 6-16, the Rotate Table Cells dialog box is displayed (see
Figure 6-17).

Figure 6-17:
The Rotate
Table Cells
dialog box.

Scale

You can change the size of the selected object, either by specifying a percentage or by changing the width and height settings in the Scale dialog box (see Figure 6-18).

Figure 6-18:
The Scale
dialog box.

Don't use the Scale dialog box to change the size of imported bitmap graphics. For those graphics, use the Set DPI button in the object properties (select Graphics➪Object Properties) instead.

Set # Sides

Create a polygon from a rectangle or oval using the Set # Sides command. In the Set Number of Sides dialog box (see Figure 6-19), specify the number of sides you want for the shape, and the angle at which you want to start the polygon.

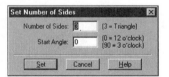

Figure 6-19:
The Set
Number of
Sides dialog
box.

This is a useful little tool for creating triangles, squares, pentagon, hexagons, and more.

Join

If you have two "open" objects (such as lines, polylines, arcs, or freehand curves) and their ends are touching, you can join them to make a single line object. Select both objects, and then select the Join command.

Object Properties

The Object Properties command displays information about the selected object. The exact dialog box you see depends on the object. Figures 6-20 and 6-21 show some variations.

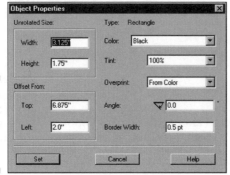

Figure 6-20:
The Object
Properties
for a
rectangle.

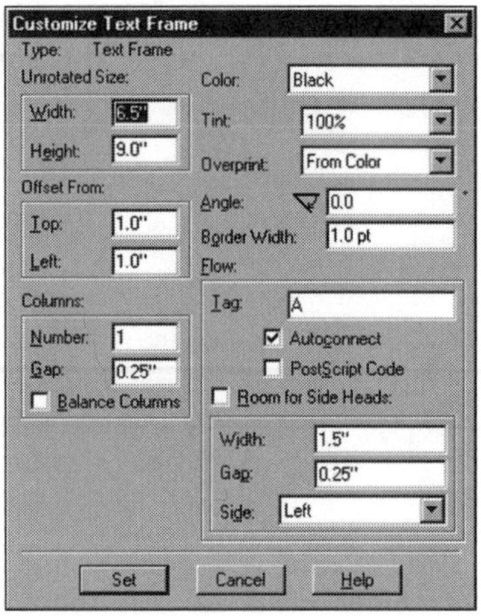

Figure 6-21:
The Object
Properties
for a text
frame.

Runaround Properties

You can set how text flows around graphic objects by using Runaround Properties (see Figure 6-22).

Figure 6-22:
The
Runaround
Properties
dialog box.

Runaround Properties work only for graphics, not for anchored frames.

Here are your options for Runaround Properties:

- ✔ **Run around Contour:** Flows text around the shape of the graphic.

- ✔ **Run around Bounding Box:** Flows text around the rectangle that makes up the box around the graphic.

- ✔ **Don't Run Around:** Doesn't run text around the graphic; text flows on top of the graphic.

Gravity

If checked on the Graphics menu, objects attract! If you move an object close to another object, the force of gravity causes the two objects to touch.

Snap

If you have this option checked, objects that you move will snap to a grid. You can set the size of the grid by selecting View➪Options and adjusting the Snap Grid Size setting.

Chapter 7

Contemplating Your Table

● ●

In This Chapter

▶ Creating tables

▶ Understanding the Table Designer

▶ Creating table definitions

▶ Customizing tables with ruling, shading, straddles, and more

● ●

*A*table is a way to show information in a grid of rows and columns. You can use lines or backgrounds to distinguish rows and columns.

In FrameMaker, the Table Designer gives you control over your table formatting. You can also do some additional formatting outside the Table Designer, for example, by adding new rows and columns, resizing column widths, and customizing individual cells. FrameMaker's table features are integrated into the application (it's not a separate editor), and you get lots of power and flexibility.

Inserting Tables

To create a new table, follow these steps:

1. **Select Table⇨Insert Table, which displays the Insert Table dialog box (see Figure 7-1).**

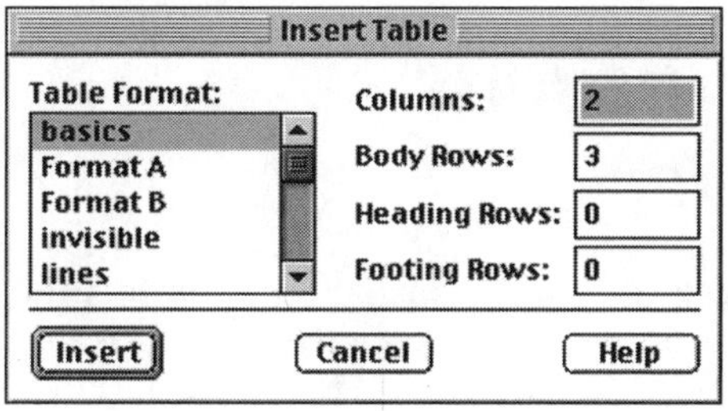

Figure 7-1:
The Insert
Table dialog
box.

Insert Table		
Table Format:	Columns:	2
basics	Body Rows:	3
Format A	Heading Rows:	0
Format B	Footing Rows:	0
invisible lines		
Insert	Cancel	Help

2. **Choose a table format (more on how to set those up later in this chapter).**

3. **Specify the number of rows and columns you want initially. (You can change this later.)**

   Heading Rows are repeated at the top of every page of the table; Footing Rows are repeated at the bottom of every page.

4. **Click the Insert button.**

   This inserts a new table. An anchor appears at your cursor location; this anchor represents the location where the table is anchored to the text. See Figure 7-2 for an example. The anchor means that the table moves with the text that it is anchored to.

You can't nest a table inside another table.

Table anchor

Figure 7-2: Every table has a corresponding anchor.

Here's a quick overview of the basic character formatting features.¶

Table 5: Character Designer quick reference.¶

To apply a character tag§	Select the text that you want to apply the tag to, then click the tag you want in the character catalog.¶ OR Press F8 (PC or UNIX) or command-\ (Mac) and type the first few letters of the character tag, then press Enter.§
To display the Character Designer§	Select the Format menu, then Character, then Designer.¶ OR Press command-D (Mac) or control-D (PC or

End-of-flow symbol in cell

Your new table has paragraph formats already applied to each cell, and columns are set to default widths. The default widths are the widths that you used the last time you saved this particular table format. You can always change the column widths (see the "Now That I Have a Table, How Do I Fix It?" section).

Creating Table Definitions in the Table Designer

The Table Designer lets you create a table format that controls the positioning, lines, and shading in your tables. To display the Table Designer, select the table whose format you want to modify, and then select Table⇨ Table Designer.

The Table Designer looks a little like the Paragraph Designer (see Chapter 4) and includes a list of the table tags (just like paragraph tags) that are available in your document.

You can't set the number of rows and columns, widths of columns, or default paragraph tags in the Table Designer. See the "Things you can't do in the Table Designer" sidebar for more on why. You change these properties manually for each table; see "Now That I Have a Table, How Do I Fix It?" later in this chapter.

Unlike the Paragraph and Character catalogs, FrameMaker doesn't supply a handy button to list the Table Catalog, so you can't display the Table Catalog on its own. However, you can view the Table Catalog in two places: in the Insert Table dialog box (refer to Figure 7-1) or in the Table Designer drop-down list (see Figure 7-3).

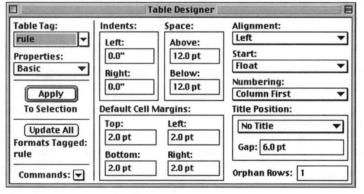

Figure 7-3: Here are the basic properties you can choose in the Table Designer.

Like the Paragraph Designer, the Table Designer has tabs available on the Windows version only. On the Macintosh version, shown in this chapter, and the UNIX version, you must change from one property sheet to another using the Properties drop-down list.

The common items (Apply button, Update All button) on the left side of the Table Designer are identical to those in the Paragraph Designer. See Chapter 4 for more information.

Table 7-1 describes Basic properties in the Table Designer.

Table 7-1	Basic Properties of the Table Designer
Item	**Description**
Indents	Sets the table's indent from the left and right margins.
	If your text column contains room for side heads, your table aligns with the text column if it is narrower than the text column and aligns with the entire column if it is wider than the text column. If you change the width of the table, it can cause the table to "jump" from one position to another, which is extremely disconcerting.
Space: Above, Below	Sets the amount of space above and below the table.
Default Cell Margins	Sets the gap between the edge of the cell and the text inside the cell. You can override these default margins by setting margins in the Table Cell properties of a paragraph tag used inside the table. See Chapter 4 for more information about Table Cell properties in the Paragraph Designer.
Alignment: Left, Center, Right, Side Closer to Binding, Side Farther from Binding	Sets the alignment of the table in the text frame.
Start	Sets where the table begins on the page.
Start: Anywhere	Means that the table can start immediately below the line where it is anchored (this is similar to the Below Current Line setting on an anchored frame — see Chapter 6 for more information).
Start: Top of Column	This setting forces the table to the top of a column. (In a page with more than one text column, this is not always at the top of the page.)
Start: Top of Page	This setting forces the table to the top of the next page.
Start: Top of Left/Right Page	This setting forces the table to the top of the next left or right page.

Item	Description
Start: Float	This setting allows the table to float to the first column that's long enough for the table. When a table is set to Float, the space left empty by moving the table is filled in with text. When you set a table to Top of Page, the space at the bottom of the preceding page is left blank.
Numbering: Row First	Any autonumbered paragraphs in the table number appear like this: 1 2 3 4 5 6
Numbering: Column First	The autonumbering flows like this: 1 3 5 2 4 6
Title Position	Controls whether the table's title appears above the table, below the table, or not at all.
Gap	Controls the space between the table title and the table itself.
Orphan Rows	The number of rows that can appear by themselves on a page. If you set Orphan Rows to 2, the table always puts at least two rows on a page.

Once you've set up your table's Basic properties (like the indents), you're ready to move on to something more exciting. The Ruling properties, shown in Figure 7-4, are described in Table 7-2. Ruling properties let you control where your table has lines and the kind of lines.

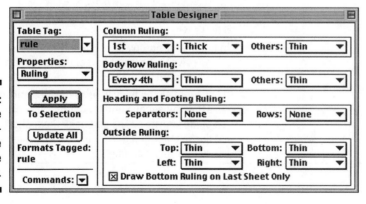

Figure 7-4:
Here are the Ruling properties in the Table Designer.

Table 7-2	Ruling Properties in the Table Designer
Item	*Description*
Column Ruling	Sets the column lines. You can set one column's line to have a different settings from all the others.
	In the first drop-down list (the options there are 1st, 2nd, 3rd, and so on), specify the line that you want to have a different setting (2nd would choose the line to the right of the second column).
	In the second drop-down list, specify the style for the special line.
	In the third drop-down list, specify the type of line for all the other column lines.
	If you want all the column lines to be the same, make sure that the second and third drop-down lists use the same line style. (The setting of the first drop-down list doesn't matter if the second and third drop-down lists use the same setting.)
Body Row Ruling	Sets the row lines. You can establish a repeating pattern of lines for your rows; for example, a thick line every third line, and thin lines everywhere else. This is, of course, *much* more efficient than putting all those lines in manually!
	In the first drop-down list (options are Every 2nd, Every 3rd, Every 4th, and so on), specify how many lines you want in your line pattern. For example, if you want to put a line after every three rows, select Every 3rd.
	In the second drop-down list, specify the line style for the repeating pattern (the line style for every 3rd row, if that's what you chose).
	In the third drop-down list, specify the line style for all the rows that are not part of the Every 2nd, 3rd, 4th, . . . pattern.
	If you want all the body lines to be the same, make sure that the second and third drop-down lists use the same line style.(The setting of the first drop-down list doesn't matter if the second and third drop-down list use the same setting.)

Item	Description
Heading and Footing Ruling	The Separators setting defines the line style for the line that's after the heading rows and before the main table body rows and the one that's after the main table body rows and before the footing rows.
	The Rows setting controls the line style used to separate rows if you have more than one heading row or more than one footing row.
Outside Ruling	Sets the ruling around the outside edge of the table. You can set the top, bottom, left, and right separately.
	Check Draw Bottom Ruling on Last Sheet only if you do not want a ruling at the bottom of the table, except on the last page. If checked, this overrides the setting in the Bottom drop-down list, except on the last page of the table.

Your table is now set up and looks spiffy with lines (ruling) where you want it. Time to jazz it up with some color, so you'll want to move on to the Shading properties, shown in Figure 7-5. Table 7-3 describes the options for the Shading properties.

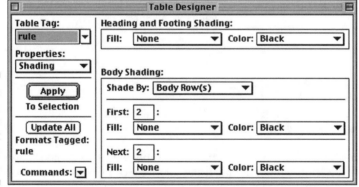

Figure 7-5:
The Shading properties let you get creative with colors.

Table 7-3	Shading Properties in the Table Designer
Item	**Description**
Heading and Footing Shading	Sets the shading for the heading and footing rows. A fill of None makes the color setting irrelevant. To set a fill of solid black, set the fill to 100% and the color to black.

(continued)

Table 7-3 (continued)

Item	Description
Body Shading	Sets the shading pattern for the main body of the table. You can set up a pattern based on columns or on rows and then specify how many times to repeat each fill setting.
	Shade By sets whether you shade rows or columns. You can only pick one.
	First sets the shading for the specified number of rows (or columns, depending on what you set in the Shade By drop-down list). For example, if you type in **3**, the first three rows or columns use the fill and color you specify.
	Next sets the shading for the specified number of rows or columns.
	By combining the First and Next settings, you can set a pattern, for example of two rows of gray followed by three rows of no fill. This pattern (in this case, five rows) repeats throughout the entire table. (And no, you can't set up a shading pattern with more than two variations.) Again, this is a very efficient way of managing your table style, because you don't have to apply the shading to each row manually.

Now That I Have a Table, How Do I Fix It?

Once you've set overall properties for a table with the Table Designer, you may need to refine a particular table further. FrameMaker gives you several different features that let you tweak your table to get it exactly right.

Changing column width

You may not like the default widths that FrameMaker assigns to your columns. To change the width of a column, select a cell in that column (Ctrl+click on the PC; Option+click on the Mac, Meta+click on UNIX). A handle now appears on the right side of the column. Click it and drag it to change the width of the column.

Table ruling and shading examples

When you create a table style with rulings, it helps to keep the following in mind:

✔ For lines between rows, you can set a repeating pattern.

✔ For lines between columns, you can set one line to be different from the rest, but you cannot set a repeating pattern.

The following figures show some table ruling examples. The first figure shows the results of a column ruling where the first column rule is thick and the rest are thin. It also includes body rows that alternate between thick and thin.

The second figure shows a table with no column ruling (all are set to None). Its row ruling has thin lines, but every third line is medium.

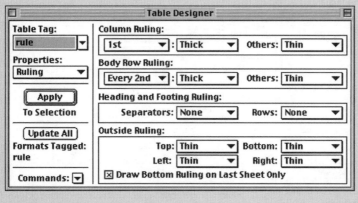

(continued)

(continued)

For table shading (or fills), things get a little more complicated. You can fill with a row-based pattern or a column-based pattern — but not both. For example, you can alternate black and white rows in a table. You can also alternate black and white columns, but you can't do both in the same table. The Shading tab in the Table Designer gives you just one place to define fills. The first figure below shows the Shading tab and a sample definition for rows. The second figure shows the Shading tab again, however this time it has a definition for columns.

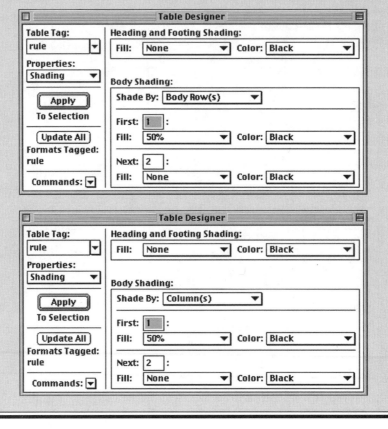

When you change the width of one cell, you change the entire column's width. You can't resize a single cell.

If you need more precise control, you can use a dialog box instead of the handle. Again, select the cell(s) you want to change and select Table⇨Resize Columns. The Resize Selected Columns dialog box (see Figure 7-6) gives you lots of different ways to change column widths.

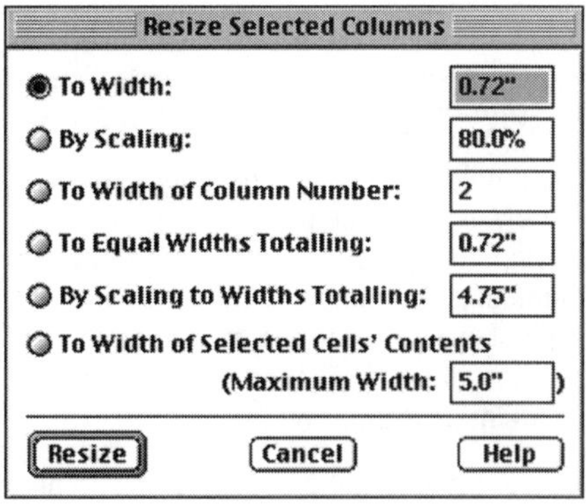

Figure 7-6:
Change
column
widths more
precisely
with the
Resize
Selected
Columns
dialog box.

Resize Selected Columns	
● To Width:	0.72"
○ By Scaling:	80.0%
○ To Width of Column Number:	2
○ To Equal Widths Totalling:	0.72"
○ By Scaling to Widths Totalling:	4.75"
○ To Width of Selected Cells' Contents	
(Maximum Width:	5.0")

[Resize]　　[Cancel]　　[Help]

All of these options change only the *selected* columns. Make sure that you select all the columns you want to change before you resize.

Table 7-4	Table Column Resizing Options
Option	*Description*
To Width	Type in a number. Each selected column is changed to the width you specify. For example, if you select three columns, and type **10 pc** (pica) in the To Width field, each of your three columns is resized to 10 pc wide, for a total width of 30 pc.
By Scaling	Type in a percentage. Your selected columns are scaled accordingly. For example, if you type in **25%**, each column is scaled down to 25 percent (one quarter) of its previous size.
To Width of Column Number	This option is useful if you already have a column that is the proper width. Type in the number of the column whose width you want to copy. Each of the selected columns will be the same width as the specified column. (The column number is counted from the left.)
To Equal Widths Totalling	This option lets you specify a total width for your selected columns. FrameMaker then makes all the columns the same width and fits them into the width you've specified. For example, if you select three columns, and type **6"** in the To Equal Widths Totaling field, each of your columns is resized to 2" wide, for a total width of 6".

(continued)

Table 7-4 *(continued)*

Option	Description
By Scaling to Widths Totalling	You specify a total width for your selected column. FrameMaker fits the column into the width you've specified but preserves the proportions among the columns. (For example, if the first column was two-thirds of the total and the second column was one-third of the total, then the new column widths will maintain that ratio.)
To Width of Selected Cells' Contents	If you want the contents of your cell to be displayed on one line, use this option.

Setting page breaks

Page breaks inside tables are handled differently than page breaks in text. If you put your cursor inside a table and attempt to create a page break (by selecting Special⇨Page Break), the Page Break option is grayed out. So you can't create a page break by changing the paragraph tag's settings (for more on setting page breaks in regular text, see Chapter 4). Instead, you have to set the page break to fall between rows.

You can't put a page break inside a table cell. Page breaks always fall between table cells.

Here are the steps to set a page break:

1. **To set a page break, click in the row that you want at the top of the page (not in the last row of the preceding page) and select Table⇨ Row Format.**

   Doing so displays the Row Format dialog box.

   By default, the Start Row drop-down list is set to Anywhere.

2. **To set a page break, change this selection to Top of Page.**

3. **Click Set.**

   The selected row is moved to the beginning of the next page.

Keeping rows together

If you want to make sure that a particular set of rows always stays together, you can set rows to keep with the next or previous row. To do so, select the row you want to "glue" and select Table⇨Row Format. Check Keep with Next Row or Keep with Previous Row, and click Set. This is useful if you want sections of your table to stay on the same page.

In the Table Designer, you can set a minimum number of rows to keep together in the Orphan Rows field. This prevents those lonesome table rows from being orphaned at the top of the last page.

Setting minimum and maximum row height

By default, each row in your table has a minimum height of zero and a maximum height of 14 inches. For most documents, these defaults work well. But if you want to change the minimum and maximum height for a row, you can. Select the row, then select Table⇨Row Format, and type the new values in the Minimum Height and Maximum Height fields. Click Set to apply these new values to the selected row(s).

Here's another FrameMaker annoyance. If your maximum height is smaller than the space required to display the information in the table, the extra content disappears!

Fortunately, once you figure out what happened, it's easy to fix. Just go back to the Row Format dialog box (select Table⇨Row Format) and increase the maximum height. See Figure 7-7.

I strongly recommend that you leave the default row height maximum (14"), which should be plenty for a regular page size. Changing the row height minimum, on the other hand, can be useful to make all your rows look even, and doesn't cause bizarre disappearing text problems.

Straddling (merging) cells

Straddling, or merging, cells lets you combine two (or more) adjacent cells. This lets you produce some interesting effects, like the one shown in Figure 7-8.

To straddle two cells, select them and then select Table⇨Straddle. The cells must be next to each other. Once you've straddled the cells, the straddled group behaves like a single cell.

To unstraddle a straddled group, select the straddled cell and then select Table⇨Unstraddle.

Figure 7-7:
Yikes! The
text
vanished
(top).
Changing
the row
height maxi-
mum makes
the text
come back
(bottom).

	heading row	
	There's lots of important information in this cell. Unfortunately, you can't see	
	footing row	

	heading row	
	There's lots of important information in this cell. Unfortunately, you can't see some of it, because the Maximum Row Height was too small.	
	footing row	

Figure 7-8:
An example
of a
straddled
heading in a
table.

The four most important food groups	
	Chocolate
	Chocolate
	Chocolate
	Chocolate
Other, less important food groups	
	Vegetables
	Grains

I need a line and a color riiiight here . . .

The table styles you create in the Table Designer give you global control over the pattern of your table's ruling and shading. But in some cases, you may need lines and fills that don't match the pattern. FrameMaker gives you the ability to set custom ruling and shading, which overrides the settings in the table style. To apply custom ruling or shading, first select the cell(s) that you want to customize. Then select Table⇨Custom Ruling & Shading to display the Custom Ruling and Shading dialog box (see Figure 7-9). Select the new settings and click Apply. Table 7-5 shows your options in the dialog box.

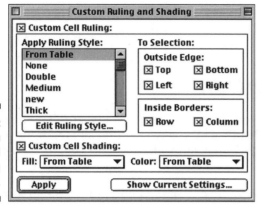

Figure 7-9:
The Custom
Ruling and
Shading
dialog box.

Table 7-5	Custom Ruling and Shading Options
Option	*Description*
Custom Cell Ruling	If checked, the custom ruling is applied to the selected cells.
Apply Ruling Style	Select the rule that you want to apply.
To Selection/Outside Edge	Each check box is a side of the rectangle made by your selection in the table. If you selected only one cell, this is the exterior of that cell. If you selected a group of cells, this is the outside edge of that cell grouping.
To Selection/Inside Borders	The inside borders are the lines that are inside your selection. You have inside borders only if you selected two or more cells.
Edit Ruling Style	Click to change the appearance of the selected ruling style.
Custom Cell Shading	If checked, the custom shading is applied to the selected cells.
Fill	Selects a fill percentage.
Color	Selects the color you want to fill with. (You can define new colors in the color catalog; see Chapter 11 for details.)
Show Current Settings	Shows the settings of the currently selected block and whether the settings are part of the table format ("From Table") or part of a custom ruling or shading. If it's a custom setting, this dialog box tells you which cell the customization is from.

The From Table setting strips any custom formatting and applies the formatting defined in the table's style.

Continuing Education

If your table is more than one page long, you might want to put the word *(continued)* after the table title on the second, third, and following pages. FrameMaker's Table Continuation variable makes this simple. Follow these steps:

1. **Position your cursor at the end of the table title on the first page of the table.**

   You can select the table title on the *first* page of the table only. (The same is true for table header and table footer rows.)

2. **Select Special⇨Variable to display the Variable dialog box.**

3. **Select Table Continuation and click Insert.**

   You don't see much of a change on page 1 of your table, but look at the next page. The word *(continued)* now appears at the end of the table title, as shown in Figure 7-10.

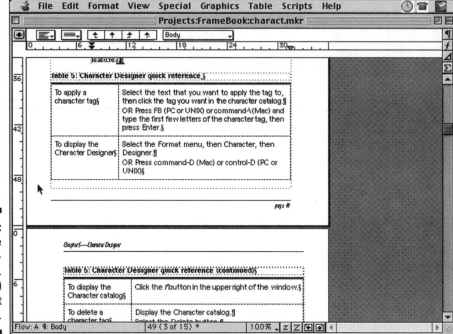

Figure 7-10: An example of table continuation . . . (continued) on the next page.

Things you can't do in the Table Designer

Although the Table Designer offers a way to set many table attributes, several are not available in the Table Designer. These are

- ✔ Number of rows and columns
- ✔ Column widths
- ✔ Default paragraph tags for each cell
- ✔ Default paragraph tag for the table title

I call these *implicit* properties — as opposed to the properties that you set explicitly in the Table Designer. (No, this is not the R-rated part of the book. Keep looking.)

Although you can't set implicit properties with the Table Designer, FrameMaker offers a sneaky way to set their defaults. Selecting Update All in the Table Designer updates your table tag and applies the settings to all tables with that tag. But selecting Update All also updates the default values for rows and columns, column widths, and default paragraph tags for that particular table tag. In other words, FrameMaker saves the currently selected table's settings for

these items as the default when you select Update All. When you create a new table, the default settings are used.

You'll find a critical difference between these default settings and the settings in the Table Designer. If you change the basic, ruling, or shading settings for a table tag and select Update All, the new settings are applied to every table in your document with that table tag, so you can change the appearance of many tables all at once. The implicit properties that are listed earlier, however, are not applied when you select Update All. You cannot use Update All to change the number of rows or columns, the column width, or the default paragraph tags for your tables.

If you have a lot of tables in your document that use similar settings, you can save a lot of time by formatting your first table perfectly and making sure you select Update All in the Table Designer to save the implicit properties. That way, whenever you create a new table, you'll get the most common settings as your default.

Adding More Rows and Columns

Although you start with a specific number of rows and columns, you aren't stuck with those . . . you can add rows and columns later. To add more rows and columns to a table, follow these steps:

1. **Position your cursor where you need the new rows or columns.**

2. **Select Table⇨Add Rows & Columns to display the Add Rows or Columns dialog box (see Figure 7-11).**

   You can use this dialog box to add more body rows and columns or to add "special rows" (for headers and footers).

   If you're adding body rows or columns, you can add rows above or below your current location or add columns to the left or right of your current location.

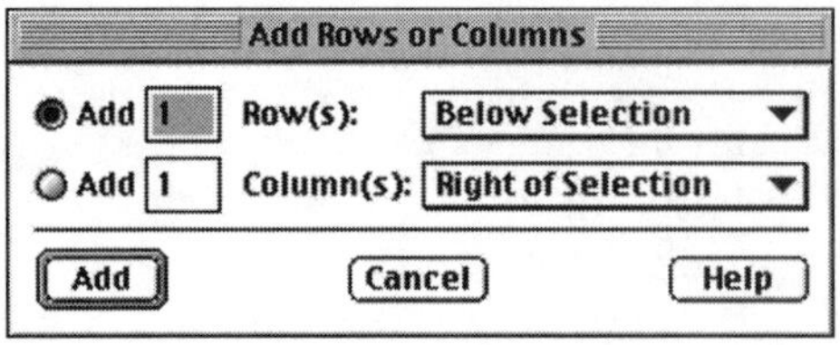

Figure 7-11:
You can add regular rows and columns or more heading rows.

Add Rows or Columns

● Add `1` Row(s): [Below Selection ▼]

○ Add `1` Column(s): [Right of Selection ▼]

[Add]　　[Cancel]　　[Help]

3. **Select the item you want from the drop-down lists and then click Add.**

   You can't add rows and columns simultaneously.

Creating Table Headings and Footers

Your tables can have *heading rows,* rows that are repeated at the top of every page of the table. Table footer rows are just like table heading rows but are repeated at the bottom of every table instead of the top. When you first create the table, you can specify how many heading and footing rows you want (refer to Figure 7-1).

If you want to add heading rows to a table, put your cursor in the table and select Table⇨Add Rows & Columns. In the Add Rows drop-down list, select To Heading. Then click Add to add the new heading row to your table. You can have as many heading rows as you want.

You can edit heading and footing rows on the *first* page of the table only.

To add footing rows, follow the same process, but select To Footing. You can have as many footing rows as you want.

Creating Table Footnotes

Footnotes are supported in tables just like in regular text. To create a table footnote, put your cursor where you want the reference, then select Special⇨Footnote. A new footnote is created at the bottom of your table and your cursor jumps to it. You can now type in the contents of the footnote.

FrameMaker automatically manages the footnote labels for you. That is, you don't have to worry about making sure that the footnotes are numbered properly.

Can I convert a body row to a heading row?

No. If you have text in a body row that you want to use as a heading row, you'll need to insert a heading row and then copy and paste the infor- mation from the existing body row to the new heading row.

By default, footnotes in tables are alphabetical; you can change this as follows:

1. **Put your cursor anywhere inside the table.**

2. **Select Format⇨Document⇨Footnote Properties to display the Table Footnote Properties dialog box.**

   If the regular Footnote Properties dialog box is displayed, your cursor is not in a table. Move it to a table and try again.

3. **Make the changes you want and click Set.**

You can't control the numbering of the table footnote by changing the format- ting of the TableFootnote paragraph format. You have to use the formatting options in the Table Footnote Properties dialog box.

Converting Text to Tables

You can convert existing text to a table. Of course, it helps if the text has some structure to it. For example, if each line of text represents a row, and the cells are marked by commas (this is usually called comma-delimited text), FrameMaker can easily convert the text to a table.

To convert text to a table, select the text, and then select Table⇨Convert to Table. This displays the Convert to Table dialog box (see Figure 7-12).

Set up the conversion options to reflect your text and then click Convert.

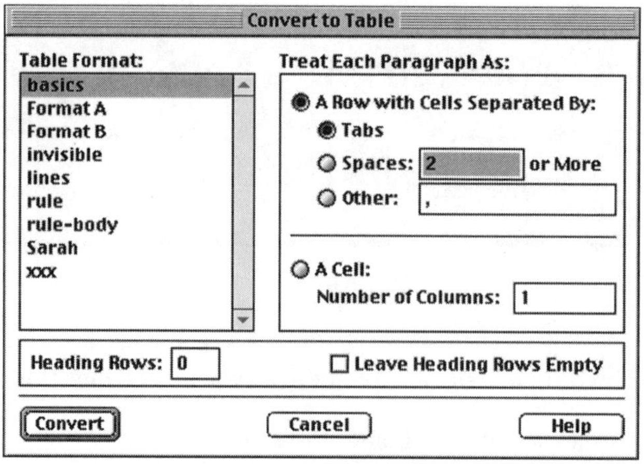

Figure 7-12:
The Convert
to Table
dialog box.

Sorting Table Information

You can sort a table's contents in ascending or descending order. To sort a table, follow these steps:

1. **Click in the table you want to sort.**

   If you want to sort only part of a table, then select the portion you want to sort. If you change your mind and decide to sort the entire table, select the Select All Body Rows button in the Sort Table dialog box (displayed after the next step).

2. **Select Table⇨Sort to display the Sort Table dialog box.**

   You can sort either by row or by column. If you sort by row, the rows are kept together and you pick a column to use for the sort. The opposite is true for a column sort.

3. **Select the type of sort you want.**

4. **In the Sort By area, select the column or row you want to use to rearrange the table information and select an ascending or descending sort.**

   For a row sort, you specify a column to sort on. For a column sort, you specify a row to sort on.

5. **(Optional) You can use the Then By sections to do second- and third-level sorting.**

For example, you could sort by last name and then by first name. Once the last names were sorted, the rows with identical last names would be sorted by first name.

6. **If you want the capitalization of words considered during the sort, check the Consider Case check box. Otherwise, FrameMaker ignores the case (which means that adams and Adams are equivalent).**

7. **Select the Sort button. This sorts the table.**

Converting tables from Word

When you import content from Microsoft Word into FrameMaker, the table formatting from the Word file is converted to FrameMaker. But instead of showing up as a table format, all the Word formatting is converted to custom table formatting. To make the table look right, you have to apply the proper table style, select the entire table, and apply the From Table setting to everything. Follow these steps:

1. **Click anywhere inside the table.**

2. **Display the Table Designer (select Table⇨Table Designer).**

3. **In the Table Tag field, select the table style you want.**

4. **Click Apply and close the Table Designer.**

5. **Select the entire table (Ctrl+triple-click in it).**

6. **Display the Custom Ruling and Shading dialog box (select Table⇨Custom Ruling & Shading).**

7. **Set every attribute in this dialog box to From Table and make sure that all check-boxes are selected.**

8. **Click Apply and close the Custom Ruling and Shading dialog box.**

You now have a well-behaved, well-formatted table.

Part III

Making FrameMaker Do the Heavy Lifting

The 5th Wave   By Rich Tennant

"It says, 'Seth - Please see us about your idea to wrap newsletter text around company logo. Production.'"

In this part . . .

This is where the fun starts! This part discusses FrameMaker's master pages, cross-references, variables, and color. Once you've mastered these features, you'll see how to design FrameMaker templates, how to produce output for any medium, and how to use a couple of advanced features: reference pages and conditional text.

By the time you finish this part, you'll be ready for action!

Chapter 8

Mastering Page Layouts

· ·

In This Chapter

▶ Getting around in the master pages

▶ Changing master page items

▶ Adding master page items

▶ Creating new master pages

· ·

*F*rameMaker's page layout capabilities, though difficult to use, are extremely powerful. (That sounds like a fine motto for the entire product: "Difficult, but powerful." I'll ask Adobe Marketing about it.)

You control page layouts using *master pages*. A master page is basically a skeleton for your regular pages *(body pages)*. They usually include a container for headers and footers and the main body text (you insert the text itself on the body pages, but you set up the container on the master pages). You can add graphics, lines, multiple columns, and other items to your master pages.

Every FrameMaker document has at least a Right master page. If your document is double-sided, you also have a Left master page. You can modify the Left and Right master pages, but you can't delete or rename them. By default, the Left master page is applied to all even pages and the Right master page to all odd pages. (In a single-sided document, the Right master page is applied to every page and there is no Left master page.)

You can create up to 100 different master pages in a single document. For an average template, you'll probably need between three and ten master pages.

Getting Around in the Master Pages

To work with the master pages in your current document, you need to display them. Select View⇨Master Pages to switch from your default body page view to the master pages.

When you go to the master pages, the status bar changes slightly. The page number area displays the name of the current master page. Instead of indicating the current body page out of all the body pages in the file (for example, 3 of 10), the status bar now indicates the name of the current master page and the current master page out of all of the master pages in the file (Right 1 of 4).

Click the master page name to display a dialog box that lets you rename the master page. But remember, you can only rename custom master pages. You can't rename the default Left or Right master pages.

Applying a Custom Master Page to a Body Page

By default, all your body pages use the Right master page, or, if your default is double-sided, the Left and Right master pages. But you can apply a custom master page to a particular page. To do so, follow these steps:

1. **Select Format⇨Page Layout⇨Master Page Usage.**

   This displays the Master Page Usage dialog box.

2. **In the Use Master Page section at the top, select the master page you want to use from the Custom drop-down list.**

   This automatically selects the Custom radio button.

3. **In the Apply To section at the bottom, select the page or pages to which you want to apply this master page.**

   The default is the current page, but you can select a range of pages and even select only the odd or even pages within a range.

4. **Click Apply.**

Changing Master Page Items

You can change the items on your master pages in many ways. For example, you can make your body text column shorter (Ctrl+click or Option+click to select it, then drag the selection handle at the bottom up), you can delete a header (Ctrl+click or Option+click to select it and then press Delete), or you can add new items to the master page.

You can also type new information in your headers and footers. Anything you put in the header or footer will be displayed on every page that uses this master page.

If you want to put information on your master pages that changes based on the information on the body page (for example, page numbers and running headers), you need to use system variables. See Chapter 10 for details on how to do this.

 In a double-sided document, you have two default master pages — Left and Right. Don't forget to change both; otherwise, the change will appear only on half your body pages! (In some cases, of course, you'll want to make changes on only one page.)

Adding Master Page Items

You can add different types of items in different ways. The next few sections give you an overview of what to do with different kinds of new content.

Imported graphics

Chapter 6 stresses the importance of using anchored frames when you insert graphics into your documents. On master pages, however, you don't need anchored frames. The primary purpose of the anchored frame is to make sure that the contents of the frame move along with the frame's anchor. (For example, if you have a graphic that belongs with a particular piece of text, you want them to stay together, and you need an anchored frame for that.) When you put a graphic on a master page, you generally want it to stay put in a particular location, so you don't need an anchored frame. (For example, you might want to put a logo at the top of every page, so you place it there on the master page.)

But importing without an anchored frame can be a little tricky. Before you try to import the graphic, make sure that you click outside the text frame on the master page to make sure that the cursor is not in your master page's text column. (Information that is in the master page's main text column isn't displayed on the body pages, because the main text column is a placeholder for the text on the body pages.) Then, you can import the graphic as usual. The graphic is dropped onto the page without a frame.

FrameMaker graphics

You can use FrameMaker's graphics tools to draw on the master pages. Any art you put on the master pages will appear on the corresponding body pages. For example, you might need thumb tabs along the right edge of your right-hand pages. You could draw a black box along the right edge of your Right master page (and maybe even create some white text to put inside it). See Chapter 6 for details on how to work with FrameMaker's graphics features.

Text frames

You can create two kinds of text frames on a master page: text frames that display information on the background of the body pages and text frames that let you insert content into them on the body pages. Confusing? Just think of headers and footers — they are background items — and the main text column — which is a placeholder for information that you insert on the body pages. You can select background items on the master pages but not on the body pages.

To create a new text column on the page, follow these steps:

1. **Click the Text Column tool on the Graphics toolbar.**

2. **Click and drag the text column cursor (a little crosshair) to create a new text column.**

   When you release the mouse, you're prompted to specify what kind of text column this is (see Figure 8-1).

3. **Select the type of text item that you want. You have two choices:**

   ✔ **Background Text:** Select the Background Text radio button to put information into this text frame on the master page and have the content displayed (but not editable) on the body pages.

   ✔ **Template for Body Page Text:** Select Template for Body Page Text to display this text column as an empty, editable frame on the body pages. Leave the default flow tag, A, unless you have multiple flows in your document. (See "I need two separate text flows" later in this chapter for an example of multiple flows.)

   When you create a new body text column, that new text column is connected to the end of the existing text column on that page. This means that once the first text column is filled with content, the content flows into the new column automatically.

Figure 8-1:
You can
choose the
kind of text
column in
the Add
New Text
Frame
dialog box.

```
┌─────────────────────────────────────────────────┐
│ ─              Add New Text Frame            ↑ □ │
├─────────────────────────────────────────────────┤
│ Add New Text Frame                               │
│ To Master Page: Right                            │
│ Text Frame Type:                                 │
│ ┌─────────────────────────────────────────────┐ │
│ │ ◆ Background Text (for headers, footers, and │ │
│ │   so on)                                     │ │
│ │ ◇ Template for Body Page Text Frame:         │ │
│ │    Flow Tag: [A    ] [▼]                     │ │
│ └─────────────────────────────────────────────┘ │
│ Columns:                                         │
│ ┌─────────────────────────────────────────────┐ │
│ │ Number: [1          ]  Gap: [18.0 pt       ] │ │
│ └─────────────────────────────────────────────┘ │
│ [  Add  ]        [ Cancel ]        [  Help  ]    │
└─────────────────────────────────────────────────┘
```

Text frames don't have to flow from left to right, top to bottom. By default, text frames flow in the order that they were *created*. You can easily create a page where text flows from a frame at the bottom of the page to a frame at the top. However, within a frame, text always flows from top to bottom and left to right.

After you create a new text column by drawing it on the page, you can align it precisely and change several of its properties. Select the text column and then select Format⇨Customize Layout⇨Customize Text Frame (or right-click the text column and select Object Properties). This displays the Customize Text Frame dialog box, shown in Figure 8-2.

Figure 8-2:
You can
change
properties
of a text
column in
the
Customize
Text Frame
dialog box.

```
┌─────────────────────────────────────────────┐
│              Customize Text Frame             │
├───────────────────────────────────────────────┤
│ Customize Text Frame                          │
│ Unrotated Size:          Type: Text Frame     │
│   Width:  [510.0 pt]     Color: [Black    ▢]  │
│   Height: [370.0 pt]     Tint:  [100%     ▢]  │
│                          Overprint: [From Color ▢] │
│ Offset From:             Angle:  ▽ [0.0]   °  │
│   Top:  [64.0 pt]        Border Width: [1.0 pt] │
│   Left: [15.0 pt]        Flow:                │
│ Columns:                  Tag: [A]            │
│   Number: [1]              ☐ Autoconnect      │
│   Gap:   [18.0 pt]         ☐ PostScript Code  │
│   ☐ Balance Columns       ☐ Room for Side Heads: │
│                             Width: [108.0 pt] │
│                             Gap:   [18.0 pt]  │
│                             Side:  [Left  ▢]  │
│   [Set]        [Cancel]          [Help]       │
└───────────────────────────────────────────────┘
```

Table 8-1 describes the properties you can set in the Customize Text Frame dialog box.

Table 8-1	Customize Text Frame Properties
Item	*Description*
Width	Sets the width of the text frame.
Height	Sets the height of the text frame.

Continued

Table 8-1	Customize Text Frame Properties
Item	*Description*
Offset From: Top	Sets the offset from the top of the page (or the top of the frame, if the text frame is inside a frame).
Offset From: Left	Sets the offset from the left edge of the page (or the left edge of the frame, if the text frame is inside a frame).
Columns: Number	Sets the number of columns inside the text frame. Columns set this way are always the same width (see "What about uneven columns?" later in this chapter for information on how to set up columns with different widths).
Columns: Gap	Sets the gap (or gutter) between the columns in the text frame.
Columns: Balance Columns	If *not* checked, FrameMaker fills the first column completely and then fills the second one, and so on. If checked, FrameMaker distributes the content across all of the columns on the page evenly.
Color	Sets the background color of the text frame. To set a color, you need to select the text frame and set the fill using the Graphics toolbar. After you do that, you can set the color either using the Graphics toolbar or with this option.
Tint	Sets the tint of the color specified.
Overprint	Sets the overprint settings for the text frame's color. The default, From Color, means that the overprint settings are retrieved from the color definition (see Chapter 11 for more information).
Angle	Sets the angle (or rotation) of the text frame. The default is 0 degrees. Handy if you want to splatter *DRAFT* diagonally across your document in very large letters!
Border Width	Sets the width of the border around the text frame. (Note that a pen setting must be specified in the Graphics palette for this border to take effect.) You can't set a border color that is different from the color of the text frame's background.
Flow: Tag	The flow tag of the text frame. The default is A, with the Autoconnect check box checked. Unless you have a very complicated document with multiple flows, you don't need to change this setting.

Item	*Description*
Flow: Autoconnect	If checked, content in this text frame automatically flows to the next available text frame that has the same flow tag (usually A). This option is checked by default and generally shouldn't be changed.
Flow: PostScript code	If checked, the contents of the text frame are included in a PostScript file as code. The information in the text frame is displayed on-screen but isn't printed. Instead, the PostScript code is interpreted (by the printer or by Acrobat Distiller if you're creating a PDF file). This is a very advanced feature. Refer to the FrameMaker documentation for more information.
Flow: Room for Side Heads	If checked, this text frame and those connected to it leave space for side head information. See Chapter 4 for more information about side heads or see "Wanna a side head?" later in this chapter.
Flow: Room for Side Heads: Width	The width of the area set aside for side heads.
Flow: Room for Side Heads: Gap	The gap (or gutter) between the side head area and the main text area.
Flow: Room for Side Heads: Side	The location of the side heads. Left or Right means that the side head is always on the specified side of the page. Side Closer to Binding positions the side head area on the right side of even pages and the left side of odd pages (toward the interior of a double-sided book). Side Farther from Binding does the exact opposite.

Changing how the text flows from column to column

If you need to rearrange the order in which columns are connected, you must first disconnect them and then reconnect them in the order you want.

1. **Select a column that needs to be moved in the sort order (Ctrl+click on PC, Option+click on Mac, Meta+click on UNIX). Then select Format⇨Customize Layout⇨Disconnect Both.**

   You'll be warned that this converts the frames (the selected one and the ones connected to it) to untagged flows.

2. **Click OK.**

   Now, you have frames on your page that aren't connected. You need to retag them in the correct order.

3. **Select the first frame in the flow, and select Format⇨Customize Layout⇨Customize Text Frame.**

4. **In the Flow Tag field, type A and check the Autoconnect box underneath the Flow Tag field.**

   This restores the A flow tag (which is the default). Text columns that are autoconnected will flow from one column to the next as the content is filled in. Now, you need to connect the first column to the second.

5. **Select the first column and then add the second column to your selection (Shift+Ctrl+click on PC, Shift+Option+click on Mac, Shift+Meta+click on UNIX). Then select Format⇨Customize Layout⇨Connect Text Frames.**

   If you can't tell that both frames are selected, don't panic. You won't always see the selection handles around both text frames (especially if you're working in the Windows version).

6. **Repeat this process with the second and third, third and fourth, and so on, until you have connected all the frames on the page in the proper order.**

Splitting a text frame

Instead of creating new text frames and connecting them, you can take an existing text frame and split it into two. The split frames are still connected, but you now have two separate text frames that you can move around on the page independently. To split a text frame:

1. **Place your cursor in the frame near where you want the split.**

2. **Select Format⇨Customize Layout⇨Split Text Frame.**

   The text frame is split into two text frames.

Creating New Master Pages

You can create a new master page from scratch or by basing it on an existing master page. It's usually faster to start with whatever master page is the closest match and then make changes as necessary.

To create a new master page, follow these steps:

1. **Go to the master pages (choose View⇨Master Pages).**

2. **Create a new master page (choose Special⇨Add Master Page).**

   Give the master page a descriptive name. Some examples include TitlePage, CopyrightPage, First, FirstAlternate, FrontMatterLeft, and GlossaryRight.

Choose the current master page that most closely resembles the new page as a starting point, or select Empty if none of the existing pages are similar.

Specify the number of columns that you want on this master page and the gap (or gutter) between the columns.

3. **Click Add to create the new master page.**

Having Fun with Master Pages

You can do all sorts of interesting and slightly twisted things with master pages. Here are a few of the more interesting ones.

Wanna add a side head?

Side heads are headings that appear in the margin and align with the body text. To make side heads work, you need to set up your main text flow to accommodate them and also set up your paragraphs as side heads.

To set up your default text flow for side heads, select Format⇨Page Layout⇨ Column Layout. This displays the Column Layout dialog box (see Figure 8-3).

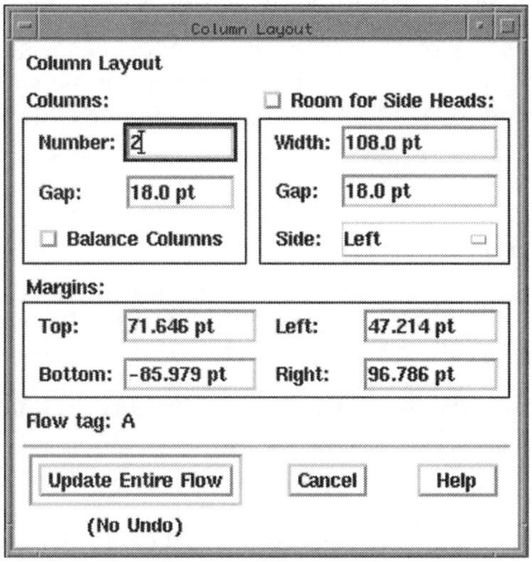

Figure 8-3:
The Column
Layout
dialog box.

Column Layout	
Columns:	☐ **Room for Side Heads:**
Number: 2	Width: 108.0 pt
Gap: 18.0 pt	Gap: 18.0 pt
☐ Balance Columns	Side: Left
Margins:	
Top: 71.646 pt	Left: 47.214 pt
Bottom: -85.979 pt	Right: 96.786 pt
Flow tag: A	
[Update Entire Flow] [Cancel] [Help]	
(No Undo)	

Check the Leave Room for Side Heads box and set the side head area. The width is the width of the side head area and the gap is the space between the side head area and the main text flow area. The width and the gap are taken out of the space allocated for the text frame. The Side setting lets you control where the side head appears on the page. You can set it to always appear on a particular side, or alternate to keep the side head on the interior side or exterior side of the page.

If you move the text frames on your master pages so that the margins on the Left and Right master pages are different, you cannot use the Column Layout dialog box. Instead, you need to select a text frame on your body pages; select Graphics⇨Object Properties and set the room for side heads there.

After you set up your text frame to leave room for the side head, you can set up different paragraph tags to use the side head area. See Chapter 4 for more information.

I need a rotated page

You can have both portrait and landscape pages in a single document. To make this work, you need both portrait-oriented and landscape-oriented master pages to work with.

Most often, you'll start with a portrait document and add landscape pages. To set up the master pages, follow these steps:

1. **Go to the master pages (select View⇨Master Pages).**

2. **Create a new master page based on your default Right master page.**

   See "Creating a new master page" earlier in this chapter for step-by-step instructions on how to do this. If your document is double-sided, you need to repeat this entire procedure for the Left master page.

3. **Name the new page RotatedRight.**

4. **Rotate the entire page (select Format ⇨Customize Layout⇨ Rotate Page Clockwise).**

   Now, you have a rotated page, but the text is still flowing in a portrait direction. Next, you have to rotate the main text frame. The headers and footers stay in the portrait direction.

5. **Select the main text frame (Ctrl+click on PC, Option+click on Mac, or Meta-click on UNIX).**

6. **Rotate the main text frame (select Graphics⇨Rotate).**

   Now that the frame is rotated, you have it aligned properly, but you need to swap the width and height settings and adjust the location of the frame on the page. See Figure 8-4 for a diagram (a picture is worth a thousand words, I hope).

   After rotating, the original width value becomes the height of the rotated page. The original height becomes the width. The original left offset becomes the top offset. The original top offset becomes the right offset, which means that you have to calculate the left offset. The new left offset is the total width of the rotated page minus the original height (new width) minus the original top offset.

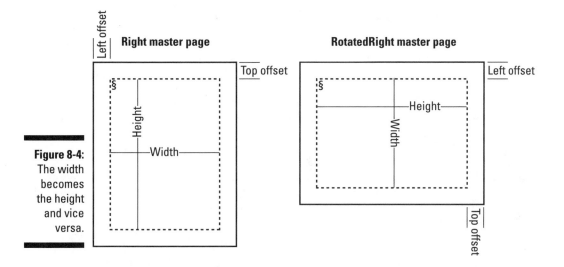

Figure 8-4:
The width
becomes
the height
and vice
versa.

7. **Check your original Right master page for the width, height, and top and left offset of the main text frame (select Format⇨Customize Layout⇨Customize Text Frame to see the value). You may want to write these down. Also find out the total height of the page.**

8. **On the RotatedRight master page, select the main text frame (Ctrl+click on PC, Option+click on Mac, or Meta-click on UNIX).**

9. **Change the width setting of the RotatedRight page to match the height setting of the original Right page.**

   Select Graphics⇨Object Properties to display the Customize Text Frame dialog box, where these settings are available.

10. **Change the height setting of the RotatedRight page to match the width of the original Right page.**

11. **Change the top offset of the RotatedRight page to match the left offset of the original Right page.**

12. **Enter the new left offset.**

    This final setting, the new left offset, is the most difficult to figure out. You have the total height of the original Right page (which is now the total width of the new RotatedRight page). You also have the original top offset, which became the right offset. So, you can calculate the left offset: it's the total original height minus the original top offset. Enter this value into the new left offset field.

Congratulations! You now have a spiffy new rotated master page, and you can apply it to any body page (just select Format⇨Page Layout⇨Master Page Usage and select the RotatedRight page there).

I need two separate text flows

On your body pages, your text automatically flows from page to page. As you add more content, FrameMaker automatically adds new pages and puts content on them. This default behavior is usually what you need. But in some cases, you may need to create content that doesn't flow in this nice, predictable pattern. For example, imagine that you have a newsletter where several articles begin on page 1 and then continue later in the newsletter (also commonly done in newspapers). An example of this is shown in Figure 8-5. To get this to work, you need to set up multiple text flows.

FrameMaker's default text flow is always named A. As a result, most framers use letters for other flows, such as B, C, D, and so on. You can name your text flow anything you want (Fred, for example); that single letter is just a habit.

To set up the flows in Figure 8-5, you can work either on the master pages or directly on the body pages. Which one you use is up to you. If your newsletter's articles always jump to the same location, you might want to set up the master pages. If you change the setup for each issue of the newsletter, it might be easier to work on the body pages. This example assumes that you work on the body pages.

1. **You need to set up the flows on the first page. Start with a blank portrait document.**

   To get a blank document, select File⇨New and then select the Portrait button.

2. **Select the default text frame on page one. Resize this text frame so that it covers only the left third of the page.**

   To select the text frame, Ctrl+click on PC, Option+click on Mac, or Meta+click on UNIX. To resize it, click and drag the selection handles.

3. **Type or paste text into this modified frame.**

   Notice that when you fill the text frame on page 1, FrameMaker automatically creates a page 2, with a default text frame filling the entire page, and your text flows onto this page. This is because you are working with the default text flow (A), which is automatically connected to the next page. For your other flows, you'll have to do this manually.

4. **Resize the text frame on page 2 and put it where it belongs.**

   Refer to Figure 8-5 for an example. Next, you need to create the text frame for the story at the top right of page 1.

Figure 8-5:
A newsletter
with several
text flows.
Story A
begins in the
top left of
page 1 and
continues in
the leftmost
column of
page 2.
Story B
begins in the
top right of
page 1 and
continues in
the middle
column of
page 2, and
so on.

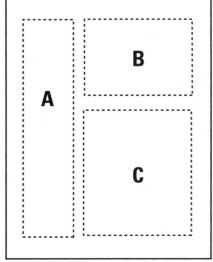

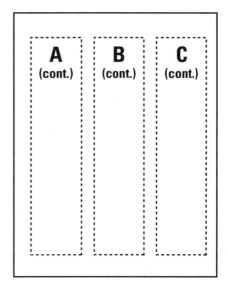

 5. **Display your Graphics tools (click the Graphics icon in the top right of your window) and select the Text Frame tool.**

6. **Click and drag the Text Frame tool to draw a text frame.**

7. **After creating the text frame, display its properties. In the Text Flow field, type a name for this flow (B).**

   To display the text frame's properties, select it and then select Graphics⇨Object Properties or Format⇨Customize Layout⇨Customize Text Frame.

   If you're working on the master pages, you can set this flow to Autoconnect, which means that the text will automatically flow from page to page. On the body pages, you have to connect the frames your-self, so autoconnecting doesn't really help you.

8. **Draw the frame where you want article B to continue on page 2. After drawing it, click the B frame on page 1, then the B frame on page 2, and then select Format⇨Customize Layout⇨Connect Text Frames.**

   The order in which you select the text frames is critical. If you select the frame on page 2 and then the frame on page 1, your text will start on page 2 and then continue on page 1. Perhaps this is the effect you want, but I doubt it.

9. **Now insert the text you want for article B, beginning on page 1.**

   When you fill the frame on page 1, the article will automatically continue to the B frame on page 2.

Use the same process to create your third article flow (C).

What about uneven columns?

You can easily create columns that are the same size using the column settings on the Text Frame properties (select Formats⇨Customize Layouts⇨ Customize Text Frame). But creating uneven columns takes a little more work.

To set up uneven columns, you need to create an individual text frame for each column and then line up those new text frames.

Use the Align and Distribute commands to get everything lined up just right. See Chapter 6 for more details.

Things you can't do

Although FrameMaker's master pages are extremely flexible and offer lots of features, there are a few things that you just can't do. They are

- ✔ **Multiple page sizes in a single file:** If you need a document that contains some pages that are, for example, 8.5x11" and some pages that are 11x17", you need to create two FrameMaker files: one for the smaller pages and one for the larger ones. You simply can't have two different page sizes in a single file. You *can,* however, mix portrait and landscape pages of the same size (for example 8.5x11" and 11x8.5").

- ✔ **Resizing columns that were created using the columns feature:** If you create a two-column page by setting a text frame to contain two columns, those columns will *always* be the same width. (To create uneven columns, see "What about uneven columns?" earlier in this chapter.) Furthermore, you cannot resize the columns within the text frame, except by changing the gap (gutter) between the columns or by changing the size of the text frame. In other words, you can't select one of the columns and drag it to change its size.

Chapter 9

Automating Cross-References

● ●

In This Chapter

▶ Defining cross-references

▶ Setting up these babies

▶ Adding new and modifying old cross-reference formats

▶ Fixing problems with unresolved cross-references

● ●

*I*n the olden days (of, say, five years ago), checking cross-references was a tedious, time-consuming task for a production editor or proofreader. Once a book was completed, her final task was to check every reference from one section to another to make sure that something like *"see more about Mrs. Higgenbotham on page 38"* actually corresponded to a heading about Mrs. Higgenbotham and actually occurred on page 38.

FrameMaker's cross-reference feature makes this incredibly boring and time-consuming process obsolete. Cross-references are maintained and updated automatically, so if you change Mrs. Higgenbotham to Miss Thistleweed and move the section from page 38 to page 45, your cross-reference updates as well.

You can create cross-references within a document or from one document to another document.

This fabulous automatic maintenance feature works only if you actually go to the trouble of creating cross-references, though. This chapter discusses how to create and format cross-references and how to fix them when they break.

Understanding Why You Should Bother with Cross-References

In FrameMaker, a *cross-reference* is a link to another part of your document. It is not regular text (you can't edit it directly), but it looks like regular text when you print it out. Cross-references are useful for many reasons, but here are the two biggest ones:

✔ They maintain page numbering and references to headings for you automatically.

✔ They are converted to hyperlinks when you convert FrameMaker files to other formats, such as HTML or PDF.

Although a cross-reference looks just like the text around it, you can easily tell whether it's a real cross-reference by clicking it. When you click a cross-reference, the entire cross-reference text is selected. By contrast, if you have regular text, you can click inside the text and edit it. If the entire text block is selected, but you're still not convinced, double-click the item instead. If it's a cross-reference, the Cross-Reference dialog box is displayed when you double-click the cross-reference.

Creating a Cross-Reference

To create a new cross-reference, you need to identify where you want the cross-reference to point to and assign a format to the cross-reference. Here's how:

1. **Open the document that you want to put the cross-reference in and the document to which you want to point (these may be the same document).**

2. **Make sure that you know what paragraph tag the target uses.**

   For example, it might be a Heading2.

3. **Click to position your cursor in the text where you want the cross-reference to occur (the location of the new "see page 123" reference).**

4. **Select Special⇨Cross-Reference to display the Cross-Reference dialog box (see Figure 9-1).**

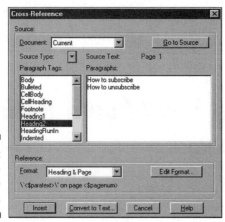

Figure 9-1: The Cross-Reference dialog box.

5. **In the Cross-Reference dialog box, identify the target for the reference.**

   - In the Document drop-down list, select the document in which the target is located. The default, Current, means that the target is in the same document as the cross-reference. (Remember, the target document must be open; otherwise, it's not available to be selected in this drop-down list.)

   - In the Source Type drop-down list, make sure that Paragraph Tags is selected.

   - In the Paragraph Tags list, select the paragraph tag of the target. When you do this, the Paragraphs list on the right lists all the paragraphs that use that paragraph tag.

   - In the Paragraphs list, select the paragraph that you want to reference.

6. **Now select a cross-reference format in the Format drop-down list.**

   FrameMaker doesn't validate your choice of cross-reference formats. It's quite possible, for example, to select a figure caption paragraph and then select a Table cross-reference format. This would lead to a cross-reference whose numbering is correct, but that reads "Table 1-1" instead of "Figure 1-1." Make sure that the cross-reference format you select makes sense for the paragraph you're referencing.

7. **Click Insert to create the new cross-reference.**

Formatting Your Cross-References

The cross-reference formats control the appearance of your cross-reference. FrameMaker gives you lots of default formats, but you can create new ones or modify the default formats if you need to.

Creating a new cross-reference format

To create a cross-reference format, follow these steps:

1. **Select Special⇨Cross-Reference.**

   This displays the Cross-Reference dialog box.

2. **Select the Edit Format button.**

   This displays the Edit Cross-Reference Format dialog box (see Figure 9-2).

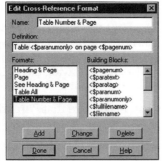

The Edit Cross-Reference Format dialog box is very similar to the Edit Variable dialog box. See Chapter 8 for a picture.

3. **In the Name field, type a name for your new cross-reference format.**

   This is the name you select when you choose a cross-reference format.

4. **In the Definition field, build the definition for your new cross-reference format. You can use three types of information in this field:**

   - **Text:** For text that is the same in every reference that uses this format

   - **Building blocks:** For text that varies based on the source of the reference

   - **Character tags:** For controlling the cross-reference's appearance

   The following sections describe these in detail.

5. **Once you have finished building your cross-reference format, select the Add button.**

   The Format list now displays the new format.

6. **Select the Done button to return to the Cross-Reference dialog box.**

   Notice that the Format drop-down list also displays your new format here.

Trying out special characters

On the Mac, you can simply type in special characters, such as em dashes, hard spaces, and curly quotes using the appropriate keyboard shortcuts (Shift+Option+hyphen, Ctrl+ space bar, and Option+[and Shift+Option+[, respectively).

On the PC and UNIX platform, you need to use the special character sequences instead. The *FrameMaker Quick Reference* (which, at 50 pages long, is not exactly quick) lists these "hex codes."

Adding text to your format

To use text in your cross-reference format, type in the text. For example, you could create a cross-reference that says, "see page" followed by the page number. You would simply type in "see page" in the Format dialog box.

Using building blocks

Cross-reference formats are based on *building blocks,* which are basically code snippets that FrameMaker replaces with content. For example, most cross-reference formats use the <$paratext> building block. When you use this format, the content of the targeted paragraph replaces <$paratext>.

Table 9-1 illustrates the other building blocks that are available.

Table 9-1	Cross-Reference Building Blocks
Building Block	*Function*
<$pagenum>	Prints the page number of the referenced paragraph.
<$paratext>	Prints the text of the referenced paragraph.
<$paratag>	Prints the name of the paragraph tag of the referenced paragraph.
<$paranum>	Prints the autonumber of the referenced paragraph.
<$paranumonly>	Prints the numeric part only of the autonumber of the referenced paragraph.
<$fullfilename>	Prints the file name of the file that contains the referenced paragraph, including the full directory path for the file.
<$filename>	Prints the file name of the file that contains the referenced paragraph. Doesn't print the full file path.

Using character tags

By default, your cross-references use the same formatting as the paragraph that you put them in. If you want to customize the formatting for the cross-reference, you can use character tags to do so.

The bottom of your list of building blocks lists the character tags in your character catalog.

If you don't have a character tag that is appropriate for your cross-reference formatting, you need to create one. Chapter 5 offers details on creating a character tag.

Once you have the appropriate character tag, select it from the list of building blocks.

Don't forget to put the <Default Para Font> building block at the end of your cross-reference; otherwise, your character tag could spill over into your regular text.

Getting Help for Unresolved Cross-References

Occasionally, you'll see the infamous "unresolved cross-references" error message. Although it looks ominous, it just means that FrameMaker can't figure out where the cross-reference is supposed to go. Here are some troubleshooting tips to hunt down these pesky unresolved cross-references.

The easiest way to locate unresolved cross-reference is to use the Find/Change feature (choose Edit⇨Find/Change). In the Find drop-down list, select Unresolved Cross-Reference and then click the Find button.

Did you move any files? Did you change any file names?

If you moved your files from one machine to another or from one place to another on the same machine, the links may be broken. Changing file names will also cause FrameMaker to lose track of cross-references.

Cross-references in HTML and PDF

Cross-references are even more critical when you're delivering material online. When you convert FrameMaker files to PDF or HTML (either through FrameMaker's built-in converter or via a third-party tool), the cross-references are preserved and become live hyperlinks. A user can click the cross-reference and jump directly to the cross-reference's target.

If you plan to deliver online, consider modifying your cross-reference formats to eliminate page numbers, which don't mean much in HTML.

For more information about converting to PDF and HTML, see Chapter 14.

To fix unresolved cross-references that are a result of files moving or file names changing, follow these steps:

1. **Open the file with the unresolved cross-references.**

2. **Select Edit⇨Update References.**

3. **Select the Commands drop-down list and then select Update Unresolved Cross-References.**

This displays the Update Unresolved Cross-References dialog box, shown in Figures 9-3, 9-4, and 9-5 (Windows, Mac, and UNIX, respectively). The PC, UNIX, and Mac versions of this dialog box are all slightly different.

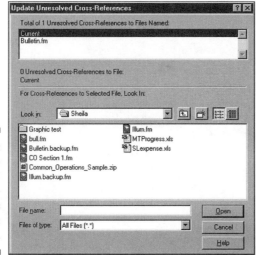

Figure 9-3:
The Update
Unresolved
Cross-
References
dialog box in
Windows.

This dialog box tells you to which files you have cross-references. If you click one of the files listed, you can find out how many of those cross-references are unresolved for each file.

4. **To resolve the cross-references, select a file that has missing cross-references and use the directory navigation to find that file on your system. Then click Update.**

FrameMaker searches the new file and attempts to resolve the cross-references. If successful, the number of unresolved cross-references drops.

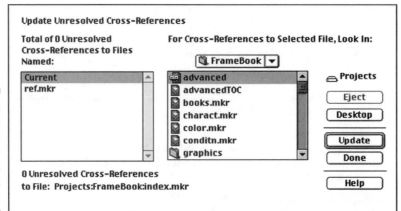

Figure 9-4:
The Update
Unresolved
Cross-
References
dialog box
on the Mac.

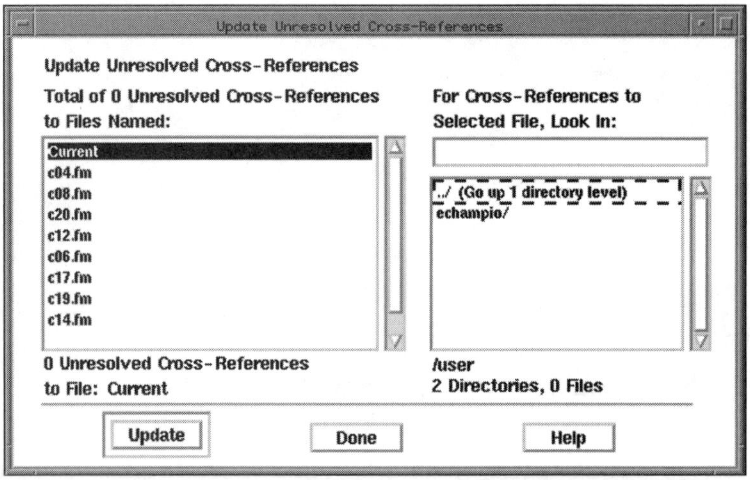

Figure 9-5:
The Update
Unresolved
Cross-
References
dialog box
on UNIX.

Did you delete information from the target document?

FrameMaker relies on cross-reference markers to locate cross-reference targets. If you delete information from the target document, you might accidentally delete the cross-reference marker. If this happens, you need to re-create the cross-reference to restore it.

TECHNICAL STUFF

The gory details about cross-references

I've said a lot about what cross-references do, but not much about how they work under the covers. If you just can't live without knowledge of how FrameMaker does cross-references, read on. If you like hot dogs, but don't really want to know what goes on at the hot dog factory, you may want to skip this section.

FrameMaker inserts a cross-reference marker at the beginning of the target paragraph when you create a cross-reference. This cross-reference marker contains a unique identifying number, the paragraph tag name, and the text

of the paragraph, like this:

```
83744: Heading1: Creating a
     cross-reference
```

Internally, FrameMaker uses only the number at the beginning of the marker to keep track of cross-references. As a result, if you delete a cross-reference marker, any cross-references to that paragraph will become unresolved. So keep an eye out for markers when you're editing your text, and make sure you don't accidentally delete them.

Is it just being ornery?

When you open a file, FrameMaker checks the cross-references in that file to make sure that they're resolved. Sometimes, this check results in a report that cross-references are unresolved when in fact, they're fine. This usually occurs because the target document contains fonts that aren't available on the current machine. To check the cross-references, FrameMaker attempts to open the file that the cross-reference points to. The "missing fonts" message causes the file-opening process to fail, and FrameMaker is unable to resolve the cross-reference. As a result, you get an unresolved cross-references message.

You can fix this problem in a couple of ways:

- Open the file with the missing fonts *before* you open the file that has cross-references to it.
- Fix the missing font problem in the target file.

If your file reports unresolved cross-references, but you can't find the unresolved references with a Find operation, the missing fonts are almost always the culprits.

Chapter 10

Variables: Saving You Time and Trouble

*I*n FrameMaker, a variable is a placeholder. Variables can actually be grouped into two distinct groups: those that perform a function (such as page numbers, running headers, and date variables) called *system variables*; and those that are placeholders for text called *user variables*.

I think Adobe should have separated these two items into two distinct features, but nobody asked me. When working with variables, keep in mind that system variables and user variables have little in common except the name (and a listing in the Variable dialog box).

What's a Variable and Why Should I Bother?

Variables are designed to save you time and trouble when you update information.

Reasons for system variables

System variables let you easily keep certain information about your document up to date. The Modification Date variable, for example, shows the date (and time if you want) that you last saved your file. You could, of course, type in the time manually every time you save the file, but it's much more efficient to insert a variable and let it do the work for you. After all, you have better things to do!

Other system variables can report information that changes from one page to another. For example, you can insert a Current Page Number variable on your master pages. On the body page, this variable always displays the page number of the current page. The running header/footer variables (you have four, starting with Running H/F 1) allow you to put the most recent heading or a chapter title into your footer.

Keep in mind when you're working with system variables that you can't change their function. You can change the formatting or the content displayed by the different variables (some are more flexible than others), but you can't change their purpose. For example, a Modification Date variable always displays the date when you last saved the file — it can't be made to display the date that the file was created.

System variables are limited to the four running header/footer variables included in FrameMaker. You can't create any additional ones, and you can't delete the existing ones, either.

Reasons for user variables

User variables are placeholders for formatted text. You can, for example, create a variable for *FrameMaker For Dummies*. Every time you need to insert that book title, insert the variable instead of typing in the whole phrase. And you can even set up the variable to italicize the text for you automatically.

User variables are convenient for text that you repeat frequently, especially if it is difficult to type. You might want to create a variable for the copyright statement that appears at the bottom of every page in your books. When the next year rolls around, you can simply update the copyright variable from 1999 to 2000, and FrameMaker will change the date everywhere you used that variable. Too bad other Y2K problems are harder to solve.

How do I know it's a variable?

If you have an item in your text and you think it might be a variable but you're not sure, double-click it. If it's a variable, the Variable dialog box is displayed (and in the Variable dialog box, the name of the variable is selected).

How do I update a variable?

Once you insert a variable, that variable will be updated for you when you open a file and before you print. If you'd like to force FrameMaker to update all the system variables, select Special⇨Variable and click the Update button.

The Basics: Inserting Variables in Text

To insert a variable into your text, select Special⇨Variable, click the variable you want, and click Insert (or Replace if you selected text).

Headers and Footers: Create Them Once and Move on with Your Life

You'll find that system variables are useful when you're setting up your basic master pages. For example, if you want to put a page number in your footer, first click in the footer where you want the page number (make sure you're on the master pages), and then select Special⇨Variable. This displays the Variable dialog box (see Figure 10-1).

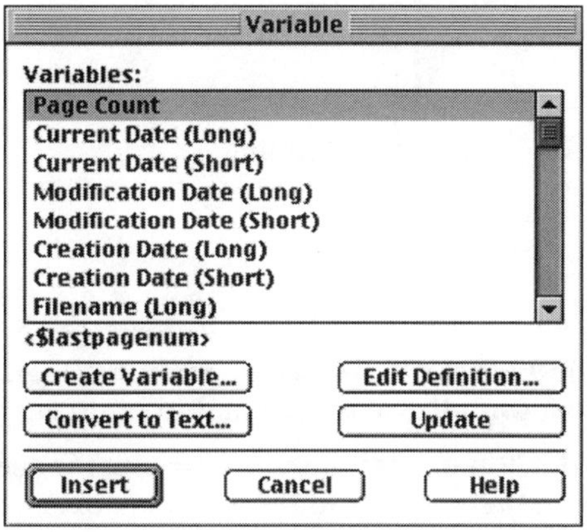

Figure 10-1:
The Variable dialog box. If you use variables often, get used to seeing this dialog box.

```
┌─────────────── Variable ───────────────┐
│ Variables:                              │
│ ┌─────────────────────────────────┐▲   │
│ │ Page Count                      │     │
│ │ Current Date (Long)             │     │
│ │ Current Date (Short)            │     │
│ │ Modification Date (Long)        │     │
│ │ Modification Date (Short)       │     │
│ │ Creation Date (Long)            │     │
│ │ Creation Date (Short)           │     │
│ │ Filename (Long)                 │▼    │
│ └─────────────────────────────────┘     │
│ <$lastpagenum>                          │
│ ┌ Create Variable... ┐  ┌ Edit Definition... ┐ │
│ ┌ Convert to Text... ┐  ┌    Update    ┐     │
│ ┌ Insert ┐    ┌ Cancel ┐    ┌ Help ┐    │
└─────────────────────────────────────────┘
```

In the list, select the Current Page Number variable and then click Insert. On your master page, you'll see a pound sign (#), but this will show up as a page number on your body pages. If you don't believe me, check for yourself . . .

Your running header/footer variables are also available on the master pages (and only on the master pages). To create a running header/footer, you first need to identify the paragraph tag that you want to repeat. For example, you might decide that you want to always print the most recent Heading1 in your header. To do this, you'll need to insert a Running H/F variable and instruct it to pick up the Heading1 information.

Here's one way to do this (I'll skip the variations):

1. **Go to the master pages (select View⇨Master Pages).**

2. **Click in the header or footer where you want to put the running information.**

3. **Select Special⇨Variable.**

   This displays the Variable dialog box (refer to Figure 10-1).

4. **Select an available running header/footer variable (that is, one that you're not using elsewhere).**

5. **Click Edit Definition to display the Edit System Variable dialog box (see Figure 10-2).**

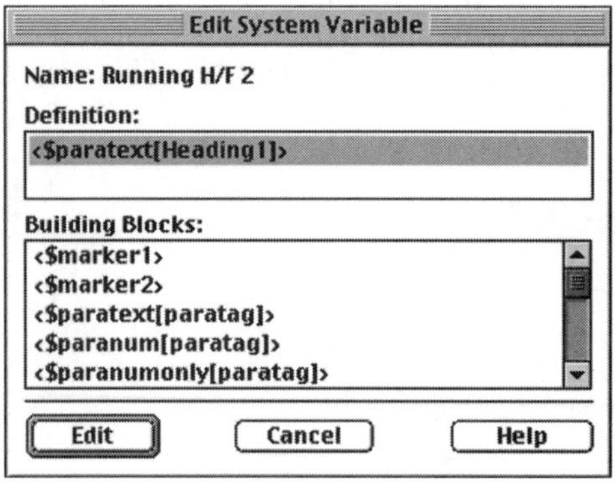

Figure 10-2:
The Edit
System
Variable
dialog box.

6. **Use the available building blocks to set up the running header/footer you want. (See Table 10-1 for a list of the available building blocks.)**

   To create a running header/footer that picks up the most recent instance of the Heading1 paragraph tag, you would insert this code:

   ```
   <$paratext[Heading 1]>
   ```

7. **Click the Edit button to define the running header/footer.**

8. **In the Variable dialog box, click Insert to insert the modified running header/footer variable at your cursor location.**

Table 10-1 lists the building blocks that are available for running header/footer variables. Keep in mind that for different types of variables, you'll have different building blocks available.

Table 10-1   Building Blocks for Running Header/Footer Variables

Building Block	Description
<$marker1>	Inserts the text from the most recent marker with a "Header/Footer $1" type. Rarely used, but quite useful if headings are too long and need to be shortened for the header.
<$marker2>	Same as <$marker1>, only it looks for the marker type "Header/Footer $2."
<$paratext[paratag]>	Inserts the contents of the most recent paragraph that uses *paratag*. For example, <$paratext[heading 1]> would look for a paragraph that uses the heading 1 paragraph tag.
<$paranum[paratag]>	Inserts the entire autonumbering definition from *paratag*. (That is, it inserts the contents of the Autonumbering field from the Numbering properties of the paragraph tag that you are referencing.)
<$paranumonly[paratag]>	Inserts only the numbered portion of the autonumbering definition from *paratag*. For example, if a figure tag had the autonumber definition, "Figure <n+>: ", <$paranumonly[figure]> would pick up only the number (1, 2, 3, and so on).
<$paratag[paratag]>	Inserts the name of the paragraph tag specified. So, if the definition is <$paratag[heading 1]>, the result is "heading 1."
<$condtag[hitag, . . . , lotag, nomatch]>	Another interesting, but obscure, building block. It checks the current page (and only the current page) for an occurrence of the specified conditional text tags. If one of those conditional text tags is used on the page, the first matching tag (from left to right) is printed. If there is no matching tag, the content of the last item in the list is printed.

According to Adobe's documentation, this building block is useful for specifying security levels on a page. If classified text is tagged with a conditional text tag matching the classification level (Secret, Top Secret, and so on), then putting those classifications in the <$condtag> building block, starting with the most classified down to the least classified, would always print the highest classification level that occurs on the page.

You can include character formats in your running headers and footers. They are available in the Edit System Variable dialog box after the list of building blocks. Using a character format lets you format the content of the variable (for example, by italicizing it).

The Dating Game: Using the Date-related Variables

Your system variables include several date-related variables. These include two Creation Date variables, two Modification Date variables, and two Current Date variables. For each group, the two variables perform the identical function, but by default one is defined with more information (the Long version) and one with less (Short). However, you can modify these variables to look exactly the way you want them.

This would probably be a good time to mention that, according to Adobe, FrameMaker 5.5.3 and later is Year 2000-compliant; however, earlier versions are not. For more information about Adobe products and Y2K issues, check out www.adobe.com/newsfeatures/year2000/prodsupport.html.

Although you can specify that a variable include the minute and even the second, the variable value is updated only when you open the file, print, or force an update. You can't use a variable to create a live clock in your document.

Table 10-2 lists the building blocks that are available for date-related variables.

Table 10-2	Building Blocks for Date-related Variables
Building Block	*Description*
<$AMPM>	Tells you whether it was updated in the morning or evening in uppercase (AM or PM)
<$ampm>	Tells you whether it was updated in the morning or evening in lowercase (am or pm)
<$dayname>	Gives the name of the day that it was updated (Monday, Tuesday, and so on)

Building Block	Description
<$daynum01>	Gives the number of the day of the month with a leading zero, if necessary (for example, 01, 02, 30, 31)
<$daynum>	Gives the number of the day of the month with no leading zero (for example, 1, 2, 30, 31)
<$hour01>	Tells you the hour it was updated with a leading zero (for example, 1:00 is 01)
<$hour24>	Tells you the hour in 0–24 military format (for example, 1:00 a.m. is 01, 11:00 p.m. is 23)
<$hour>	Gives the hour in normal form (for example, 1:00 a.m. is 1, 11:00 p.m. is 11)
<$minute00>	Gives the minute with leading zero (for example, 01, 02, 58, 59)
<$minute>	Tells you the minute without leading zero (for example, 1, 2, 58, 59)
<$monthname>	Tells you the name of the month that the file was updated (for example, January)
<$monthnum01>	Tells you the number of the month with leading zero (for example, January is 01)
<$monthnum>	Gives you the number of the month without a leading zero (for example, January is 1)
<$second00>	Tells you the second with leading zero (for example, 01, 02, 58, 59)
<$second>	Gives you the second without leading zero (for example, 1, 2, 58, 59)
<$shortdayname>	Gives you the three-letter abbreviation for the name of the day (for example, Monday is Mon)
<$shortmonthname>	Gives you the three-letter abbreviation for the name of the month (for example, January is Jan)
<$shortyear>	Gives you the two-digit number of the year (for example, 1999 is 99 and 2000 is 00)
<$year>	Tells you the four-digit number of the year (for example, 1999 or 2000)

You can include character formats in your date/time variables. They are available after the list of building blocks.

Table Talk: Variables in Tables

FrameMaker includes two variables that are available only in tables: Table Continuation and Table Sheet.

Table Continuation

If you have a table that spans multiple pages, you need the Table Continuation variable. When you insert this variable into a table's title or heading row, the initial results are underwhelming. You may notice that a hard space is inserted, but it doesn't look as though anything else happens. Check the second and subsequent pages of the table. Where you insert the Table Continuation variable, you now see *(continued)*. But the word doesn't appear on the first page of the table. Pretty cool, eh?

No, you can't insert this automatically into every table. And yes, this is a sad state of affairs.

Table Sheet

The Table Sheet variable is like a page count, but it's for tables. Insert this variable into a table, and it'll tell you which page of the table you're currently on and how many total pages (or sheets) the table has. If you put the variable in a heading row or in the table title, every page of the table displays the sheet count.

Another Work Elimination Technique: Creating User Variables

Although user variables don't quite have the same coolness factor as system variables, user variables can also help you avoid work. (And that's what this is all about, after all. For your boss, you could reword this in boss-speak . . . the key phrase is *increased productivity*.)

It's wise to create variables for text that repeats often and is likely to change. These days, this probably includes your company name and your job title.

To create a user variable for your company name, follow these steps:

1. **(Optional) Click where you want to insert the variable.**

   If you just want to set up the variable definition without inserting it, you don't need to click where you want the variable.

2. **Select Special⇨Variable to display the Variable dialog box (refer to Figure 10-1).**

3. **Click Create Variable to display the Edit User Variable dialog box (see Figure 10-3).**

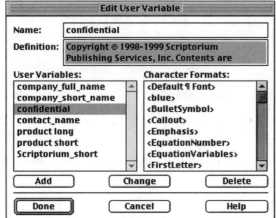

Figure 10-3:
The Edit
User
Variable
dialog box.

4. **In the Name field, type a name for the new variable.**

   This is the name that you use to retrieve the variable, so you might want to make it generic; for example, *company name du jour.*

5. **In the Definition field, type the text that you want to display when you insert this variable.**

   You can use character formats in this definition but not building blocks. Building blocks are available only for system variables.

6. **Click Add to create the variable.**

   If you want to create more variables, go to Step 3.

7. **Click Done.**

8. **(Optional) Click Insert to insert the variable at your cursor position.**

Some practical uses for user variables

My favorite variable example is for your company name. For those of you who toil at small high-tech companies, mergers, reorganizations, and other Dilbertian events are common. Set up your company name as a variable and use the variable consistently. This can save your sanity if (when) your company changes names twice in three months and then again the following week.

Another good variable is your confidentiality statement. You may be required to put a statement like this at the bottom of each page:

> Contents are proprietary and confidential. Do not photocopy.

Your corporate lawyers will modify this statement approximately once every six months; you might as well set up a variable so that you can change it quickly.

In the medical or pharmaceutical industry, consider using variables for long, hard-to-spell drug names. Set up the variable using the informal name as the variable name and with the official, difficult name in the variable definition. This way, you have to spell the drug correctly once — when you set up the variable. After that, just insert the variable and all is well.

A brand name with complicated formatting, such as small caps or italics on only part of the name, might also be worthwhile setting up as a variable. Because you can embed character formats into the variable definition, you can do all the formatting once — instead of having to format the name every time you type it.

Chapter 11

Managing Color

● ●

● ●

A desktop publishing package without color capabilities would be, well, gray and boring. If you want to add a splash of color to your documents, read on.

Seeing the World in Color

In the printing world, colors are created with inks. For some print jobs, the ink is mixed before printing and then used on the press. This is called *spot color.* In other projects, the printer uses several different colors and combines them on the press to create the color you need. This is called *process color;* the final color is created during the printing process. Spot color is good for projects that require only two or three colors; process color lets you create a full-color printed document.

The most common process color system is called CMYK, which includes four colors: C for cyan, M for magenta, Y for yellow, and K for black. (Black is the most important, or *key,* color in printing.)

Computer monitors use a combination of red, green, and blue (RGB) to create the colors on-screen. As a result, the colors on your monitor don't match the colors you see in print.

If you're creating a color project, check your colors against a reliable source, like a swatch book. The major color system vendors (like Pantone) provide swatch books that contain all their colors, so that you can see what those colors look like when they are printed. Use these swatch books to pick a color; don't rely on what you see on-screen!

Working with Color Definitions

Color definitions, like everything else in FrameMaker, are part of a catalog. Your color catalog includes a few default colors; you'll need to add color definitions if you're working in color.

Why create a color definition instead of just applying color willy-nilly? If you decide that you don't like a particular shade of green, you can adjust its color definition . . . and every place where you use that color is automatically updated with the new shade. This includes text (paragraphs and characters), graphics, and anywhere else you used a color.

To help you set up colors quickly, FrameMaker provides several *color libraries,* which are long lists of colors that are already defined. If you want to use one in your document, you just select it from the library and add it to your document.

Adding Color Definitions

To create a new color definition, select View⇨Color⇨Definitions. This displays the Color Definitions dialog box (see Figure 11-1).

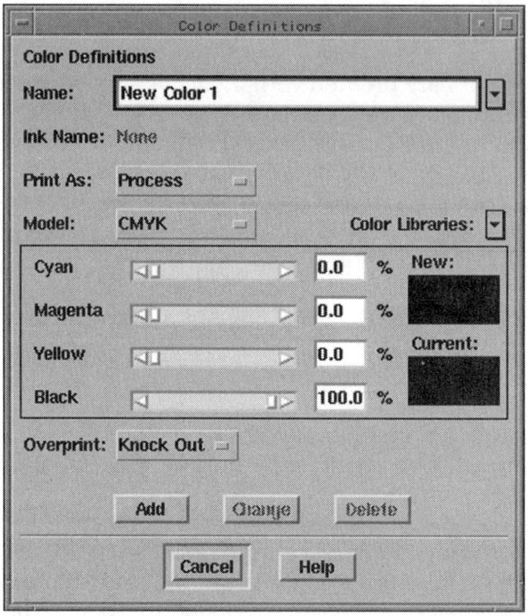

Figure 11-1:
The Color
Definitions
dialog box.

The type of color that you need depends on the output medium for this document. Do you intend to print the document in color? If so, focus on spot and process colors that are based on the printing color models (like CMYK). These include Pantone, Trumatch, and several other color libraries provided. If you plan to deliver the document online, consider the Online color library, which includes the 216 colors that display properly on all Web browsers. Table 11-1 briefly describes the color libraries available in FrameMaker.

Table 11-1	Color Libraries	
Library	*Color Model*	*Description*
Apple Color Picker (Mac)		Lets you choose a color using the Macintosh system color palette. *Not recommended for print.*
Color (Windows)		Lets you choose a color using the Windows system color palette. *Not recommended for print.*
Crayon	RGB	Provides frequently used colors with descriptive names, just like a box of crayons. *Not recommended for print.*
DIC	CMYK	Commonly used in Japan.
FOCOLTONE	CMYK	Includes 860 process colors.
Greys	CMYK	Includes grey in 1 percent increments, defined for both process and spot colors.
MUNSELL	HSL	Uses hue, lightness, and saturation to define colors.
PANTONE	CMYK	Several libraries, some with spot colors, some with process colors. Separate libraries for coated and uncoated paper.
TOYO	CMYK	Commonly used in Japan. 1,000 colors based on printed inks in Japan. Intended for coated paper.
TRUMATCH	CMYK	Includes 2,000 process colors that cover the CMYK spectrum.

Selecting a color from a library

If the color you want is defined in a color library, follow these steps to create a color definition for it.

1. **In the Color Definitions dialog box (refer to Figure 11-1), select the Color Libraries drop-down list and select the color library that contains the color you want.**

   The library's color list is displayed.

2. **Locate the color you want and select it by clicking it. You can use the Find field at the top of the window to locate the color you want quickly.**

   If your document is intended for print, use the swatch books provided by the color vendors (like Pantone and Trumatch) to choose a color. Don't rely on the colors shown on your monitor.

3. **Click Done to return to the Color Definitions dialog box.**

   Notice that all the information about the color is now shown here (see Figure 11-2).

Figure 11-2:
After you choose a color, FrameMaker fills in the color settings for you. In this case, the color is 0 percent cyan, magenta, and black and 100 percent yellow.

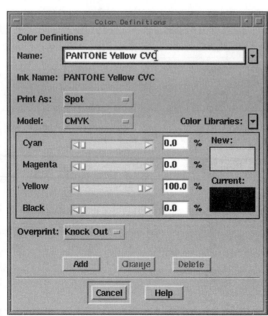

4. **(Optional) Give the color a descriptive name in the Name field at the top of the window.**

Your new color definition is now available in the color catalog. See "Wondering where Color Definitions Appear" later in this chapter for details about where the colors now show up.

Creating a color from scratch

To create a color without using a color library, follow these steps:

1. **Display the Color Definitions dialog box (select View⇨Color⇨Definitions).**

2. **In the Name field, type a name for your new color.**

3. **In the Print As field, specify how you want the color printed.**

   A spot color is printed on a single press plate; a process color is printed by combining the four press colors (cyan, magenta, yellow, black). If you select "Don't Print," you create a color that you can use in your document and see in FrameMaker, but that will not print.

4. **Select the color model you want to use.**

   Your choices are

   • **CMYK:** Cyan, magenta, yellow, black. Used in offset printing.

   • **RGB:** Red, green, blue. Used for online documents.

   • **HLS:** Hue, lightness, saturation. Used for online documents.

   The color model you choose determines the available settings. See Figure 11-3 for an example of CMYK settings.

5. **Change the CMYK, RGB, or HLS values to create the color you want.**

   You can see a preview of the new color next to the old color in the color block on the right.

6. **Set the Overprint setting.**

   This is necessary only for offset printing. If you want this color to print on top of overlapping colors, choose Overprint. If you don't want this color to print where it would cover other colors (so it leaves a hole where the other colors are), choose Knock Out.

7. **Click Add to add the new color to the Color Catalog.**

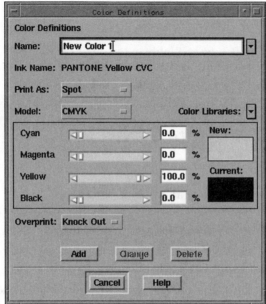

Figure 11-3:
If you select
CMYK as
your model,
then you set
values for
cyan,
magenta,
yellow, and
black to
create your
color.

Creating a tint

A *tint* is a percentage of a color. For example, a medium grey is a tint (per-haps around 40 percent) of black. You can create tints based on colors in the color catalog.

To create a new tint, follow these steps:

1. **Display the Color Definitions dialog box (select View⇨Color⇨Definitions).**

2. **In the Name field, type a name for your new color.**

3. **In the Print As drop-down list, select Tint.**

   Notice that the lower half of the dialog box changes (see Figure 11-4).

4. **In the Base Color drop-down list, select the color for which you want to define a tint.**

   Only colors defined in your color catalog are available as base colors.

5. **Type in a percentage for your tint (or move the slider).**

   The color boxes on the right show the new tint (top box) and the base color (bottom box).

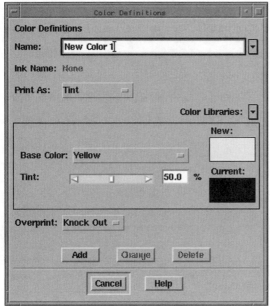

Figure 11-4:
To create a
tint, choose
a base
color and
adjust the
percentage
to get the
shade you
want.

6. **Set the Overprint setting.**

   This is necessary only for offset printing. If you want this color to print on top of overlapping colors, choose Overprint. If you don't want this color to print where it would cover other colors (so it leaves a hole where the other colors are), choose Knock Out.

Wondering Where Color Definitions Appear?

Your color catalog is available in some places where you'd expect it and in others that might be a little surprising.

Graphics

When you think of using color, graphics are probably the first item that springs to mind. You can apply color to your graphic objects in two ways: from the Graphic toolbar or from the Object Properties dialog box (select Graphics⇨Object Properties). Figure 11-5 shows where the color catalog appears in each.

Tint versus color definition. And what about the Graphics tools' Tint setting?

If you create a tint based on an existing color and then change the underlying color, the tint changes as well. This makes it easier to manage all your colors.

Instead of setting the tint in your color definition, you could use the Tint setting on the Graphics tools. But this has a couple of disadvantages:

✔ Unless the tint is defined as a separate

color, you can't use it for a paragraph tag or character tag color setting.

✔ If you use the Tint setting on the Graphics tools, you have to set the tint manually every time you apply the color. If you set up a color definition, the correct tint percentage is built in.

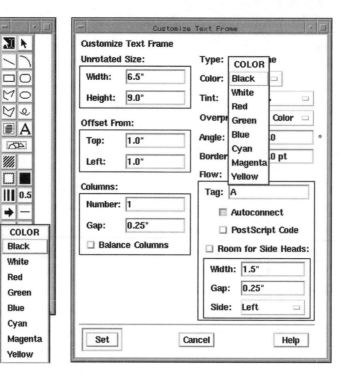

Figure 11-5: For graphics, you can use either the Graphic tools (left) or the Object Properties dialog box (right) to apply color from the color catalog.

Text

You can set up text to use color either through a paragraph tag or a character tag.

For paragraph tags, the Color attribute in the Default Font properties lets you assign a color to a paragraph tag (see Figure 11-6). To display the Default Font properties, display the Paragraph Designer (by selecting Format⇨ Paragraphs⇨Paragraph Designer) and then select the Default Font properties in the Properties drop-down list.

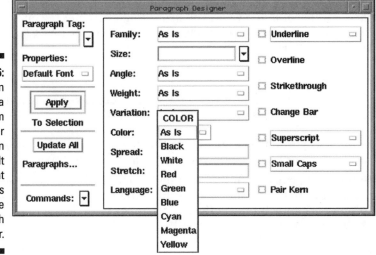

Figure 11-6: You can assign a color from the color catalog in the Default Font properties of the Paragraph Designer.

For character tags, a similar Color attribute is available in the Character Designer (select Format⇨Characters⇨Character Designer).

Because you can insert character tags into definitions for variables, cross-references, and other items that use building blocks, colored character tags make it possible to apply color within almost any special text in your document.

Autonumbering

If your autonumber uses the Default Para Font setting (that is, the same font settings as the paragraph tag), then it uses the same color as the rest of the paragraph. If you want to use a different color for the autonumber, you need to set up a character tag with the appropriate color setting and then assign that character tag to the autonumber in the Numbering properties (see Chapter 4 for details).

Conditional text

When you edit a conditional text tag or create a new tag, any of the colors in the color catalog are available. Just select the color you want from the drop-down list. (See Chapter 16 for details about conditional text.)

Cross-References

You can add color to your cross-reference. Set up a character tag that uses the color you want and then insert that character tag into the cross-reference format definition. (See Chapter 9 for details about cross-references.)

Variables

Like cross-references, variables can use color. Again, you'll need a character tag that uses the color you want. You insert that character tag into the variable definition. This works for system and user variables. (See Chapter 8 for details about variables.)

Index markers

To create an index with entries in blazing color, you'll need to include the color in one of two places:

- **In the paragraph tags in the index file:** If you set up your paragraph tags in the index with color, your entire entry will be colorful.

- **In the index markers:** If you want just a word or a few characters in an index entry to be in different color from the rest of the entry, you'll need to set up a character tag in the index marker itself. For details about creating index markers, see Chapter 19.

Deleting Color Definitions

If you end up with extra color definitions that you don't need, you can delete them from your document. You cannot, however, delete the default color definitions — Black, White, Red, Green, Blue, Cyan, Magenta, and Yellow.

To delete a color definition, follow these steps:

1. **Display the Color Definitions dialog box (select View⇨Color⇨Definitions).**

2. **In the Name field, select the color you want to delete.**

3. **Click the Delete button at the bottom of the dialog box.**

4. **Click Done.**

If the color you are deleting is used by any items in your document, those items will revert to black. A dialog box prompts you to confirm this.

If you need to delete several colors, consider saving the file to MIF (Maker Interchange Format) and deleting the colors there (you can open the MIF file in a text editor). It's much faster than going through the Color Definitions dialog box. For more information about MIF, refer to the FrameMaker user documentation.

Chapter 12

Working with Modular Text

● ●

In This Chapter

▶ Defining text insets

▶ Understanding why you should use text insets

▶ Creating a text inset

▶ Updating text insets

▶ Deleting text insets

● ●

A *text inset* is a FrameMaker document that has been inserted into another document. You can use any FrameMaker document as a text inset or as a container for text insets.

FrameMaker's text inset feature makes it possible to embed content from one file in another file. (It's similar to importing a graphic, but instead of importing just a graphic, you import an entire FrameMaker file.)

Using text insets makes it possible to create truly *modular documents*. This has nothing to do with houses — a modular document is a document that is assembled from smaller parts (or modules). You can use and reuse the content modules in different ways.

The most obvious advantage of text insets is to reuse modules. For example, if you create a small document that contains information about tempering chocolate, you could include that information both in your big, comprehensive book on cooking techniques and in your candy-making cookbook. You would maintain the information about tempering chocolate in a single file and import that file into both books. Using a text inset means that you update the information once and use it in more than one location.

 Instead of using text insets, you can insert files into book files selectively (see Chapter 17 for more information). But text insets have a big advantage over the book file approach: You *don't* have to start a text inset on a new page. With a book file, each file must start on a separate page.

Creating a Text Inset

To create a text inset, you first need to put the information you want to use as a text inset into its own file.

You can't use a text inset to import a portion of a file. It's all or nothing. If you want to import a single paragraph, consider using a cross-reference instead (see Chapter 9).

Once you've created a file that contains the information you want to embed, you're ready to create a text inset. Follow these steps:

1. **Open the file in which you want to create the text inset and put your cursor where you want to start the text inset.**

2. **Select File➪Import➪File to display the Import dialog box.**

3. **Select the file that you want to import by reference.**

   This file must be a FrameMaker file. (You can import other files, but you cannot import them by reference and create text insets.)

4. **Select the Import by Reference button.**

   The Copy into Document button doesn't create a text inset; it just makes a copy of the text!

5. **Select the Import button to import the file.**

   FrameMaker scans the file and displays the Import Text Flow by Reference dialog box (see Figure 12-1).

Figure 12-1:
When you insert the imported flow, FrameMaker gives you several options.

6. **Select the flow you want to import.**

   Generally, you'll want to import the main text flow (A). But you can also import other flows from the document or flows from the reference pages.

7. **Specify how you want to format the imported flow.**

   You have three choices:

   - **Reformat Using Current Document's Formats:** The current (container) document overrides the formats from the source document, *if* the format names are identical. You can also strip manual page breaks and other overrides.

   - **Reformat as Plain Text:** This displays the source document's information without any formatting.

   - **Retain Source's Formatting:** This displays the source document the same way as it looked in the original file.

8. **Specify whether you want to update the imported flow automatically or manually.**

   Generally, you'll want to set this to update automatically. Manual updates give you more control over when the text insets are updated, but you have to remember to do it!

9. **Select the Import button to import the text inset.**

If you're not sure whether something is a text inset or not, click it. You can't edit a text inset in the container file; you have to edit the source file instead. If clicking the text selects a block of text, you're dealing with a text inset. (Double-click to display the text inset's options.)

A few text inset "quirks"

If you're going to use a lot of text insets, you should know about a few "quirks" (some of them are bugs):

✔ **Search and replace:** The Find/Change command will not locate information in the text insets when you search in the container file. To find information in a text inset, you have to open it and search inside the text inset file.

✔ **Importing formats:** If you change any formats, the changes generally must be imported to every text inset file as well as the container files. Some users create a "utility" book, which contains only the text insets, to make this process easier.

✔ **Stacking text insets:** If you're going to import two insets in a row, make sure you leave a blank paragraph between the two. You can create a Separator paragraph tag that's very small (2 points) to minimize the effect on your text. If you stack text insets without the "separator" paragraph, you will see some unexpected (and unpleasant) formatting problems.

✔ **Cross-referencing information in a text inset:** You can create a cross-reference to information in a text inset as if it were regular text in your container file. (That is, you don't have to point to the source file for the text inset; the cross-reference can point to the "current" document, which contains the text inset.) But when you create the cross-reference, the cross-reference marker is not inserted in the text inset. As a result, when you update the text inset, the cross-reference marker is removed and your cross-reference becomes unresolved. To avoid this problem, it's best to insert cross-reference markers into the text insets where needed and then use those cross-reference markers to build your cross-references.

Here's how to do it:

1. **In the text inset file, position your cursor in the paragraph to which you want to create a cross-reference.**

2. **Select Special⇨Marker to display the Marker dialog box.**

3. **Select Cross-Ref as your marker type and type something descriptive in the Marker text box. (This marker name must be unique for this file.) Save your file.**

4. **In the container file, create the cross-reference. Select Special⇨Cross-References to display the Cross-Reference dialog box.**

5. **Create the cross-reference as usual (see Chapter 9 for instructions). The paragraphs inside the text inset are listed as paragraphs in the current document.**

Alexia Prendergast and Melanie Johnson provided these tips.

Updating Text Insets

The beauty of text insets is that when you modify the source file, all the places where that source file is used as a text inset are updated. It's just like a graphic that's imported by reference, but for text insets you actually have more options. (A referenced graphic is always updated immediately, but you can control when text insets are updated.)

You can update every text inset in your file (or in an entire book), or you can update just a single text inset.

When you update a text inset, the information displayed in the container document is refreshed with the new information from the original source file. (It's like reimporting the document.)

If you have set up text insets for automatic updates, opening the container file will update the insets in that file. If your container file is part of a book file, updating the book file updates the text insets in every file in the book. But in addition to these "automatic" updating features, you can also update text insets manually. If you have set up text insets for manual updates, then you must use one of the techniques described below. For automatically updated text insets, these techniques force the text inset to be updated yet again.

Updating one text inset

To update a single text inset, display the inset's options by double-clicking it (refer to Figure 12-2). Click the Update Now button to update the inset. This updates any text inset, regardless of whether it's set for automatic or manual updates.

Updating all text insets in a book

You can update text insets for a book. Go to the book file and update the book (select File⇨Generate/Update). This updates the text insets marked for automatic updates only; the insets marked for manual updates are *not* updated.

Updating all text insets in a file

Text insets set for automatic updates are updated whenever you open the container file. To update text insets set for manual updates (or to update the ones set for automatic updates again), select Edit⇨Update References to display the Update References dialog box (see Figure 12-2).

Figure 12-2:
Update the
text insets
marked for
manual
updates
separately
from those
for
automatic
updates.

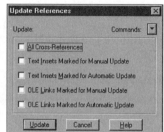

In the dialog box, check the text insets you want to update and then click Update.

Preventing Automatic Updates

You can suppress the automatic updates that occur when you open a file or update a book file. To do so, select Edit⇨Update References to display the Update References dialog box (refer to Figure 12-2). Click the Commands drop-down list and select Suppress Automatic Updating. Make sure the check box for suppressing automatic updating of text insets is checked and then click Set. This prevents FrameMaker from updating any text insets when you open the file.

Removing a Text Inset

To remove a text inset, click it. This selects the entire text inset. Then press the Delete key to delete the text inset.

Be sure you have the right text inset; you get no confirmation message when you press Delete. The text inset disappears immediately. You can, however, undo the deletion (select Edit⇨Undo).

Converting a Text Inset to Regular Text

Converting a text inset to regular text removes the link from the container document to the source document; instead, you have regular, editable content in your container document.

To convert a text inset to regular text, double-click the text inset to display the properties for the text inset. Select the Convert to Text button to display the Convert Text Insets to Text dialog box.

You can't undo a conversion to regular text!

You can convert just the selected text inset to regular text or all the text insets in the file. Choose the option you want and then select Convert. This removes the link from the container document to the original file that contains the text inset. Instead, you now have regular text, which you can edit in the container document.

A real-life example

At VERITAS Software, documentation manager Alexia Prendergast creates modular documentation using text insets. Each discrete topic (usually a procedure, concept, or reference material) is stored in a separate file; typically, these files are one to three pages long. To create a book, Alexia imports the modules into container documents (which become chapters). The chapter files, in turn, become part of a book file. The book file includes information that is specific to that book, such as a table of contents and introduction, but over 95 percent of a typical book is made up of text insets.

This modular approach has allowed VERITAS to reuse information efficiently. For example, a certain product might have a light and a professional version. With the modular approach, the light documentation discusses all the basic features and the pro documentation includes information about the additional features.

And, perhaps most importantly, if a module is updated, the changes dynamically appear in all the books that use that particular module.

Alexia estimates that using text insets has doubled production (rule of thumb estimates for creating modular documentation are four to ten pages per day). At the same time, the documentation has become more usable because writers spend more time planning and structuring information and less time writing it.

Chapter 13

Designing FrameMaker Templates

● ●

In This Chapter

▶ Understanding templates

▶ Copying formats from a template

▶ Organizing your template

● ●

*O*nce you start designing FrameMaker templates, you'll really begin to appreciate the power that FrameMaker offers. This chapter explains the concept of a template, discusses how to copy formats from a template, and provides some hints on how to design a template.

Understanding Templates

A *template* is a framework. It doesn't provide much content, but it gives you a starting point. You could think of a child's coloring book as being full of templates. Each page provides an outline drawing, and kids can fill the outlines with lots of different colors.

In FrameMaker, a template is a regular document file that contains a collection of tags (paragraph tags, character tags, master pages, cross-reference formats, and so on). It may also contain placeholder or boilerplate content. You use the structure in the template as a foundation for the documents you create.

You don't need a special document for a template. You can use any ol' FrameMaker document with tags as a template — you just import the formats from that document to your file.

The strong tagging structure in FrameMaker helps you automate and accelerate your document development. Once you create, for example, a table format, you can use that table format over and over in your document. You can insert a table that matches the format of the first table you created, and be confident that the tables will have the same look and feel.

You can also make changes to the various catalogs. When you do so, you can choose to update every item in your document that uses that particular format. This makes global updating very simple.

Once you have a file that you use as a template, you can import the formatting catalogs in this file to other files. This makes it possible to create many documents that all use the same template — and thus all are formatted consistently. You can also import formats from a single file into some or all of the files in a book at once, which is a useful shortcut.

Generally, creating a document "the right way," by setting up the appropriate catalogs will save you time — even if the document is relatively short. The longer and more complicated the document, the more time you'll save (and the more aggravation you'll avoid). And if you plan to reuse the template for other files, a solid template is absolutely critical.

If your template will be used by more than one person, create a guide where you explain all the different styles in the template and how to apply them correctly.

Copying Formats from a Template

A template is useful only if you can copy the formats in the template to other files. Follow these steps:

1. **Open the template file and the file that you want to copy the formats into.**

2. **Put your cursor in the file that you want to import to (the nontemplate file) and select File⇨Import⇨Formats.**

   This displays the Import Formats dialog box (see Figure 13-1).

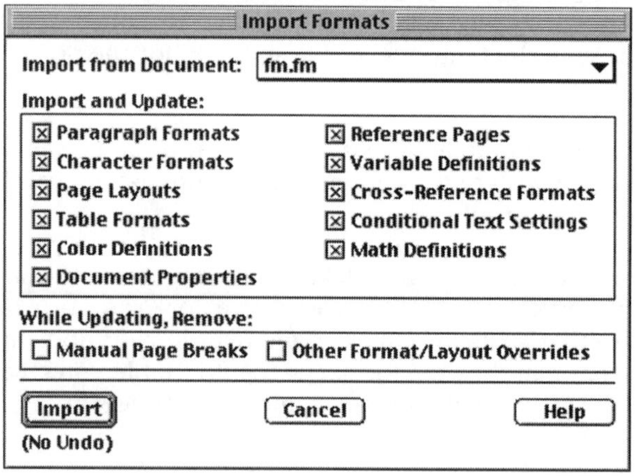

Figure 13-1:
The Import
Formats
dialog box
lists the
items that
are copied
when you
transfer
formats
from one file
to another.

Import Formats

Import from Document: fm.fm ▼

Import and Update:

☒ Paragraph Formats   ☒ Reference Pages
☒ Character Formats   ☒ Variable Definitions
☒ Page Layouts   ☒ Cross-Reference Formats
☒ Table Formats   ☒ Conditional Text Settings
☒ Color Definitions   ☒ Math Definitions
☒ Document Properties

While Updating, Remove:

☐ Manual Page Breaks   ☐ Other Format/Layout Overrides

[Import]   (Cancel)   (Help)
(No Undo)

3. **In the Import From Document drop-down list, select your template file.**

   Only files that are currently open are available in this list (this is why you had to open the template file earlier).

4. **Select the items for which you want to import formats.**

5. **Select the overrides that you want to remove.**

6. **Click Import.**

   The template file's formats are copied into the current file.

When you import formats from one file to another, FrameMaker does an *additive merge,* which means that the tags in the original document aren't deleted. The tags from the template document are added to the original document, and where the template document contains a tag with the exact same name as the tag in the original document, the *template* tag overwrites the original tag. See Figure 13-2 for an example.

Because the tags are case-sensitive, you end up with both Body and body and RegularText (no space) and Regular Text in your document. But Heading, Step1, and Step2+ in file B are overwritten by the information from file A, because the format names are exactly the same. This process occurs for all the different formatting catalogs, not just the paragraph tags.

File A formats	**File B formats**	**Importing formats from file A to file B results in this**
Body	*body*	Body
Heading	*Heading*	*body*
RegularText	*Regular Text*	Heading
Step1	*Step1*	RegularText
Step2+	*Step2+*	*Regular Text*
		Step1
		Step2+

Figure 13-2:
The process of merging two formatting catalogs.

Organizing Your Template

Developing an effective template means that you need to think carefully about your document's requirements, such as tables and figures, and then take advantage of FrameMaker's power to automate the design you want as much as possible.

Paragraph tags

Paragraph tags are the most visible and perhaps most-used component of your template. To create an effective list of paragraph tags, you need to analyze your document requirements. For example, ask yourself:

- How many heading levels and types of body text does the document need? Is the first paragraph after a heading formatted differently from other paragraphs?
- How many levels of indents does the document need?
- Do you need numeric and alphabetic numbered steps? How many types of numbered lists? How many levels of indent for the numbered lists?
- How many types of bulleted items does the document need? How many levels of indent for the bulleted items?
- What about formats for headers and footers?
- Do you need a numbering scheme for the document? Will the chapters or major sections be numbered? Will there be appendixes that are numbered alphabetically?
- Do you need notes, cautions, warnings, and other asides?
- Do you need separate styles for table information?
- What are the document's dimensions?

Take advantage of the features that FrameMaker can automate for you. For example:

- Use autonumbering to automate your steps, notes, and other repeated text.
- Use the Next Paragraph setting (in the Basic properties) intelligently. For example, you probably want to set the next paragraph after a heading to be a body tag. The tag after Step1 should probably be Step2.
- If a certain kind of heading always starts at the top of a page or column, make sure the Paragraph Designer does this automatically.
- Don't forget about the Advanced properties, where you can get hyphenation and graphics above and below the paragraph.

✔ The Language attribute on the Default Font properties control what dictionary you use to spell-check that paragraph. Remember that a language of None causes the paragraph to be skipped by the spell-checker.

Your paragraph tags use and depend on other template components, including

✔ **Reference pages:** The reference pages store the graphics called by the Frame Above and Frame Below settings in the Advanced properties.

✔ **Character tags:** The autonumbering format is a character tag.

✔ **Master page layouts:** If you use columns or side heads, those have an effect on the settings in the Pagination properties.

✔ **Table tags:** The Table Cell properties interact with the Table tag settings.

✔ **Color definitions:** Only the colors in your color catalog are available for the Color attribute in the Default Font properties.

Character tags

Character tags let you format a few characters or words within a paragraph consistently. Many other template components also use them to create formatting inside those components. To create a list of character tags, review this list:

✔ **Formatting inside paragraphs:** The most common requirements are boldface and italics.

✔ **Variables:** You can include character tags inside variables to format them automatically.

✔ **Autonumbering formats:** Remember that you can apply a character tag to the autonumbering in the Paragraph Designer.

✔ **Cross-references:** If you're delivering a PDF file, a format that creates blue, underlined text may be needed.

✔ **Generated files:** The specifications on the reference pages use character tags.

✔ **Index markers:** You can use character tags inside index markers, so you can, for example, use italics in an index entry.

✔ **Text lines:** When you create a text line (the *A* tool on the Graphics palette), you'll need a character tag to apply formatting to the text line.

Here are some tips and tricks to keep in mind:

- For most character tags, it's best to use the As Is setting throughout, except for the item that you want to change.

- The Language attribute of the character tag overrides the language of the paragraph for the tagged words.

- Consider naming your character tags by function, instead of by formatting. For example, if you create a character tag called *Syntax,* template users will know to use that tag for code samples. If you name the character tag *Courier,* you're only describing the formatting that the character tag applies, not the type of information that it should be applied to.

- Because you have to type in character tags in many places (index markers, reference pages, cross-reference, variables), make the names short. You might even create special one-letter tags to minimize typing, such as *I* for italics and *B* for bold.

If you want to use color in your character tags, you need to define the color in the color catalog to make it available in the Color drop-down list.

Page layouts (master pages)

The master pages control the basic appearance of your files. Use them to set page margins, columns, side head spacing, and more. By default, your documents use the Left and Right master pages, but you can apply custom master pages when necessary. Here are some things to consider when creating master pages:

- You are limited to 100 master pages. (If this is a problem for you, I'd really like to hear about your template; it must be a monster!)

- Whenever FrameMaker automatically creates new pages, those pages will use the default Left and Right master pages. Try to work with the Left and Right pages as much as possible, so that you don't have to apply other master pages when you add new pages to your document.

- If you're creating a template for a double-sided book (which uses left and right pages), make sure that the outside and inside margins are set up properly.

- Importing the page layout settings also imports the change bar settings, the page number style (Format⇨Document⇨Numbering), page size information (Format⇨Layout⇨Page Size), and the view options (View⇨Options).

The master pages you set up will depend on other template components. Make sure that you coordinate master pages with these components:

- ✔ **Paragraph tags:** The Paragraph Designer's Pagination tab lets you control various attributes that interact with the page layouts, such as starting a paragraph at the top of a column or a page. Most importantly, you can set up master pages to include a side head area, but you'll also need to modify the paragraph tags to take advantage of the side head space.

- ✔ **Variables, especially system variables:** Most master pages require page numbers and running headers and footers. To automate these, you need to use variables.

Table formats

Before you begin creating table tags, think about what types of tabular information you'll need in your document. You may want to create a table tag for each type of information, or you might just create three or four table tags with different ruling and shading styles and name them according to the formatting.

I strongly recommend that you create a table definition that has no lines or shading (I call mine *Invisible*). This table is very useful for setting up information across multiple columns. For example, if you have 20 short bulleted items, instead of listing all 20 down the left side of the page, you might put them in 4 columns. For this, the invisible table is perfect.

The table formats use a few other template components:

- ✔ **Paragraph tags:** The information in the Table Cell properties from the Paragraph Designer affects how paragraphs are displayed in a table. Furthermore, you can set up your table to use certain paragraph tags as a default. For more information, see Chapter 7.

- ✔ **Page layouts:** The positioning of the table on the page depends on the master page layouts. If you have a side head area, things get funny. If the table is narrow enough to fit into the main text area (excluding the side head area), it is lined up in the main text. If the table is too wide to fit in the main text area, it is aligned with the beginning of the side head area. As a result, a small change in table width could cause your table to "jump" from one location to the other.

- ✔ **Color definitions:** The color catalog stores the colors that are available for your table rules and shading.

- ✔ **Variables:** It's not exactly a dependency, but your two table-specific system variables, Table Continuation and Table Sheet, could be useful when you're creating your tables. See Chapter 10 for details.

Color definitions

The color definitions contain the colors that are available for your document. If you want to use a color anywhere for anything, you'll need to define it in the color catalog first.

Here are some color guidelines:

✔ Do your homework on color and the output you plan. If you're creating a full-color document that's going to be printed professionally, talk to your printer early and often.

✔ FrameMaker supplies some default colors. You can't change their definitions or delete them. Color names are, however, case-sensitive, so if you really want to, you can add *black* along with FrameMaker's default Black.

✔ The color definitions can be used throughout your document but don't have any dependencies on other template components.

Paragraph tags, character tags, graphics (not strictly a template item, but very important nonetheless), table tags, and variables, cross-references, reference pages, and other items use the color definitions via the character tags with color settings.

Document properties

The document properties are a collection of miscellaneous components. When you import these formats, the following items are updated:

✔ Acrobat Setup settings (but not the bookmark settings)

✔ The characters for which line breaks are allowed (Format⇨Document⇨Text Options)

✔ Custom marker types

✔ Footnote properties (Format⇨Document⇨Footnote Properties)

Reference pages

FrameMaker's reference pages store formatting information for generated files (such as tables of contents and indexes), along with HTML and XML conversion information, and named frames used in the Paragraph Designer (Advanced properties).

In addition to the "official" purpose of the reference pages, consider storing frequently used content there. For example, if you have certain graphic elements that you use in many different line art drawings, you might place copies on the reference pages so anyone who has the template also receives the graphics. This makes it easier to keep graphics drawn in FrameMaker consistent. Some users also store text on the reference pages.

The reference pages depend greatly on two components:

✔ **Paragraph tags:** The specifications for generated files determine what information you include in the generated files, but you need paragraph tags to determine the appearance of the information.

✔ **Character tags:** Use character tags inside the specifications for generated files to format information within the generated paragraphs.

The HTML conversion information is created from settings in the HTML Setup dialog box (select File⇨Utilities⇨HTML Setup), but the reference pages give you more control than the dialog box.

Don't open the HTML Setup dialog box while you're looking at the HTML reference pages (or vice versa). It can corrupt your reference pages.

Variable definitions

You need to set up the system variables and use them where appropriate. Many (but not all) system variables are best used on the master pages. Running headers and footers and page numbers, for example, are only available on the master pages. Again, the key to creating useful variables is to analyze your document and identify the items that would benefit from variables.

Here are some things to consider when setting up variables:

✔ Which system functions can you automate? Running headers and footers? Page numbers? Date and time stamps?

✔ What information could benefit from a user variable? Confidentiality statements? Copyright information? Book names?

✔ Do your documents contain product names or other information that changes frequently and could be maintained with a variable?

Variables depend on several other components:

✔ **Character tags:** You need character tags to embed formatting information in variable definitions.

✔ **Paragraph tags:** The <$paratext> building block pulls information from specific paragraph tags in your document.

✔ **Conditional text tags:** The <$condtag> building block pulls information from specific conditional text tags in your document.

Cross-reference formats

Cross-references are an important part of any document, but if you're planning to deliver information online, they are critical because FrameMaker cross-references become live hyperlinks when you convert to HTML or PDF format.

FrameMaker supplies some default cross-reference formats, but you'll probably need additional ones. Here are some items that you might need:

- References to chapter and appendix titles (for example, see Chapter 7 on page 18 or see Appendix B)
- References to major sections (for example, see "Heading" on page 29)
- Page-only references (for example, see page 88)
- References to other elements, with and without page numbers (for example, see Figure 8, see Table 19, see Example 12, see Figure 9 on page 27, see Table 2 on page 10, see Example 4 on page 100)

Cross-references depend on a few other components:

- **Character tags:** You need character tags to embed formatting information in cross-reference definitions.
- **Paragraph tags:** The <$paratext> and <$paranum> building blocks pull information from specific paragraph tags in your document.

Conditional text settings

Conditional text tags let you embed information in your document that isn't always displayed. This is a critical feature if you're single-sourcing information for multiple deliverables (print, PDF, online) out of a single file. It's also useful if you need to produce slightly different versions of the same content. For example, imagine that you have a manual that discusses a product that has two versions: a light version and a professional version. If the light version is a subset of the professional version, you should be able to flag all the information that is specific to the professional version as conditional text. When you hide that information, you have the light version of the manual; when you display it, you have the professional version.

Here are some thing to consider as you create conditional text tags:

- Try to limit your conditions to five or six. If you use more than that, things start to get confusing and difficult to manage.
- Be sure to use different colors for each condition type. This will help you keep track of what's what when you're looking at the entire document.

✔ Give your conditional text tags descriptive names. ProfessionalVersionOnly is much more intuitive than PVO.

✔ Be considerate of template users who are color-blind and provide cues in addition to the colors (like underlines or strikethrough).

✔ Try to avoid using multiple conditional text tags on the same piece of content. It's possible, but it's confusing.

Conditional text tags are almost completely independent of other template components, except for color definitions. When you pick a color for your conditional text, you can only use colors defined in the color catalog.

Math definitions

Math definitions let you set up formatting catalogs for your equations. This is an advanced (and quite interesting) feature and is unfortunately beyond the scope of this book. If you need information about equations, check Adobe's FrameMaker documentation.

Chapter 14

Creating Output in Many Media

. . . .

. . . .

Creating output from your FrameMaker files is probably one of your top priorities. After all, the stellar content that you've created doesn't do much good if you can't deliver it! This chapter examines different forms of output and how to create them from your FrameMaker files.

Printing a Hard Copy

Ten years ago, this chapter would have been entitled "Printing" — online help, HTML, PDF, and other media didn't exist. (FrameMaker existed, but just barely.) But today, print is only one of many output options.

Black and white

Black and white print is a nice, safe place to start, so I'll begin here.

Printing in the (home) office

Printing to a printer in your office should be just like printing from any application. Make sure that the printer is connected to your computer or to the network and then select the printer as the current printer. Select File⇨Print to display the Print dialog box. Depending on your platform and your selected printer, your dialog box may or may not look like the ones shown in Figures 14-1 and 14-2. Select the options you want (see Table 14-1 for your options) and then click the Print button. Your document is printed on the selected printer.

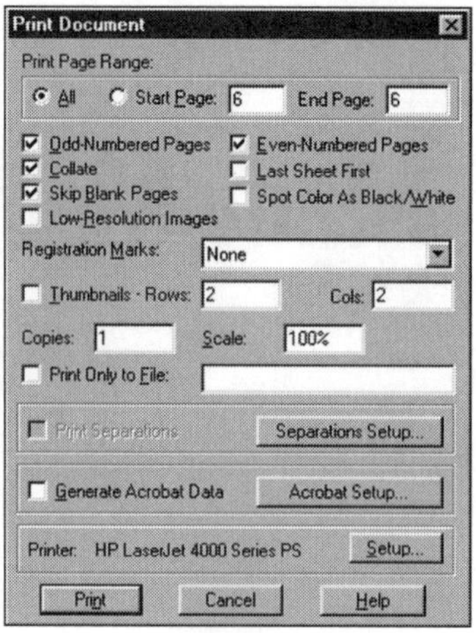

Figure 14-1: The Print dialog box gives you lots of printing options. The Windows version shown here is similar to the UNIX version.

Figure 14-2: On a Mac, the appearance of the Print dialog box depends greatly on the selected printer. The dialog box has different sections where you can select print-specific options.

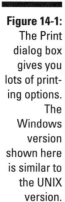

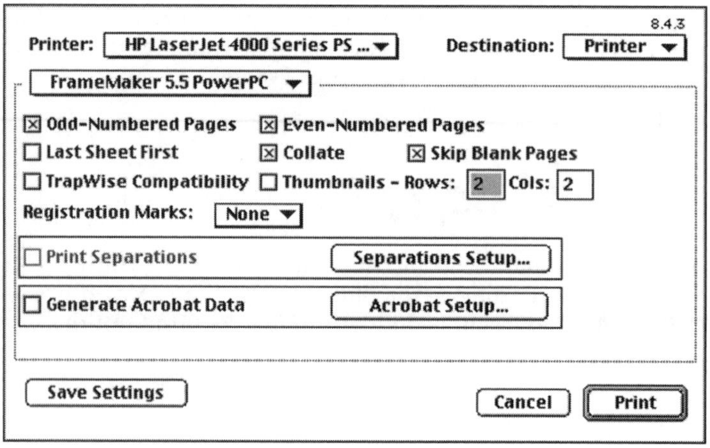

For more information about printing in your operating system, refer to *UNIX For Dummies,* 4th Edition, by John Levine and Margaret Levine Young, *Macs For Dummies,* 6th Edition, by David Pogue, or *PCs For Dummies,* 6th Edition, by Dan Gookin (all published by IDG Books Worldwide).

Table 14-1	FrameMaker Printing Options
Option	*Description*
Odd-Numbered Pages	If checked, odd pages are printed (1, 3, 5, . . .).
Even-Numbered Pages	If checked, even pages are printed (2, 4, 6, . . .).
Last Sheet First	If checked, the document prints starting with the last page. (Useful if your printer stacks pages in reverse order.)
Collate	If checked and you print multiple copies, the entire document is printed before beginning the second copy. If not checked, all copies of page 1 are printed, followed by all copies of page 2, and so on.
Skip Blank Pages	If checked, pages with no information on them are not printed. Master page items count as content; the page must be completely blank to be skipped.
TrapWise Compatibility (Mac)	If checked and you're printing a PostScript file, the PostScript file will be usable in TrapWise software (which provides trapping features). *Trapping* is a printing technique that is sometimes required when two colors are very close together in the printed document. It ensures that there are no unsightly gaps between the colors.
Thumbnails	If checked, FrameMaker prints multiple pages on a single page, using the row and column settings you specify. The defaults, two rows and two columns, would display four pages on one printed page.
Registration Marks	If checked, registration marks (also called crop marks or printer marks) are included on the printout. Western and Tombo (Japanese) crop marks are available.
Download Fonts (UNIX)	Lets you control whether fonts are included in the print job.
Destination (UNIX)	Lets you specify whether you print, create a PDF file, or print to PostScript.

(continued)

Table 14-1 *(continued)*

Option	Description
Print Separations	If checked, color separations are printed using the settings from the Separations Setup dialog box.
Spot Color as Black/White	If checked, spot colors are printed in pure black or pure white.
Separations Setup	Available only if the selected printer supports color output. For details about color separations, see "Understanding color separations" later in this chapter.
Generate Acrobat Data	If checked and you create a PostScript file, the PostScript file contains all the information required to maintain your cross-references as hyperlinks, create bookmarks for the file, and more. For more information, see "Creating PDF files" later in this chapter.
Acrobat Setup	Lets you set up the bookmarks for your Acrobat file. For details, see "Creating PDF files" later in this chapter.
Printer Setup	Lets you select a printer.

Commercial printing

If you need to print your content commercially, you have several options. Offset printing is considered the traditional printing process and is usually a good choice if you need to print at least 1,000 copies of your document (or book). Offset printing has high setup costs, but as you increase the number of copies you print, the per-copy cost decreases. Offset printing also offers the highest quality available.

If you plan to use offset printing, choose your print vendor carefully. At a minimum, your print vendor should accept PostScript files. A printer who uses and understands FrameMaker files is ideal, but can be difficult to find.

Other factors to consider depend on your project's requirements. Here's a list to think about:

- What will the shipping and delivery costs be?
- What is the turnaround time for the project?

✔ What is the cost? (Printers specialize in different niches; some will be more competitive for large runs of 100,000 or more; others specialize in short-run jobs of 5,000 or fewer.)

✔ Does the printer accept files electronically (FTP or e-mail)?

Color

The biggest difficulty in creating printed materials in glorious color is actually your monitor. Because colors are created differently on paper than on-screen, the colors you see on your monitor are usually noticeably different from the paper output. Here are some techniques to minimize color problems:

✔ Don't rely on the color shown on your monitor.

✔ Get swatch books (your printer should have them) that show you examples of the colors on paper. Use these to pick the right color.

✔ Do a press check. When your printer begins to run the job, go to the printing plant and take a look at the first few copies coming off the press to make sure that the colors are correct. (While you're there, get a tour. Printers have lots of very cool equipment.)

Selecting a color print vendor

In addition to the criteria listed for commercial printers in the black and white section earlier, you need to consider some additional factors for color print vendors:

✔ How many colors does the printer support? How many colors can the press print in one pass? (For example, you can do four-color work on a two-color press, but it requires sending each piece of paper through the press twice: once for the first two colors and again for the second two. A four-color press usually will provide better results.)

✔ How many colors do you need? In many cases, adding just one color to the basic black can help you create an effective document.

✔ Is tight registration required and can the print vendor handle it? (*Registration* is the alignment of each color on the page. If the registration is slightly off, the colors don't quite line up. If you have space between one color and another, this isn't a problem, but if you need to print colors that adjoin or overlap, registration needs to be very accurate.)

Understanding color separations

If your printer works directly with FrameMaker files, you don't need to do anything special for files that contain color. But if you plan to ship PostScript files, you'll need create color separations.

A *color separation* is a file in which each page contains only the information required for a specific color. The most common printing setup is to use four colors: cyan, magenta, yellow, and black, which is abbreviated to CMYK. (I know, I know. The black gets a K because it is the *key* color.) So, for a CMYK printing process, you need four color-separated pages for each page in the document. The printer combines those separations on the press to create the full-color image.

The process you use to create color separations varies depending on what platform you're working on, but here are the basics:

- ✔ Install a printer driver that will support the printer's equipment (your printer can help you figure out which driver to use).
- ✔ Print a PostScript file using this driver and with color separations turned on.

The PostScript file will contain four pages for every page in your document. Those four pages will be the separations: one cyan, one magenta, one yellow, and one black. And don't worry — each separation is labeled with its color.

Printing color separations

If you're ready to create your separated PostScript file, here's how to do it:

1. **Open the book file or the document file that you want to print.**

2. **Make sure that the appropriate printer is selected.**

3. **Select File⇨Print to display the Print dialog box (refer to Figures 14-1 and 14-2).**

4. **Click the Separations Setup button to display the Set Print Separations dialog box (see Figure 14-3).**

   For a CMYK print project, all color definitions should be in the Print As Process list.

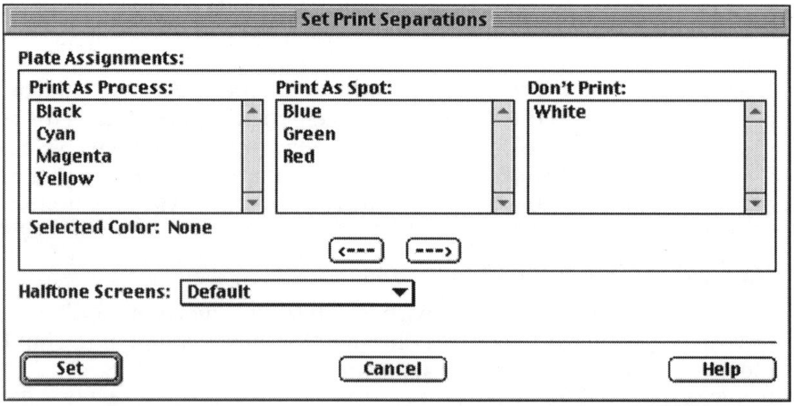

Figure 14-3:
Setting up color separations on a Macintosh printer driver.

Set Print Separations

Plate Assignments:

Print As Process:	Print As Spot:	Don't Print:
Black	Blue	White
Cyan	Green	
Magenta	Red	
Yellow		

Selected Color: None

(<---)   (--->)

Halftone Screens: Default ▼

(Set)   (Cancel)   (Help)

5. **Click Set to return to the Print dialog box.**

6. **Set up the printer to print a PostScript file, and then click Print (or Save).**

Understanding spot color

If you don't need a full-color piece, consider *spot color*. Spot color means that you specify the colors you want to use on the press (instead of using the CMYK inks). For example, you could create a document that uses only black and purple. In a four-color (CMYK) process, the printer would create that purple with a combination of four colors, so you'd need a four-color press. But with a spot color, you would only need two: black and purple (the purple is mixed before you go to print). The printer would set up the press to use those specific inks. Spot color is usually more economical than a four-color process, and you can create some very attractive output with it.

It's possible to use a four-color process *and* spot colors in the same document. You might, for example, create a full-color document that includes a metallic color (and metallic colors can't be created using CMYK inks), so you could set up your document for CMYK plus a metallic spot color. (This would require a press that supports at least five colors.)

The key to printing both spot and process colors is to set up the colors you are using in your color definitions (see Chapter 11). Make sure that the metallic color is defined as a spot color and that all the other colors are defined as *process*. (A process color is a color created by combining various inks.)

Finally, make sure that you set up the metallic color to print as a spot color in your separations.

Understanding trapping

Commercial printers use *trapping* to work with different colors that are very close together. A detailed discussion of trapping is beyond the scope of this book, but I'll give you the short version. On a printing press, each color is put on the page separately. You print color separations with registration marks to help the printer line up all the printing plates (with the different colors). Small registration problems will result in colors that don't quite meet up at the edges. These alignment problems are particularly noticeable where you have two very different colors that adjoin (or meet up) on your page. If the two colors are off slightly, you might end up with a small white line between the two, where no color was printed at all.

To avoid this problem, printers use trapping software. Trapping sets one of the two colors to print a little extra to overlap (or a little less for overlapping colors). Figuring out which color to trap and how much is actually quite complicated, so graphic designers and commercial printers use trapping software to help with the process.

PostScript basics

PostScript is a language developed by Adobe. It describes the contents of a page and is designed to be platform-independent (the same across Windows, Macintosh, UNIX, and other operating systems) and device-independent (the same PostScript file can be used on different printers). In the real world, some customization is usually required to make the file work on a specific platform and with a specific printer. Almost all commercial printers (digital and offset) use PostScript to create output. Some office printers also use PostScript.

You'll need PostScript for any commercial printing. A few printers accept FrameMaker files, but if you send the FrameMaker files, you also need to include any referenced graphics and all the fonts you used in the document. With PostScript, you can create a single (very large) file that includes all your content, your graphics, and your fonts. (Fortunately, PostScript files compress well.) PostScript is also important if you're creating PDF files, because you create PDF files by first creating a PostScript file and then processing that file to create a PDF file.

FrameMaker provides limited support for trapping. You can create a separated PostScript file with no trapping information, which a printer can then feed into trapping software. On the Macintosh, one of the options in the Print dialog box is to generate PostScript with TrapWise compatibility. TrapWise is dedicated trapping software and checking this option means that your PostScript file will include some extra information to help TrapWise analyze where you need trapping.

Creating PDF Files

Adobe's Portable Document Format (PDF) is the format used by Acrobat files. Adobe Acrobat lets you create a file that looks just like your original FrameMaker file but can be viewed without owning a copy of FrameMaker. The person who wants to view the file just needs a copy of Acrobat Reader software, which is free from Adobe's Web site (www.adobe.com).

Originally, Adobe marketed PDF as a replacement for the old "print it out and overnight it to the client" review process. But in addition to electronic reviews, PDF format has become an important part of the World Wide Web, because you can make a PDF file available online and be sure that it will look the same for every user. (This in contrast to HTML, where you can never be sure exactly what might happen in different browsers.) As a result, PDF is widely used when the appearance of the document is critical.

To create a PDF file, you need to generate a PostScript file from your FrameMaker file and distill the PostScript file into PDF format.

When you "save as" PDF, the same process takes place (print to PostScript, distill the PostScript), but you don't have an opportunity to check your settings; the defaults are used. For this reason, I strongly recommend that you create your PDF files manually instead of using Save As PDF — at least until you're certain that your settings are working.

Make sure that you have a PostScript printer driver installed on your system. You don't need the actual PostScript printer; you're just going to fake out your computer and pretend that you have one attached to your machine.

The next few sections discuss how to configure your system with a PostScript driver, generate the PostScript file, and finally distill the PostScript file into a PDF file.

Setting up a PostScript driver

The FrameMaker CDs provided by Adobe include the AdobePS printer driver, but more up-to-date versions of AdobePS are available from Adobe's Web site (www.adobe.com/prodindex/printerdrivers/main.html).

This Web site also includes a downloadable PDF file with instructions on how to install and use the PostScript printer drivers. Download and install the appropriate printer driver for your platform and then proceed to the section for your platform.

You don't need to install the Adobe PostScript driver on a UNIX machine, because UNIX by default includes a PostScript driver.

Macintosh

After installing the AdobePS driver, you need to assign the proper PostScript printer description (PPD) file. Go to the Chooser (select Apple menu⇨ Chooser) and click the AdobePS driver icon.

Click the Setup button on the right side of the window to display the setup options.

Click Select PPD, and select the Acrobat Distiller (PPD) file on your system. Generally, this file is in the System Folder, under Extensions, under Printer Descriptions. Click the Select button. Click OK to return to the Chooser.

Your AdobePS driver is now set up and ready to generate PostScript files.

Windows

During the AdobePS driver installation process, you'll be prompted to supply the PostScript printer description (PPD) file. You should have the Acrobat Distiller 3 or 4 PPD on your system.

Don't use the generic PostScript driver that's installed with Windows to create PostScript files for distillation. This is a driver provided by Microsoft, and the PostScript files it creates will not work in Distiller.

The default PostScript driver settings should work for you, but they don't always behave properly on a Windows machine. If you're having trouble with your files, go to the print options (right-click the printer in your Printers folder), and in the PostScript tab, change the PostScript setting to Optimize for Portability (see Figure 14-4).

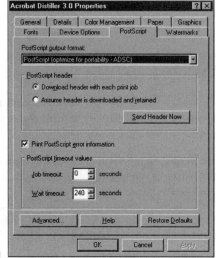

Figure 14-4:
A single change in the printer driver settings often eliminates distillation headaches.

Creating the PostScript file

Once you've set up the PostScript printer driver, you need to use that printer driver to create a PostScript file. During this process, instead of sending a stream of instructions to an actual printer, you capture the printer instructions in a file. These instructions are in the PostScript printer language, so the file is called a PostScript file.

To create the file, first select the PostScript printer driver as your printer. Then go to FrameMaker and open the file (or book) for which you want to create a PDF file. Print the file (select File⇨Print). In the Print dialog box, make sure that Print to File is selected. The exact setup varies depending on your operating system, see Figures 14-5 and 14-6.

Figure 14-5:
To print to
file on a
Windows
machine,
select the
Print Only to
File check
box and
specify the
file name.
(The UNIX
version is
very similar.)

Figure 14-6:
On a
Macintosh,
select the
File
dropdown
item. Notice
that the
Print button
changes to
Save. When
you click the
Save button,
you're
prompted to
specify the
file name.

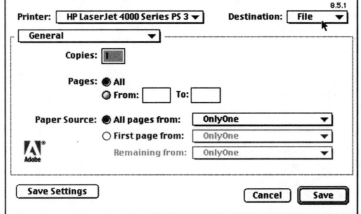

For other Macintosh printer drivers, the selection may be a radio button on a single Print dialog box instead of a drop-down list.

What about the PDFWriter?!?

When you install Adobe Acrobat on a Windows or Macintosh system, you acquire a new printer driver called PDFWriter. The PDFWriter lets you "print" from FrameMaker (or any other application) and create a PDF file directly, without going through the distillation process. Sounds great, but unfortunately, it has some limitations.

Problems with PDF files created with PDFWriter include the following:

✔ You cannot embed fonts.

✔ EPS graphics look terrible, because the low-resolution preview image is rendered (instead of the high-resolution EPS file that you get when you distill).

Because of these (and other) limitations, I strongly recommend that you avoid using PDFWriter. It's okay for quick previews, though.

Setting up Acrobat Distiller

When you first install Acrobat Distiller, its settings, by default, are to make the PDF file as small as possible. Unfortunately, this typically results in files where the graphics are fuzzy. This problem has been fixed in Acrobat version 4, so if you're using Acrobat 4, you can skip this section. To set up Acrobat Distiller version 3, follow these steps:

1. **Open Acrobat Distiller.**

2. **Select Distiller⇨Job Options to display the Job Options dialog box (see Figure 14-7).**

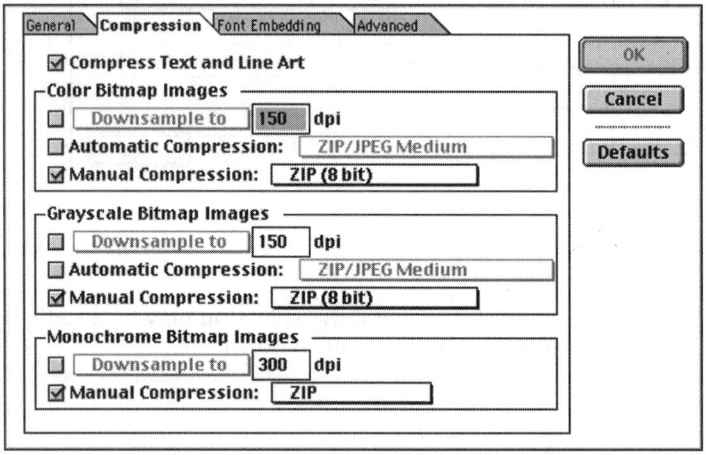

Figure 14-7: The Job Options dialog box lets you adjust compression to avoid the fuzzy graphics problem.

3. **Change the job options.**

   Make them match the settings in Figure 14-7 — no downsampling, manual compression using ZIP 8-bit for color and grayscale images, and ZIP for monochrome images.

4. **Click OK to save the new job options.**

Distilling the PostScript file into PDF

Finally, you're ready to distill the PostScript file. Open Acrobat Distiller, check the settings, then select File⇨Open and select the PostScript file you want to distill. Distiller immediately begins processing the file.

Creating HTML Files

Hypertext Markup Language (HTML) is the language used on the World Wide Web. FrameMaker includes an HTML converter, and several third-party tools are also available.

FrameMaker's converter

The built-in FrameMaker converter lets you save a FrameMaker file as an HTML file (or files). To do so, you select File⇨Save As and select HTML as the file type.

To adjust the HTML output, you can change HTML mapping. Select File⇨Utilities⇨HTML Setup to display the HTML Setup dialog box (see Figure 14-8).

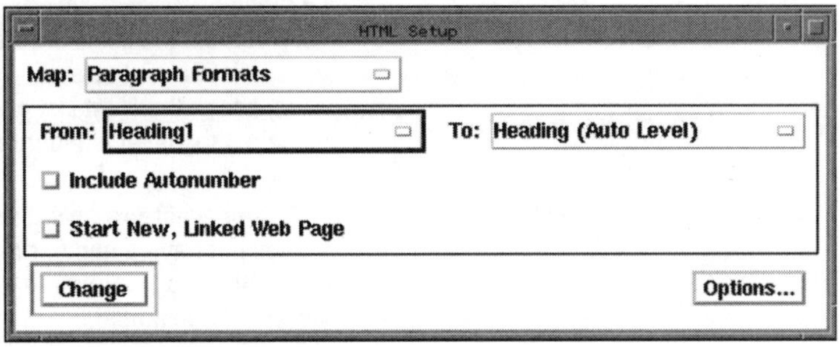

Figure 14-8: Set up your initial mappings in the HTML Setup dialog box.

HTML Setup

Map: Paragraph Formats

From: Heading1   To: Heading (Auto Level)

☐ Include Autonumber

☐ Start New, Linked Web Page

Change   Options...

Mapping paragraph formats

You start by mapping the FrameMaker paragraph formats to HTML equivalents. The HTML Setup dialog box lists the FrameMaker formats on the left (in the From drop-down list) and the HTML equivalents on the right (in the To drop-down list). For each paragraph format, select an HTML mapping.

Table 14-2	HTML Mappings for Paragraphs	
HTML Mapping	*Result*	*What It Means*
Heading (auto level)	<H1>, <H2>, . . ., <H6>	An HTML heading tag is inserted for this paragraph. The level of the paragraph is determined by the Headings Table, which you'll find on the reference pages. For more information, see Chapter 15.
Paragraph	<P>	An HTML paragraph is created for this paragraph.
Preformatted Text	<PRE>	The paragraph is converted to preformatted text.
Address	<ADDRESS>	The paragraph is converted to address text.
Block Quote	<BLOCKQUOTE>	The paragraph is converted to a block quote.
List Item	<OL> or <UL>	Depending on the autonumber in the paragraph, FrameMaker automatically assigns either a bulleted list (<UL>) or a numbered list (<OL>). (You can override FrameMaker's choice, but you have to use the HTML reference pages to do so. See Chapter 15 for details.) By default, the list is created as a first-level list. If the list is not a first-level list, check the Nest List check box and specify the level of indentation for this list
	<LI>	Creates a paragraph within a list that does not have a number or a bullet. Useful for explanatory text between steps, for example.

HTML Mapping	Result	What It Means
Data Term	<DT>	Creates a data term item.
Data Definition	<DD>	Creates a data definition item.
Data Definition (continued)		Creates a data definition continuation item.
Throw Away		The paragraph is not converted to HTML. The content of the paragraph is eliminated from the HTML output.

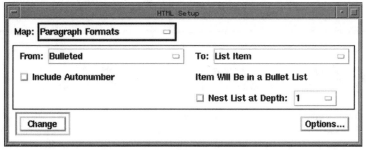

Figure 14-9:
When you select List Item as your mapping, the dialog box changes slightly.

Advanced HTML mapping

In addition to the options available in the HTML Setup dialog box, you can work with the settings in the HTML reference pages. For details, see Chapter 15.

Creating XML Files

In version 5.5.6, FrameMaker has added an XML export feature. XML stands for Extensible Markup Language — it's supposed to be the Next Big Thing. To create an XML file, select File⇨Save As and select XML as the format.

For more information about XML, see *XML For Dummies,* by Ed Tittel, Norbert Mikula, and Ramesh Chandak (IDG Books Worldwide, Inc.).

For HTML conversion, you have a convenient HTML Setup dialog box. But for XML conversion, all the settings are on the XML reference pages; no nifty XML Setup dialog box. For details on configuring the XML reference pages, see Chapter 15.

The importance of being structured

When you create HTML output, *structure* suddenly becomes critical. For print and PDF output, you can get away with using creative formatting tricks and overriding the template periodically. But all the HTML filters use the formatting tags (paragraph tags, character tags, and more) in your document to assign HTML equivalent tags. If you use formatting overrides, they can get you in big trouble when you create HTML output.

Imagine, for example, that someone (certainly not you) used the Format menu to modify the font, font size, and other attributes of a paragraph with a Body tag. Although the paragraph still has a Body paragraph tag, it now looks just like a Heading1. Unfortunately, this distinction is lost on the HTML converter. It converts the mangled paragraph based on the tag (Body), not based on the appearance (Heading1, more or less). This can cause some unpleasant surprises. I strongly recommend that you avoid paragraph overrides if at all possible, especially in documents that will be converted to HTML.

Creating RTF and WinHelp Files

Windows online help, or WinHelp, is based on rich text format (RTF), which is a Microsoft format that is read by Microsoft Word. FrameMaker includes an RTF export filter, but the output generated by that filter is — and I say this with the greatest of respect — awful. If you need to reuse your FrameMaker content in online help, consider investing in a third-party export tool that produces better RTF output. Your choices include the following:

- ✔ Filtrix by Blueberry Software (www.blueberry.com)
- ✔ MIF2RTF by Omni Systems (www.omsys.com)
- ✔ WebWorks Publisher by Quadralay (www.quadralay.com)

You will recoup the investment almost immediately because you'll eliminate a lot of tedious clean-up work.

If you decide to stick with the built-in RTF export, be prepared to wait. For complex FrameMaker files, the RTF export process on Windows can take a long time — as much as several hours!

Chapter 15

Understanding Reference Pages

● ●

In This Chapter

▶ Setting up a graphic frame

▶ Understanding generated files

▶ Setting up HTML conversion

▶ Preparing for XML conversion

▶ Adding a new reference page

▶ Deleting a reference page

● ●

*L*ike most desktop publishing packages, FrameMaker includes body pages and master pages. The body pages are where you create content; the master pages are the templates (or skeletons) for the body pages. Generally, the master pages include items such as page numbers, headers and footers, and a placeholder for the text that you insert on the body pages.

FrameMaker adds a third type of page: the reference page. You can use reference pages to store information that is called (or *referenced*) in other places in your document. It's possible to associate a particular graphic with a paragraph tag; the graphic is stored on the reference page in a graphic frame. You also store information about generated files (such as tables of contents and indexes) and HTML conversion settings on the reference pages.

This chapter looks at the various reference page items and how to set them up.

Setting Up a Graphic Frame

As part of a paragraph tag definition, you can specify that the paragraph includes a frame above or below the paragraph. This lets you insert a line under a heading or a graphic above a paragraph tag. This option is available in the Advanced properties of the Paragraph Designer (see Figure 15-1).

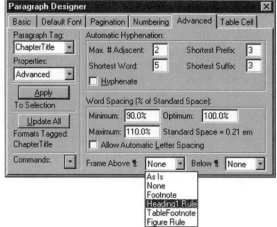

Figure 15-1:
The Frame
Above and
Frame
Below
options let
you
automatically
insert
graphics
with each
paragraph.

The items listed in the Frame Above and Frame Below options correspond to the frames defined on the reference pages (see Figure 15-2).

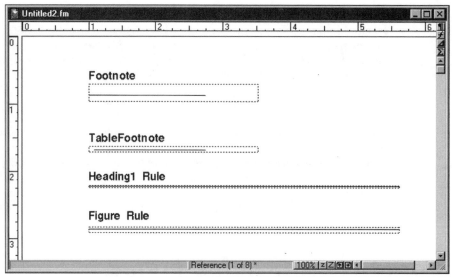

Figure 15-2:
This
reference
page
contains the
frames
that are
available for
use in your
paragraphs
(compare
with
Figure 15-1).

You can create new graphic frames for use in the Paragraph Designer and rename the existing ones. The following sections describe how.

Creating a graphic frame

To create a new graphic frame:

1. **Go to the reference pages (select View➪Reference Pages).**

   Find a reference page with available space or add a new one to make room for the new frame (see "Adding a New Reference Page," later in this chapter).

2. **Select the Graphic Frame tool and draw a frame on the page.**

   Every frame on a reference page must have a name, so when you release the mouse, you're prompted to name the new frame.

3. **Type a name in the Name field, and then click Set.**

   If you leave the Name field blank, the frame is not created.

   The new frame appears on the reference page. You can import graphics into this frame and use the graphic tools to draw in the frame. The frame is now listed in the Advanced properties of the Paragraph Designer in the Frame Above and Frame Below options.

To help keep track of reference frames, it's probably a good idea to add a text label that identifies that frame. Put it outside the frame so that it's not included when you use the frame elsewhere. (The labels *aren't* created automatically.)

Identifying a reference frame

The default frames provided in FrameMaker files include labels above the frames that identify them. But Adobe provides these labels as a convenience to you; they aren't part of the reference frame. To check the name of a frame, select it by clicking it. The name of the frame is displayed in the status bar.

Renaming a graphic frame

You can change a frame's name after creating it. Select the frame, and then click in the status bar where the frame name is displayed. This displays the Frame Name dialog box. Type in a new name and click Set.

If you change the name of a frame that's used by a paragraph, the paragraph will lose its referenced frame! You'll have to adjust the Paragraph Designer for that paragraph tag to use the new frame name. (For more information about the Paragraph Designer, see Chapter 4.)

Modifying Generated File Definitions

The most common generated files are tables of contents and indexes, but you can generate other files, such as lists of imported graphics, lists of markers, and much more.

Each generated file has a two- or three-digit file extension: TOC for the table of contents, IX for the index, and AML for alphabetical list of markers. When you generate a file, FrameMaker automatically creates a flow on the reference pages (on a new page) that controls the formatting of the generated information. The name of this flow corresponds to the file extension. So, for example, a generated table of contents contains a flow on the reference pages named TOC.

To customize the appearance of a generated file, you modify the information on the reference pages. Chapter 18 discusses how to set up the table of contents, including the reference page information; Chapter 19 discusses the index.

One useful generated file that doesn't get much attention is the list of references. It lets you create a list of imported graphics, fonts, and other items for a file. Take a look at the Generate/Book dialog box (select File⇨Generate/Book) for the list of generated files that are available. Each one has a slightly different reference page definition; Figure 15-3 shows the definition for the list of references (LOR).

Figure 15-3:
The specification for a list of references (LOR) is simple.

```
openObjectId <$relfilename>:<$ObjectType> <$ObjectId>
<$referencename> <$pagenum>
```

Setting Up HTML Conversion

FrameMaker stores settings for HTML conversion on the reference pages. You can configure some of the HTML conversion settings in the HTML Setup dialog box (select File⇨Utilities⇨HTML Setup), but if you want to go beyond the basics, you need to work with the information on the reference pages. For basic information about the HTML Setup dialog box, see Chapter 14.

Don't attempt to work in the HTML Setup dialog box with the HTML reference pages displayed (or vice versa). This can cause some serious FrameMaker pain because changing the settings in the dialog box changes the information on the reference pages (and vice versa).

This section discusses how to use the HTML reference pages to fine-tune your HTML conversion and use the advanced features, which are available only from the reference pages.

If you want to do any serious work with the HTML converter, I recommend that you learn some basic HTML coding. Check out *HTML For Dummies,* 3rd Edition, by Ed Tittel and Stephen James (IDG Books Worldwide, Inc).

Although the XML converter uses a separate set of reference pages (labeled XML), most of the settings described in this HTML conversion settings are identical to the settings used in the XML conversion settings. The "Setting Up XML Conversion" section discusses the differences.

Creating HTML output

To create HTML files from your FrameMaker file, select File⇨Save As and select HTML as the output format. Don't forget to give the file a .html or .htm extension.

After creating the initial HTML output, use the techniques described in the next few sections to fine-tune your conversion. As you make changes, resave the files to see how things are working.

Creating HTML reference pages

The FrameMaker templates provided with version 5.5 include HTML reference pages, so if you create files based on those templates, the new files should automatically include HTML reference pages. But for files that were originally created in older versions of FrameMaker (or using a template that doesn't include HTML reference pages), you may not have any HTML reference pages initially.

If the HTML reference pages are missing, force FrameMaker to create them. Fortunately, this is a simple process. Just go to the HTML Setup dialog box (select File⇨Utilities⇨HTML Setup) and click Change.

You don't have to make any changes to the settings in the HTML Setup dialog box.

FrameMaker now creates the HTML reference pages with the default settings. Figure 15-4 shows the first page of the HTML reference pages.

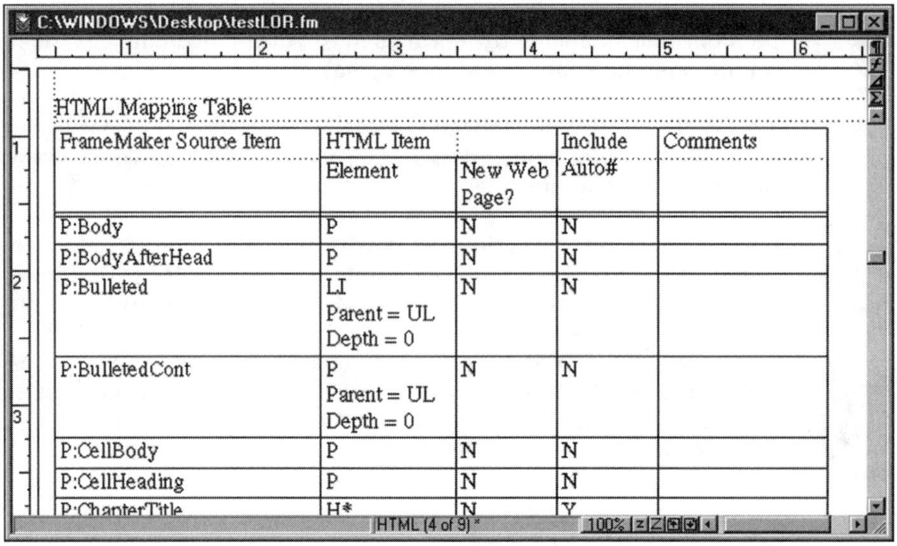

Figure 15-4:
The HTML
reference
pages let
you modify
the same
information
as the HTML
Setup dialog
box, but the
reference
pages
provide
additional
options that
aren't
available in
the dialog
box.

Setting up paragraph mappings

The HTML reference pages contain several tables that store your mappings. The first table, the HTML Mapping Table, controls several conversion settings, including your paragraph mappings. The HTML Mapping Table lists the paragraph mappings first.

Table 15-1 describes each column in the HTML Mapping Table.

Table 15-1	HTML Mapping Table Items
Column Name	*Description*
FrameMaker Source Item	Lists the item being mapped. A P: entry indicates a paragraph tag, a C: entry indicates a character tag, and an X: entry indicates a cross-reference format.
HTML Item/Element	Lists the HTML element to which the item is converted.
HTML Item/New Web Page?	Options are Y or N. Controls whether the paragraph tag generates a new web page (Y) or not (N).

Column Name	Description
Include Auto#	Options are Y or N. Controls whether the paragraph's autonumber is included (Y) or not included (N) in the HTML output.
Comments	Not used in conversion. The Comments field lets you include explanatory information about your mappings. It's a good idea to describe what you did in the conversion settings here.

Understanding heading mappings

In the HTML Mapping Table, a heading paragraph uses the H* mapping element. The asterisk (*) indicates that the heading level isn't specified. But later on the reference pages, you'll find a Headings Table (see Figure 15-5), where the heading levels are set up.

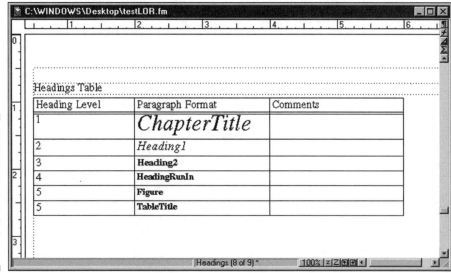

Figure 15-5:
The Headings Table is where you set up the hierarchy for your headings.

The Headings Table resides on a reference page named Headings, in a flow named Headings (seems like overkill, don't you think?).

Table 15-2 lists the columns available in the Headings Table.

Table 15-2	Headings Table Items
Column Name	*Description*
Heading Level	This number determines the heading level in the HTML output of the paragraph listed in the paragraph format column.
Paragraph Format	Specifies the paragraph tag. By default, FrameMaker uses the corresponding paragraph tag in this column (for example, the text "heading 1" is actually in heading 1 format). Seems like more of that overkill to me.
Comments	Not used in conversion. The Comments field lets you include explanatory information about your mappings.

The numbers that you set up in the Headings Table are what replaces the asterisk that you've specified for a heading in the HTML Mappings Table. So, for example, if you have three main headings in your chapters (named ChapterTitle, Heading1, and Heading2), you would want the Headings Table to look like this:

Heading Level	Paragraph Format	Comments
1	ChapterTitle	Used for chapter titles. Only one per chapter.
2	Heading1	Main headings within a chapter.
3	Heading2	Subheadings within a chapter.

Understanding bulleted and numbered list mappings

HTML code contains two list types: bulleted or unordered lists (UL) and numbered or ordered lists (OL). Unlike FrameMaker, HTML ordered lists don't support complicated, multipart autonumbering. As a result, you may have some difficulties in converting your files if, for example, you have a set of steps labeled 1a, 1b, 1c.

If you set up your paragraph mappings through the HTML Setup dialog box, you don't have any control over whether a list is exported as a bulleted or numbered list. FrameMaker examines the autonumbering scheme for each list paragraph tag and decides for you which type of list is appropriate. But in the reference pages, you can set the numbering scheme that you need.

Take a look at the example shown in Figure 15-6. For regular paragraphs, you only have a single line in the Element column, but for a list item, more information is required.

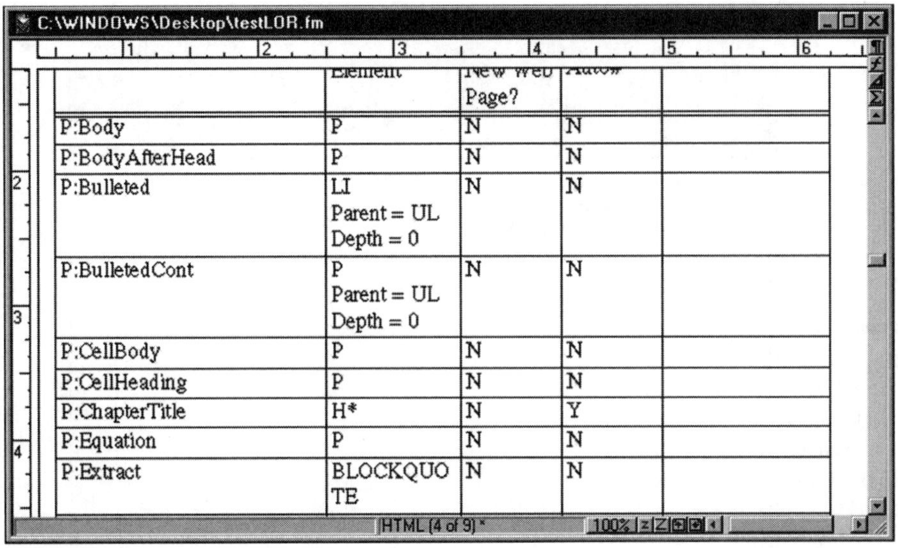

	Element	New Web Page?	
P:Body	P	N	N
P:BodyAfterHead	P	N	N
P:Bulleted	LI Parent = UL Depth = 0	N	N
P:BulletedCont	P Parent = UL Depth = 0	N	N
P:CellBody	P	N	N
P:CellHeading	P	N	N
P:ChapterTitle	H*	N	Y
P:Equation	P	N	N
P:Extract	BLOCKQUO TE	N	N

Figure 15-6: For a list item, you must specify the HTML code, the parent HTML code, and the depth (indentation level) for the list.

On the first line of the table cell, you provide the HTML element. (For a bulleted or numbered list, this is usually LI, but you might also set up definition lists this way.)

On the second line, you provide the parent HTML element. All HTML lists are nested and have tags for the list itself and for each list item. For example, a bulleted list would look like this:

```
<UL>
<LI>first bulleted item
<LI>second bulleted item
<LI>third bulleted item
</UL>
```

The <UL> and </UL> tags identify the beginning and end of the unordered list. The <LI> tags identify each bullet item. Figure 15-7 shows the result.

On the third line of your list item definition, you must set the depth of the list. A first-level list would have a depth of 0, a second-level list a depth of 1, and so on.

Setting up character mappings

Character mappings work much like paragraph mapping, but because character tags are less complicated, there's less to do. Character mappings are set up in the HTML Mappings Table. Figure 15-8 shows an example of character tag mapping.

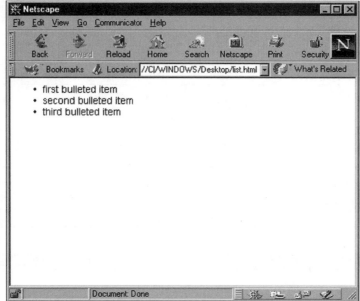

Figure 15-7:
The HTML
<UL> ele-
ment and
<LI> tags
look like this
in a
browser.

Figure 15-8:
Emphasis is
mapped to
the HTML
<I> element,
which
results in
italic text in
the Web
browser.

FrameMaker Source Item	HTML Item		Include	Comments
	Element	New Web Page?	Auto#	
C:BulletSymbol	THROW AWAY	N	N	
C:Callout	EM	N	N	
C:ChapterNumber	EM	N	N	
C:Emphasis	I	N	N	
C:EquationNumber	THROW AWAY	N	N	
C:EquationVariables	EM	N	N	
C:PageNumber	THROW AWAY	N	N	
C:StepNumber	THROW AWAY			

HTML Mapping Table

Although you could set up a character tag to generate a new Web page, it's probably not a good idea unless you have a very unusual document!

Setting up cross-reference format mappings

With cross-reference formats, Adobe has come up with yet another mapping scheme. Even though the cross-reference formats are mapped in the HTML Mappings Table, they work differently from the paragraph and character mappings. Each FrameMaker format is mapped to an HTML conversion macro. Figure 15-9 shows an example of a cross-reference format mapping (note that the cross-reference mappings all begin with X:).

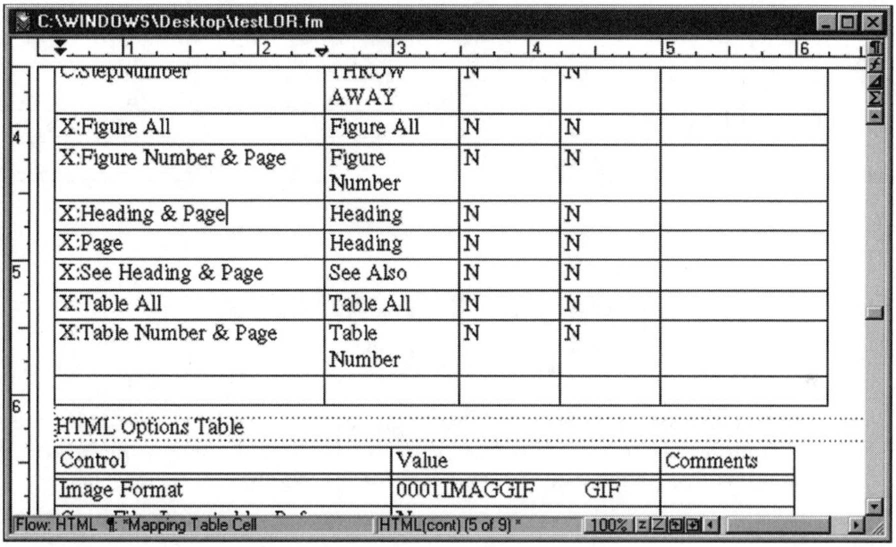

Figure 15-9:
The item listed in the second column (Heading) is actually an HTML conversion macro.

You'll find the HTML conversion macros on the HTML reference pages in a table labeled Cross-Reference Macros. Figure 15-10 shows a sample table.

Typically, you need to change your cross-references to eliminate page numbers from the HTML output.

The first item in the Cross-Reference Macros Table is the macro name. This item is used in the HTML Mappings Table. The second item is the cross-reference definition that you want to use instead of the original cross-reference format. In these definitions, you use the same building blocks as in the regular cross-reference formats. (Check out Chapter 9 for more information about cross-reference building blocks.)

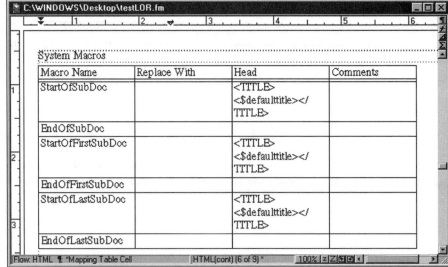

Figure 15-10:
The Cross-
Reference
Macros
Table lets
you change
your cross-
reference
formats to
make them
more useful
for online
delivery.

Setting up page templates and navigation bars

You can set up HTML code to begin and end each HTML page. The page
template information is stored in the System Macros Table on the HTML
reference pages. See Figure 15-11 for an example.

Figure 15-11:
The System
Macros
Table lets
you set up
the code for
the
beginning
and end of
each page.

FrameMaker provides several different system macros; Table 15-3 describes them.

Table 15-3	System Macros for HTML Conversion
Macro	**Inserts HTML Code Where?**
StartOfDoc	At the beginning of the main HTML document.
EndOfDoc	At the end of the main HTML document.
StartOfSubDoc	At the beginning of the HTML subdocuments (except the first and last).
EndOfSubDoc	At the end of the HTML subdocuments (except the first and last)
EndOfFirstSubDoc	At the end of the first HTML subdocument.
StartOfLastSubDoc	At the beginning of the last HTML subdocument.
EndOfLastSubDoc	At the end of the last HTML subdocument.

In addition to HTML code, you can use several FrameMaker building blocks in your conversion mappings. Table 15-4 explains available building blocks.

Table 15-4	Building Blocks Available in the HTML Conversion Macros
Building Block	**Replaced With What During Conversion?**
<$paratext>	The text of the current paragraph.
<$paratag>	The name of the current paragraph tag.
<$paranum>	The autonumber definition of the current paragraph tag.
<$paranumonly>	The numeric portion of the autonumber definition of the current paragraph tag.
<$variable[variablename]>	The definition of the variable named variablename.
<$defaulttitle>	The text of the most recent paragraph tag that is tagged as a heading. (That is, it must be identified as a heading in the HTML Mappings Table.)
<$nextsubdoc>	The file name of the next document in the HTML output.

(continued)

Table 15-4 *(continued)*

Building Block	Replaced With What During Conversion?
<$prevsubdoc>	The file name of the previous document in the HTML output.
<$parentdoc>	The file name of the document that is at the next higher level in the HTML output hierarchy.

Processing special characters

FrameMaker must process certain special characters (for example, the copy-right symbol ©) to ensure that they appear in your HTML files. HTML files support a limited set of characters, far fewer than those you can create in a FrameMaker file. (For more information, refer to *HTML For Dummies*.)

For the special characters that don't work in the HTML files, you need to set up a replacement in the Character Macros Table (see Figure 15-12).

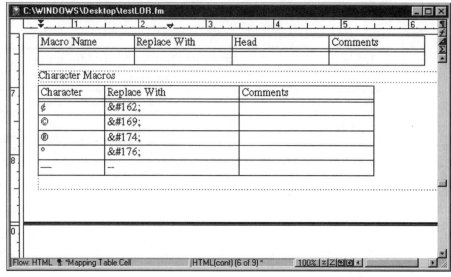

Figure 15-12:
The Character Macros Table lets you take care of those pesky characters so that they work in HTML.

Table 15-5	Character Macros Table Items
Column Name	*Description*
Character	A special character that isn't part of the regular HTML character set.
Replace with	The code to use in the HTML file. Often, this is an HTML entity code (such as ® for a registered trademark).
Comments	Not used in conversion. The Comments field lets you include explanatory information about your mappings.

Understanding the CSS file

FrameMaker produces CSS-based HTML. Depending on the HTML that you need to deliver, this is either very good or very bad. CSS stands for Cascading Style Sheets, which allows you to store formatting information about your HTML file in an external file. In theory, this makes it easier to maintain your HTML file. If every HTML file references the same CSS file, then when you change the CSS file every HTML file automatically picks up the formatting changes. Sounds great, right? Unfortunately, CSS is not fully supported in every browser. As a result, the formatting information that you include in your CSS file may or may not be used when your end users look at your Web pages. Here's a sample of how the CSS file lists the specifications for some styles:

```
H1.Heading1, H2.Heading1, H3.Heading1, H4.Heading1,
          H5.Heading1, H6.Heading1 {
display: block;
text-align: left;
text-indent: 0.000000pt;
margin-top: 36.000000pt;
margin-bottom: 8.000000pt;
margin-right: 0.000000pt;
margin-left: 0.000000pt;
font-size: 22.000000pt;
font-weight: Bold;
font-style: Regular;
color: #000000;
text-decoration: none;
vertical-align: baseline;
text-transform: none;
font-family: "Futura";
```

Although this code specifies Futura as the font, that font is used only if it is installed on the system of the person viewing the file. Generally, it's better to stick with generic fonts, but the FrameMaker-generated CSS file uses the same fonts as the original document.

A detailed discussion of the advantages and disadvantages of CSS is beyond the scope of this book, but you should be aware of the issues. If you know exactly what browsers you need to support, the decision should be fairly simple.

The CSS file typically has the same name as your main output file, but with a .css extension instead of a .html extension.

Advanced conversion information

Once you've mastered a simple HTML conversion, you can make things more complicated. Instead of converting a single file, you can convert an entire book, and you can copy settings from one file to another.

Converting a book

To convert a FrameMaker book to HTML, select the book file, then select File➪Save As, and select HTML. The first file in the book stores the conversion settings. Instead of the HTML reference pages, the reference pages for this first file contains BookHTML reference pages. (Actually, it may contain both, but the BookHTML reference pages contain the settings for the book conversion.)

Using file-level conversion settings for a book conversion

If you have created conversion settings for a file already that you want to use for the book, copy the information on the HTML reference pages and paste it on the equivalent BookHTML reference pages. I know it sounds ridiculous, but it does actually work.

Copying conversion settings from one file to another

Because the HTML conversion settings are stored on the reference pages, you can copy the settings from one file to another by importing formats for the reference pages.

Inserting custom code into the HTML output

Instead of using the basic HTML codes (like <P> and <H1>) for your output, you may want to create more complicated mappings. First, you create a general macro, which contains the code you want to use. Locate the General Macros Table in your HTML reference pages (see Figure 15-13).

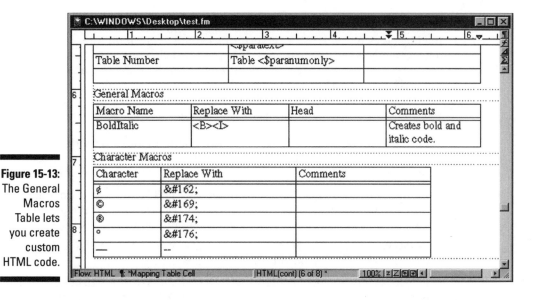

Figure 15-13:
The General
Macros
Table lets
you create
custom
HTML code.

In the first column, name the macro and then insert the HTML code in the
second column.

You can now use the macro's name (in the first column) as a mapping in your
HTML Mappings Table.

If you want to insert HTML code at an arbitrary location, you define the code
the same way in the General Macros Table. In your FrameMaker document
(on the body pages), insert a marker (select Special⇨Marker) or type **HTML
Macro** into your text where you want to insert the code and type in the name
of the macro as the marker text.

HTML Mappings table versus HTML Macro marker

Once you've defined a general macro, you can
use it both in the HTML Mappings Table and in
an HTML Macro. So, why would you choose one
instead of the other?

If you use a general macro in the HTML
Mappings Table, you can set up a particular
paragraph tag to use that macro. Every time the
specified paragraph tag occurs in your document, the macro is run to insert HTML code.

If you use the HTML Macro marker, the code is
inserted only where you insert the marker.

The bottom line is this: If you want to execute
your custom macro whenever a particular paragraph tag is used, map it in the HTML Mappings
Table. If you want to execute the custom macro
only in a few specified locations, insert the
HTML Macro marker (with the macro name as
the marker text) where you want the macro.

Fixing problems with the built-in HTML converter

FrameMaker's save as HTML converter has some major limitations; as a result, you may want to consider a third-party HTML converter. See the "Decisions, decisions: other choices for converters" sidebar for a list of popular HTML converters.

The problems with the FrameMaker converter include the following:

- ✔ **Limited conversion options:** The HTML Mapping table provides basic mapping, but more complex mapping schemes are difficult or impossible to implement here.

- ✔ **Limited formatting options:** To embed extra HTML code in a document, Adobe recommends inserting a marker with a reference to the appropriate macro. This can cause a significant amount of extra work.

- ✔ **Reliance on CSS:** The HTML converter always creates a CSS file. If you cannot use CSS for your output, difficulties ensue.

- ✔ **Users have reported problems with HTML macros not working:** Many users have found it impossible to get the HTML system and general macros to work. These problems are difficult to pin down and don't appear to be easily reproduced. If the macros work for you, count your blessings.

For most large-scale projects, you need a third-party converter.

Decisions, decisions: other choices for converters

For most users, the built-in HTML converter is appropriate and useful for conversion of short, simple FrameMaker documents. But if you need to convert a large document (or multiple documents) or if FrameMaker dependence on CSS formatting is unacceptable, some third-party tools are available to help. They include the following:

- ✔ WebWorks Publisher
- ✔ MIF2RTF
- ✔ Filtrix
- ✔ HTML Transit

Demo or evaluation versions for some of these tools are included on the CD at the back of this book.

Setting Up XML Conversion

In version 5.5.6, FrameMaker provides conversion to XML (Extensible Markup Language) for the first time. XML conversion is handled very much like HTML conversion. In fact, most of the mappings that you set up for XML are identical to the mappings for the HTML output. The next few sections discuss some of the differences, but before you try XML conversion, be sure to review the HTML information for more details. I've noted where the information differs in this section.

Creating XML output

To save your FrameMaker file to XML, select File⇨Save As and select XML as the format.

The output is a CSS file (very similar to the CSS file generated for HTML output) and an XML file. Because each XML file uses tagging based on the paragraph and character tags defined in your specific catalogs, it's impossible to predict what your file will look like. Here's a typical example:

```
<?xml version="1.0" encoding="UTF-8"?>
<?xml:stylesheet href="color.css" type="text/css"
          charset="UTF-8"?>
<XML>
<TITLE> Colors</TITLE><DIV>
<Title>
<DIV>
<IMAGE xml:link="simple" href="color-1.gif" show="embed"
          actuate="auto"/>
</DIV>
Colors</Title>
<DIV>
<Heading1>
Quick reference</Heading1>
<Body>
Here are some of the basic color features.</Body>
 </DIV>
...
</XML>
```

Like HTML, the FrameMaker paragraphs are mapped to tags in XML. But in XML, you can create your own output tags, whereas in HTML you can use only the (relatively limited) tags available in HTML.

Creating XML reference pages

The first time you save a file to XML, the reference pages for that file are created automatically. Unlike the HTML conversion with its HTML Setup dialog box, you don't have an XML Setup dialog box available.

Setting up paragraph mappings

The XML reference pages contain several tables that store your mappings. The first table, the XML Mapping Table, controls several conversion settings, including your paragraph mappings.

The XML Mapping Table first lists the paragraph mappings. Figure 15-14 shows a typical entry in the XML Mapping Table. By default, each paragraph tag is mapped to an XML entity with the same name.

The XML Mapping Table has the same columns as the HTML Mapping Table. For a description of each column, refer to Table 15-1.

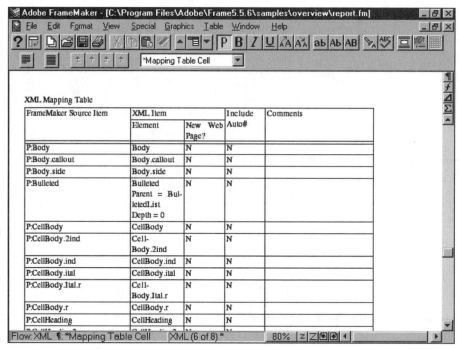

Figure 15-14: The Body paragraph is mapped to a corresponding Body entity.

What's all the fuss about XML?

XML is supposed to be the Next Big Thing. It's similar to HTML but is much more customizable. The biggest disadvantage to HTML is that you have a limited number of tags to work with. XML eliminates that problem, because with XML you define your own set of tags.

As this book goes to press, practical applications of XML are not yet available. This makes discussing the potential uses for XML a bit of an academic exercise.

Setting up character mappings

Character mappings, like paragraph mappings, are set up in the XML Mappings Table.

Setting up cross-reference format mappings

An XML hyperlink (which is what you create from your cross-references) looks like a distant cousin of a regular HTML hyperlink. Here's the XML version:

```
<A href="BBPresentation.xml#id(67202)" xml:link="simple"
          show="replace" actuate="user" CLASS="XRef">
```

The XML Mappings Table contains cross-reference mappings, which let you change the appears of the hyperlinked text in the XML output. For details, see the section "Setting up cross-reference format mappings" in the previous HTML section.

Setting up page templates and navigation bars

The procedure for setting up page templates and navigation bars is the same as for HTML. Of course, you need to use XML syntax instead of HTML. See the corresponding HTML section for more information.

Processing special characters

Again, special characters work the same way in XML as in HTML. See the corresponding HTML section for more information.

Understanding the CSS file

The CSS file for your XML file is basically the same as the CSS file for your HTML file except that in the XML, the tag itself matches the style in the CSS file. For example, in the XML, you might have something like this:

```
<Heading1>Index markers</Heading1>
```

In the CSS file, you have an entry that describes the Heading1 style:

```
Heading1 {
  display: block;
  text-align: left;
  text-indent: 0.000000pt;
  margin-top: 16.000000pt;
  margin-bottom: 6.000000pt;
  margin-right: 0.000000pt;
  margin-left: 0.000000pt;
  font-size: 14.000000pt;
  font-weight: Bold;
  font-style: Regular;
  color: #000000;
  text-decoration: none;
  vertical-align: baseline;
  text-transform: none;
  font-family: "Frutiger";
}
```

For HTML, the CSS file would look the same, but the HTML file would have slightly different syntax:

```
<H1 CLASS="Heading1">Index markers</H1>
```

So the HTML CLASS tag is (sort of) equivalent to the actual XML tag name.

Adding a New Reference Page

To create a new reference page, first go to the reference pages (select View➪References Pages), then select Special➪Add Reference Page. This displays the Add Reference Page dialog box. Type a name for the new reference page and click Add.

Each reference page must have a unique name. If you're not feeling creative, you could try Reference 2, Reference 3, Reference 4, and so on.

Deleting a Reference Page

To delete a reference page, go to that page and select Special⇨Delete Page. (The command will include the name of the page.)

Deleting a reference page breaks all the items that use information from that reference page. Make sure you don't need any of the items on the reference page. For example, if the graphics on that reference page are used by paragraph tags, the graphic frames will disappear from your body pages.

Chapter 16

Maintaining Multiple Versions with Conditional Text

● ●

In This Chapter

▶ Planning your conditional text

▶ Applying a condition tag

▶ Removing a condition tag

▶ Setting up a condition tag

▶ Deleting a condition tag

▶ Making conditional text look like regular text

● ●

Conditional text lets you maintain two or more versions of the same document in a single file. By tagging different parts of your document with condition tags, and then showing and hiding the condition tags in various combinations, you change the information that is displayed in your document.

For example, if you're an instructor developing an exam for one of your classes, you could set up your file so that you could create both the exam and the answer sheet for the exam in the same file. In this scenario, you would apply a condition tag, perhaps called exam_answers, to the answers in your exam. Then, you could hide the exam_answers tag to print out the exam for your students (without answers) and display it to print out your answer key.

You can apply more than one condition tag to an item, but these multiple condition tags can cause headaches when you try to figure out the results. If at least one of the tags applied to a piece of text is set to Show, the text is displayed. That means that if you hide a certain condition tag, and you have text with that condition tag plus another condition tag applied to it, that text *won't* be hidden.

Planning Your Conditional Text

Before you create condition tags and start making your document conditional, it's probably a good idea to do some planning:

- ✔ **If possible, tag entire paragraphs as conditional:** Conditional paragraphs are much easier to maintain than conditional sentences or words.

- ✔ **Tag spaces consistently:** If you're tagging sentences or words, be consistent in whether you tag the space before or after the conditional part. If you are not consistent, when you hide the conditional text you will have difficulties with missing spaces or two spaces in a row in your document.

- ✔ **If it's in every version, don't use conditional text:** You don't need to apply conditional text to information that appears in every version of your document.

- ✔ **It's not just for text:** You can make graphics, markers, and other items conditional text, too.

Applying a Condition Tag

Conditional text tags are completely separate from other tags. You can't, for example, make a particular paragraph tag always use a certain condition. You have to apply the paragraph tag and the condition tag separately.

To apply a conditional text tag, follow these steps:

1. **Select the text (and graphics) that you want to make conditional.**

   You can apply a conditional text tag to an anchored frame. This means you can show and hide graphics along with regular text.

2. **Select Special⇨Conditional Text.**

   This displays the Conditional Text dialog box (see Figure 16-1).

3. **Move the condition tag that you want into the In list.**

   Select the tag, then click the left arrow button to move it to the In list.

4. **Click the Apply button.**

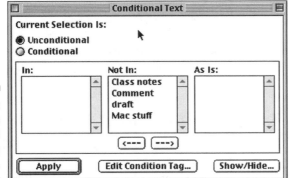

Figure 16-1:
The
Conditional
Text dialog
box.

You can also apply a conditional text tag this way:

1. **Select the text that you want to make conditional.**

2. **Press Ctrl+4.**

   The lower left of the status bar displays a ?:.

3. **Type in the first few letters of the condition tag or use the arrow keys to scroll through the list of condition tags. When the tag you want is displayed in the status bar, press Enter.**

What's your condition?

After you start applying conditional text tags, you'll want to keep track of what content uses what tag. FrameMaker offers a couple of ways for you to do so:

✔ **Color:** Use different colors for each condition. If possible, try to set up each condition with a unique color or text effect (underline, strikethrough, and so on).

✔ **Settings in the Conditional Text dialog box:** If you select a chunk of conditional text and then display the Conditional Text dialog box (select Special⇨Conditional Text), it'll show the conditional settings for the selected text.

✔ **Status bar:** If you select a chunk of conditional text and look in the status bar, the conditional text tag is shown, in parentheses, before the flow, paragraph tag, and character tag information.

Removing a Condition Tag

You can apply more than one condition tag to a single piece of text, and you can remove conditions one at a time or all at once.

Removing a single condition tag

To remove just one condition tag, follow these steps:

1. **Select the text from which you want to remove the condition tag.**

2. **Select Special⇨Conditional Text.**

   This displays the Conditional Text dialog box (refer to Figure 16-1).

3. **Move the condition tag that you want to remove into the Not In list.**

   Select the condition tag, then click the right arrow button to move it over to the Not In list.

4. **When you're finished, click the Apply button.**

You have another way to go about this:

1. **Select the text from which you want to remove the condition tag, and press Ctrl+5.**

   The lower left of the status bar displays an upside-down question mark.

2. **Type in the first few letters of the condition tag or use the arrow keys to scroll through the list of condition tags. When the tag you want to remove is displayed in the status bar, press Enter.**

Removing all conditional text tagging

You can also remove all the conditions from some text. Here's how you do it:

1. **Select the text you want to make unconditional, and select Special⇨Conditional Text.**

   This displays the Conditional Text dialog box.

2. **Select the Unconditional radio button.**

3. **Click Apply.**

A quick way to do the same thing is to select the text you want to make unconditional and press Ctrl+6.

Setting Up Conditional Text Tags

The default FrameMaker template contains a Comment conditional text tag, but you can create your own conditional text tags.

Once you have analyzed your text and figured out what condition tags you need, you're ready to create those tags. To create a condition tag:

1. **Select Special⇨Conditional Text.**

   This displays the Conditional Text dialog box.

2. **Select the Edit Condition Tag button.**

   This displays the Edit Condition Tag dialog box.

3. **In the Tag field, type a name for the condition tag.**

4. **Set the condition indicators. You can set this conditional text to use a particular style, such as an underline, and a particular color.**

   In the Style drop-down list, select a style for this condition tag. If you do not want to use a style, select As Is.

   In the Color drop-down list, select a color for this condition tag. If you do not want to use a color, select As Is.

   The colors and styles you use for your condition tags can be suppressed, so you can print your document with or without the special effects that indicate conditional text. For details, see "Blending In: Making Conditional Text Look Like Regular Text," later in this chapter.

5. **Select the Set button to create the condition tag.**

Once you create the condition tag, you can apply it to content in your document.

Deleting a Condition Tag

When you delete a condition tag from your document, this tag is removed from the text that uses it. If a particular piece of text uses more than one condition tag, the deleted tag is simply removed. If your text has only one condition tag (the one you're deleting), you're given the option of either deleting the text or making it unconditional.

To delete a condition tag, follow these steps:

1. **Select Special⇨Conditional Text.**

   This displays the Conditional Text dialog box.

2. **Select the tag that you want to delete.**

3. **Click the Edit Condition Tag button.**

   This displays the Edit Condition Tag dialog box.

4. **Click the Delete button.**

5. **Select Make the Text Unconditional or Delete the Text.**

   When you delete the conditional text tag, the tag is stripped from any content that uses it. If a particular section uses the to-be-deleted condition tag and another tag, the to-be-deleted tag is simply stripped. But if text somewhere in your document uses only the tag you want to delete (no other condition tags), you must choose between deleting that text or making it unconditional.

   This makes sense in a twisted way. If the text starts out conditional because of this tag, and you remove the tag, then the text either is no longer conditional or it should be deleted. Imagine if you have a manual with conditional text that discusses a particular product add-on. If you discontinue this add-on item, you would probably want to delete all the conditional text, because the add-on item is no longer relevant. But if you made the add-on item a part of the base product line, you would want to keep the text but make it unconditional.

6. **Click the OK button to delete the condition tag.**

Showing and Hiding Conditional Text

After spending all this time tagging your text as conditional, it's time to admire your handiwork. You can show or hide each conditional text tag. To change the settings, follow these steps:

1. **Select Special⇨Conditional Text.**

2. **Click Show/Hide.**

   This displays the Show/Hide Conditional Text dialog box (see Figure 16-2).

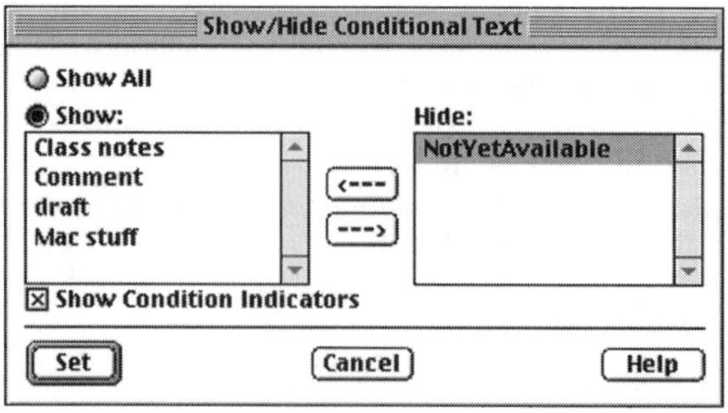

Figure 16-2:
Show/Hide
Conditional
Text dialog
box.

Show/Hide Conditional Text

○ Show All
● Show:

Show:		Hide:
Class notes		NotYetAvailable
Comment	(←---)	
draft		
Mac stuff	(---→)	

☒ Show Condition Indicators

[Set]   (Cancel)   (Help)

3. **Move the conditions that you want to show to the left side of the dialog box and the conditions you want to hide to the right side using the left arrow and right arrow buttons.**

4. **Click Set.**

   Your document now changes. The conditional text that you hid disappears (but don't worry, you can get it back). Once you hide conditional text, you don't have to repaginate; FrameMaker automatically reflows the content that is still showing.

To show hidden conditional text, just go back to the Show/Hide dialog box, move the tag from the Hide list to the Show list, and click Set.

Blending In: Making Conditional Text Look Like Regular Text

When you create your conditional text tags, you can specify a color and a style for each conditional text tag (see "Setting Up Conditional Text Tags" earlier). These style and color indicators are very useful while you're editing a file because you can see at a glance where you have conditional text. When you finalize your materials, however, you may want your conditional text to blend into the surrounding text.

FrameMaker lets you toggle the display of the condition indicators. Changing the display doesn't change the condition tags; it just changes whether FrameMaker displays the condition indicators.

Some tips for using conditional text

In tables, you can use conditional text to tag entire rows of tables. But you cannot do any of the following:

✔ You can't apply conditional text to a column in a table.

✔ You can't apply conditional text to a cell or a group of cells in a table (unless the group happens to be a complete row).

For graphics, you can make an entire graphic conditional by applying a condition tag to the anchored frame. You can also make any text within a text frame in the graphic conditional. The following limitations apply to condition tags in graphics:

✔ You can't apply a condition tag to an actual graphic, only to the anchored frame that contains the graphic.

✔ You can't apply a condition tag to a text line or a part of a text line.

✔ You can't apply a condition tag to an unanchored frame.

To toggle your condition indicators, follow these steps:

1. **Select Special⇨Conditional Text.**

   This displays the Conditional Text dialog box.

2. **Click the Show/Hide button.**

   This displays the Show/Hide Conditional Text dialog box.

3. **Check the Condition Indicators check box to display your condition tag indicators. Uncheck the check box to remove the condition indicators.**

4. **Click Set.**

Part IV
Working with Books

The 5th Wave   By Rich Tennant

"Great goulash, Stan. That reminds me, are you still creating your own table of contents?"

In this part . . .

FrameMaker is all about long documents, and I mean *long* documents. Documents of 1,000 pages are not uncommon, and many people use FrameMaker to create content that's much longer than that!

If you're in this category (or just in the 200 to 400 page category), the book features in FrameMaker are going to be very important to you. Books let you manage lots of related files (for example, a bunch of chapters that together make up a book). With books, you can manage pagination across lots of files and generate bookwide tables of contents and indexes.

Chapter 17

Building a Book

In This Chapter

▶ Understanding book features

▶ Creating book files

▶ Adding, moving, and deleting book components

▶ Opening, closing, and saving files in a book

▶ Printing from a book file

A *book file* is a list of files that make up the book. This includes the major sections (often chapters), as well as the front matter (preface, table of contents, cover page) and the back matter (appendixes, glossary, index). If you want to create a table of contents or index for your entire book, you first need to set up a book file.

Creating a book file automates several book maintenance tasks. When you update the book file, the following things happen:

✔ FrameMaker updates cross-references in every file in the book.

✔ FrameMaker updates the book's pagination. (For example, if Chapter 1 shrinks from 20 pages to 10 pages and your book is numbered straight through from 1 to 400, when you update the pagination, the starting page number for every chapter after Chapter 1 is decreased by 10 pages.)

✔ FrameMaker regenerates generated files, such as tables of contents and indexes. FrameMaker scans every file in the book and updates the items in the generated files and their page numbers.

It's also useful to look at what a book is *not*. When you add files to a book file, you *don't* make a copy of the file; you're simply creating a pointer to the existing file. You can open a file by double-clicking it in the book file list, but this is identical to opening the file directly without going through the book file.

Book files *don't* update dynamically; you must update the book to update pagination, cross-references, and generated files. For example, after adding new sections to a document, you must regenerate the book file to update the pagination and have the entries for those sections added to your table of contents.

Creating a Book File

To create a new book file, start with a file that needs to become a component of the book and follow these steps:

1. **Select File⇨Generate/Book to display the Generate/Book dialog box (see Figure 17-1).**

Figure 17-1:
The
Generate/
Book dialog
box.

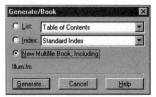

2. **In the Generate/Book dialog box, select the New Multifile Book radio button and click Generate.**

   Your new book file is created and displayed with its one file (see Figure 17-2).

Figure 17-2:
A brand-
new book
file.

You should notice a couple of important things about this new book file:

✔ When you create the book file, it uses the same name as the file you started with, but with "book" or ".book" appended to its name.

✔ A book file with only one file in it is quite pointless. To make the book file do useful table of contents compilation or pagination, you need at least two files in the book.

If you want to change the name of your book file, now would be a good time to do so.

After you add generated files, such as lists of figures, indexes, and tables of contents, to your book file, changing your book's file name will break the generated files. It's possible to fix this, but it's a real hassle, so save yourself some trouble and set a name for the book file right after you create it (and before you create any generated files).

Managing the Contents of Your Book File

Once you create the book file, with its sad and lonely single file, you'll probably want to start adding more files. Read on. . . .

This section explains how to add "regular" files, such as chapters, appendixes, prefaces, and other chapters with content. If you need to add a file whose information is based on the chapter files, such as a table of contents, list of figures, or index, see "Setting up generated files" later in this chapter.

Adding new chapter files

To add a new file to your book, first make sure that the book file is the active window. (It should be the topmost window.)

Then select File⇨Add File to display the Add File to Book dialog box (shown in Figures 17-3, 17-4, and 17-5).

The Add File menu choice is available only when a book file is the active window. The same is true for the Rearrange Files menu choice. If they're not on your File menu, your book file isn't selected.

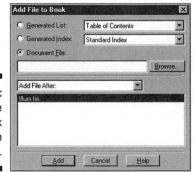

Figure 17-3:
The Add File
to Book
dialog box in
Windows.

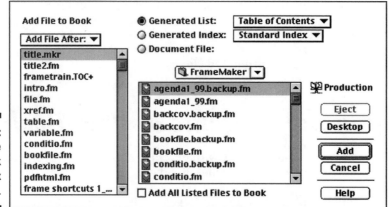

Figure 17-4:
The Add File
to Book
dialog box
on a Mac.

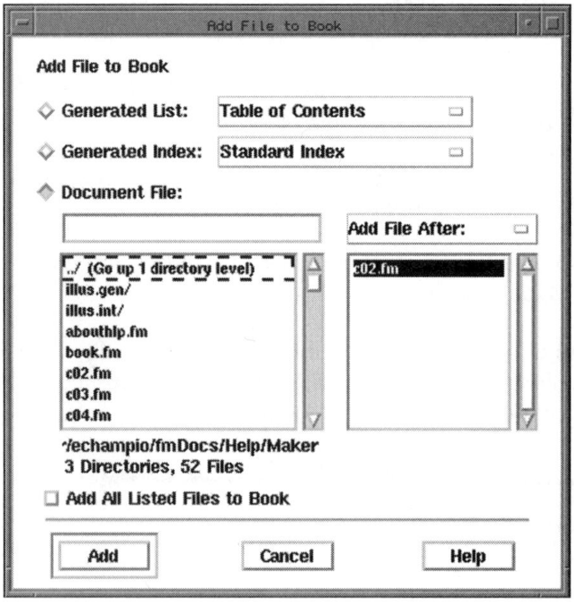

Figure 17-5:
The Add File
to Book
dialog box in
UNIX.

The Add File to Book dialog box is slightly different for each platform, so follow the instructions for your platform.

Windows

To add a file in the Windows environment, follow these steps:

1. **Click the Document File radio button.**

2. **Click the Browse button to display a directory navigation window, locate the file, select it, and click Add.**

If you know the file's name and it's in the same directory as the book file, you can just type in the name.

You can add several files at once by selecting them in the directory navigation list. Ctrl+click each file that you want or Shift+click to select a sequential list of files.

3. **To position the new file in your book, select the file that follows your file and select Add File Before from the drop-down list. Or, select the file that precedes your file and select Add File After from the drop-down list.**

4. **Select the Add button to add the file.**

5. **Repeat Steps 1-4 to add additional files. When you are finished, click the Done button.**

The Done button doesn't show up until you've added at least one file.

Macintosh

To add a file on a Macintosh, follow these steps:

1. **Select a file in the list on the left, and then specify whether you want to add the new file before or after the selected file by selected from the drop-down list at the top left.**

2. **Select the Document File radio button.**

3. **In the lower right, select the file that you want to add.**

To add every file in the directory to your book at once, check Add All Listed files to Book. The files are added in alphabetical order, so you'll probably need to rearrange them to get their order right, but it's a convenient shortcut.

4. **Select the Add button to add the file.**

5. **Repeat Steps 1-4 to add additional files. When you are finished, click the Done button.**

UNIX

To add a file in a UNIX environment, follow these steps:

1. **Click the Document File radio button.**

2. **If you know the file name, type its name in the Document File field; otherwise, use the directory navigation list on the left to find the file and select it.**

To add every file in the directory to your book at once, check Add All Listed Files to Book. The files are added in alphabetical order, so you'll probably need to rearrange them to get their order right, but it's a convenient shortcut.

3. **To position the new file in your book, select the file that follows your file and select Add File Before from the drop-down list. Or, select the file that precedes your file and select Add File After from the drop-down list.**

4. **Select the Add button to add the file.**

5. **Repeat Steps 1-4 to add additional files. When you are finished, click the Done button.**

Setting up pagination and other options for a chapter file

After you add a new file to your book file, you can adjust the pagination and other settings for that file. To do so, follow these steps:

1. **Make sure you select the book file and you select the file you want to set up in the book file list.**

2. **Select File⇨Set Up File. This displays the Set Up File dialog box (see Figure 17-6).**

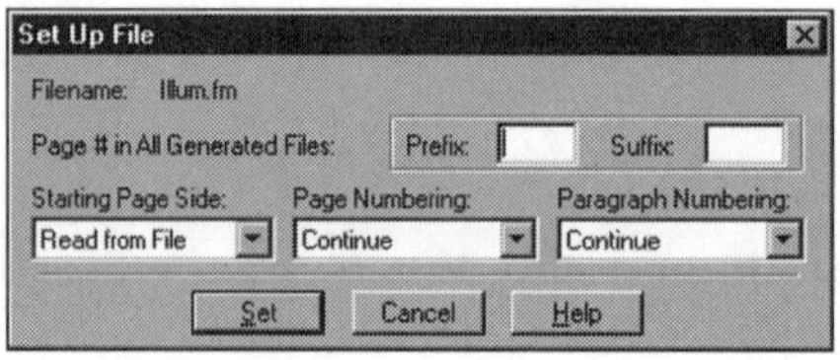

Figure 17-6:
The Set Up File dialog box for a chapter file.

Set Up File

Filename: Illum.fm

Page # in All Generated Files: Prefix: [ ] Suffix: [ ]

Starting Page Side: Read from File   Page Numbering: Continue   Paragraph Numbering: Continue

Set   Cancel   Help

3. **Choose from the options in the Set Up File dialog box.**

   • **Page # in All Generated Files, Prefix:** Sets the prefix that is included in front of the page number when you create generated files (like tables of contents and indexes). Even if you set up a multipart page number (for example, 1-1, 1-2, 1-3) as part of your page number definition, you must also specify the prefix (1-) here. When FrameMaker creates generated files, it extracts only the basic page number (1, 2, 3) and not any additional content from the page number variable. To ensure that the page numbers are displayed with the proper information, you have to specify the prefix here. If you are numbering by folio (that is, if every chapter begins with page 1 and has a chapter identifier — 1-1, 1-2, . . ., 2-1, 2-2, . . . — then you must set 1- as the prefix for Chapter 1, 2- as the prefix for Chapter 2, and so on. If you rearrange your chapters, you'll have to correct the chapter prefixes manually.

If you are using regular sequential numbering (1, 2, 3, . . ., 300, 301, . . .), you can leave the prefix blank.

- **Page # in All Generated Files, Suffix:** Sets the suffix that is included after the page number when you create generated files. See the description of the prefix setting above for more details about why this is required.

- **Starting Page Side:** Sets the page side (left or right) on which the first page of this document begins. The default, Read from File, means that FrameMaker checks the pagination settings inside the file (select Format⇨Page Layout⇨Page Size) and uses the side specified there. Next Available Side means that if the previous file ended on a left page, this file begins on a right page and vice versa. A setting of Left or Right forces the file to begin on that page side. If the required page side is not the next available side, then FrameMaker inserts a blank page at the end of the *preceding* document.

- **Page Numbering:** Sets the page numbering for this file. The default, Continue, means that this document uses the next available page number. If the previous document ended on page 20, then this document begins on page 21. If you want pagination for this file to begin on page 1, set Page Numbering to Restart at 1. A setting of Read from File means that FrameMaker checks the first page number setting inside the file (Format⇨Document⇨Numbering) and uses the page number specified there for the first page in the document. If you are numbering each chapter separately (2-1, 2-2, 2-3, . . . 3-1, 3-2, 3-3), you'll need to set this to Restart at 1 for every file.

- **Paragraph Numbering:** The default, Continue, means that paragraph autonumbering is continued from the previous file to this one. If your chapters' numbers are set using autonumbers, you need to set Paragraph Numbering to Continue so that FrameMaker can automatically manage the page numbers. Setting Paragraph Numbering to Restart means that every paragraph numbering series will be reset to 0 at the beginning of this file.

I rarely use this option, because it's usually more efficient to set up the autonumbering sequences to manage the restarts.

Deleting files

Because you add files with a menu choice on the File menu, logically there should be a Delete File choice as well, right? Well, yes, but there isn't. To delete files from a book file, you have to go to the Rearrange Files dialog box.

To delete a file from a book, follow these steps:

1. **Make sure your book file is selected.**

2. **Select File⇨Rearrange Files. This displays the Rearrange Files dialog box (see Figure 17-7).**

Figure 17-7:
Use the
Rearrange
Files dialog
box to
reorder or
delete files
from the
book.

3. **Select the file you want to delete, and click the Delete button. Repeat this step to delete several files at once.**

4. **When you are finished deleting files, select the Done button. Your book file is displayed without the files you deleted.**

Deleting files from your book file does *not* delete them from your system. Only the entry in the book file is deleted.

Rearranging files

Rearranging files lets you change the order of the files in your book file. To rearrange files, follow these steps:

1. **Make sure your book file is selected.**

2. **Select File⇨Rearrange Files. This displays the Rearrange Files dialog box (refer to Figure 17-7).**

3. **Select a file that you want to move, and then select the Move Up or Move Down button to move it in the list of files. Repeat this step for each file you need to move.**

4. **When you're finished rearranging files, select the Done button. Your book file is displayed with the files in the new order.**

Setting up generated files

A _generated file_ is a file that contains information created by scanning the files in the book and extracting information. This process takes place when you update your book file.

The most commonly generated files are tables of contents and indexes; however, you can also use FrameMaker to create lists of figures or tables, lists of imported graphics, lists of fonts, lists of markers, and more.

To create a new generated file, you add the file. But although adding the file creates a line item in the book file for the generated file, the file itself doesn't exist until you regenerate the book file. In other words, you are adding a file that doesn't exist yet!

Table of contents

To add and set up a table of contents, follow these steps:

1. **Make sure your book file is selected.**

2. **Select File⇨Add File to display the Add File dialog box.**

   Refer to Figures 17-3 through 17-5 for Mac, Windows, and UNIX versions of the dialog box.

   Do not select a file from the directory list.

3. **Select the Generated List radio button and make sure Table of Contents is selected in the drop-down list.**

4. **Select Add. This displays the Set Up Table of Contents dialog box (see Figure 17-8).**

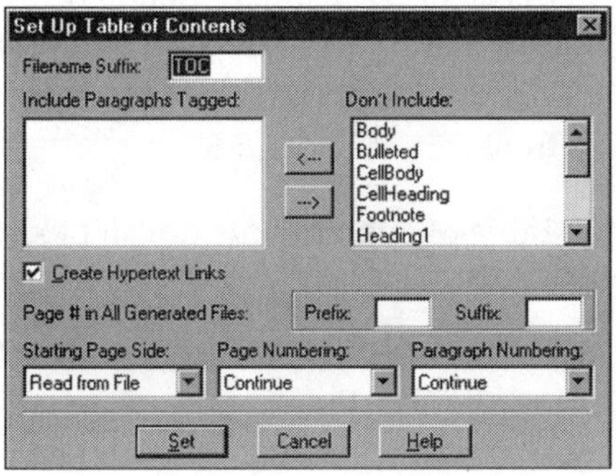

Figure 17-8:
The Set Up
Table of
Contents
dialog box.

Don't change the default suffix, TOC, unless you have a *very* good reason. (For example, if you have two TOC files and need to label them to keep track of them.)

5. **Select the paragraph tags that you want to include in the table of contents and move them to the Include Paragraphs Tagged list.**

   You can either double-click a paragraph to move it or you can select it and click the ← button.

   Generally, you want to include your chapter title and one to three levels of subheadings.

   The Create Hypertext Links check box is checked by default. It creates hypertext links from the table of contents entries to the source paragraphs in the chapter files. If you plan to convert your files to online formats, you must check this to ensure that your table of contents becomes hyperlinked.

   The hypertext links are useful for spot-checking the references and navigation in a book or chapter while you're working. On a Windows machine, hold down the Ctrl and Alt keys to change your cursor to a little hand and click one of the entries to jump to that point in the text. On a Mac machine, hold down the option and command keys and click. On a UNIX machine, a keyboard shortcut is not available to use the hyperlinks directly, but you can make the document view-only by pressing Esc Shift+f l k (that's a lowercase letter *L* in there) and then click the entries, which are now live hyperlinks. To make your document editable again, press Esc Shift+f l k again.

   For details about the other settings in this dialog box, see the "Setting up pagination and other options for a chapter file" section.

6. **Click Set to save your table of contents settings.**

7. **Select the Add button, then select the Done button to add the new table of contents to your book.**

8. **Make sure the book file is selected, then select File⇨Generate/Update to update your book and create your new table of contents.**

   The TOC file now appears in the Generate/Update dialog box. Make sure that it's on the left side in the Generate column before you update the book.

9. **Select Update to update the book.**

Until you generate your book, the table of contents file doesn't exist, even though you have defined all its settings.

Once you create your initial table of contents, you'll need to refine its formatting. For details on that process, see Chapter 18.

Can I put the same file in multiple books?

Yes. When you update a book file, you don't make any irrevocable changes to the chapter files. However, if a file is used in two (or more, if you're brave!) book files, you do need to update more often. The file that's included in several book files always uses the pagination that is appropriate for the book file that was last generated. Therefore, you need to be very careful to regenerate if there is any chance that the "other" book file might have changed the pagination.

Index

The index is generated from index markers, which are hidden (nonprinting) text. Setting up and generating the index will result in a completely blank index unless you have index markers in your document. See Chapter 19 for information on how to create index markers.

To add and set up an index file, follow these steps:

1. **Select your book file.**

2. **Select File⇨Add File to display the Add File dialog box.**

    Refer to Figures 17-3 through 17-5 for Mac, Windows, and UNIX versions of the dialog box.

    Do not select a file from the directory list.

3. **Select the Generated Index radio button and select Standard Index in the drop-down list.**

4. **Select Add.**

    This displays the Set Up Standard Index dialog box (see Figure 17-9).

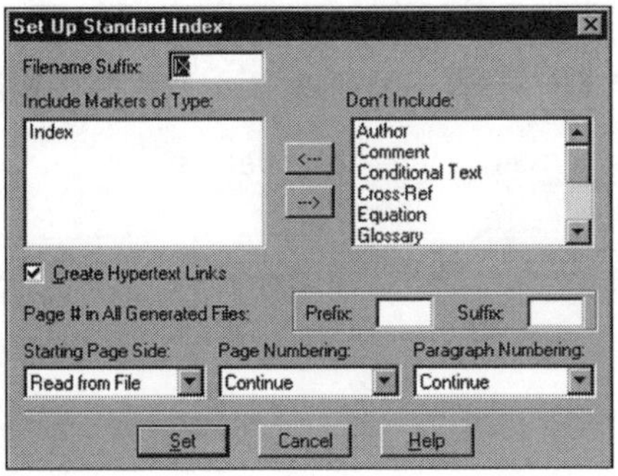

Figure 17-9:
The Set Up Standard Index dialog box.

Don't change the default suffix, IX, unless you have a *very* good reason. If you have two generated indexes, you'll need two different suffixes.

You now specify marker types that you want to include in the index. Most of the time, the default (include only index markers) should be fine.

For details about the other settings in this dialog box, see the section "Setting up pagination and other options for a chapter file" and the Technical Stuff note in the table of contents setting above.

5. **Click Set to save your index settings.**

6. **Select the Add button, then select the Done button to add the index file to your book file.**

7. **Select the book file, then select File⇨Generate/Update to update your book and create your new index file.**

You'll notice that the index file now appears in the Generate/Update dialog box. Make sure that it's on the left side in the Generate column before you update the book.

8. **Select Update to update the book.**

Opening, Closing, and Saving Files in a Book

Instead of opening each file in a book by double-clicking it, you can open every file in the book at once. To do so, hold down the Shift key and then select the File menu. Several of the choices in the File menu now change. Select Open All Files in Book and FrameMaker will do just that. You can also choose Save All and Close All.

Can I put the same file in the same book twice?

No. But you could make a copy of the file and insert the copy. You could also use a text inset. See Chapter 12 for details.

Printing from a Book File

You can print some or all of the files in a book in a single group. To do so, select the book file, and then select File⇨Print. Instead of the "normal" Print dialog box, the Print Files in Book dialog box (see Figure 17-10) is displayed.

Figure 17-10:
You can print all the files in the book or select the files you want to print.

Double-click files to move them from the Print to the Don't Print section (and vice versa). When you have the list of files you want in the Print list, select the Print button. Now, you'll see the Print dialog box and can proceed as usual.

If you want to print a single PostScript file for a book, you must print from the book file. (You can also automatically print individual PostScript files for each file in the book.) See Chapter 14 for more information.

Chapter 18

Refining the Table of Contents

· ·

In This Chapter

▶ Deciding what goes into the TOC

▶ Formatting the TOC

▶ Adding introductory information

▶ Setting up dot leaders

▶ Controlling line breaks in the table of contents

· ·

Chapter 17 discusses how to create a basic table of contents. If you like the way FrameMaker formats your table of contents and don't want to change a thing, you don't have to read this chapter. But if you would like to adjust the table of contents' formatting, read on.

Deciding What Goes into the TOC

The entries in your table of contents are always based on paragraph tags. When you set up the table of contents, you specify the paragraphs for which you want to include entries.

If you want to change the items in the table of contents, open your book file, select the table of contents file, and select File⇨Set Up File to display the Set Up File dialog box. In this dialog box, you can add and remove paragraph tags from the list of items that are included. See Chapter 17 for detailed information about how to do this.

Can I exclude certain Heading1s and include the rest?

Not exactly. If you include the Heading1 paragraph tag when you set up the table of contents, every paragraph that uses Heading1 is included in the table of contents. If you want to exclude particular Heading1 paragraphs, you need to create another paragraph tag, for example Heading1noTOC, which looks identical to the Heading1 paragraph tag. Apply the Heading1noTOC tag to the paragraphs you want to exclude from the table of contents. Make sure that Heading1 is included in the table of contents paragraph list and that Heading1noTOC is excluded. Every paragraph tag that uses Heading1 is still included in the table of contents — you've just changed the paragraph tags of the paragraphs you want to exclude.

Formatting the Content

Once you specify which paragraphs to include in the table of contents and generate the file, a table of contents file is created. (See Chapter 17 for details.) This file has all the same formatting catalogs (paragraph tags, character tags, master pages, reference pages, and so on) as a regular content file. In fact, aside from the fact that the information in the file is automatically generated, this *is* a regular file. So, for example, you can modify the master pages to make the table of contents look the way you want it to.

But if you want to change the generated content, it's better not to work directly with the content. You could edit the text directly, but every time you regenerate the file, your edits disappear because completely new content is generated.

If you directly edit the table of contents listing, do it at the very last minute, after you generate the file for the last time.

To make changes to the TOC entries that "stick" in the file even after you regenerate, you'll need to work with two entities: the reference pages and the paragraph tags.

The new content affects the text in your file, but not other settings. For example, any changes you make to the master pages are preserved when you regenerate.

Understanding reference pages in the table of contents

Most page layout programs have two types of pages: body pages (where you put content) and master pages (which are the formatting outlines for the body pages). FrameMaker adds a third type of page: the reference page. Reference pages contain information for your file that is used (or *referenced*) elsewhere. (See Chapter 15 for a detailed discussion about reference pages.)

TOC Specification

For a table of contents file, the reference pages contain something called the TOC Specification (see Figure 18-1). This is a text frame that contains information about what content to put in the table of contents.

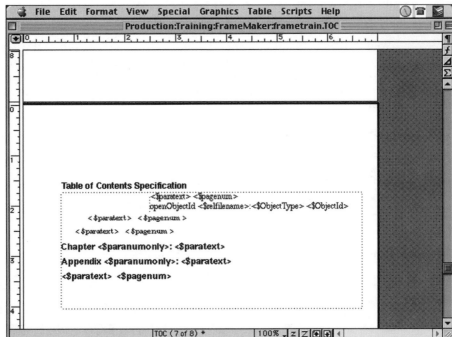

Figure 18-1:
A typical
TOC
Specification
looks fairly
cryptic.

Text shown in the figure:

Table of Contents Specification

<$paratext> <$pagenum>
openObjectId <$relfilename>:<$ObjectType> <$ObjectId>

<$paratext> <$pagenum>

<$paratext> <$pagenum>

Chapter <$paranumonly>: <$paratext>

Appendix <$paranumonly>: <$paratext>

<$paratext> <$pagenum>

TIP

You can usually locate the TOC Specification just by flipping through the reference pages. To be absolutely sure that you have the correct text frame, check the flow tag of the text frame (select the text frame and select Graphics⇨Object Properties and look in the Flow Tag field or on the status bar at the bottom left). For a TOC specification, the flow tag is always TOC. More generally, the flow tag for the specification for any generated file is the same as the three-digit suffix for that file.

When you first generate your table of contents, FrameMaker creates a default TOC specification for you. This specification includes a line for each paragraph tag that you've included. For example, I'll assume you included the following paragraph tags in the table of contents:

- chapter_heading
- heading 1
- heading 2
- heading 3

Your TOC specification would then include a line for each of those paragraph tags. Each line is formatted with a unique paragraph tag, which corresponds to the original tag name with TOC added to the end. For the preceding sample tags, your TOC specification would include lines for each of the following formats:

- chapter_headingTOC
- heading 1TOC
- heading 2TOC
- heading 3TOC

Building blocks

The contents of each line look something like this:

```
<$paratext><$pagenum>
```

Chapters 9 and 10 discuss these codes (FrameMaker calls them building blocks). The reference pages can use the following building blocks:

Building block	Information pulled from referenced paragraph
<$paratext>	Text
<$paranum>	Complete autonumber
<$paranumonly>	Numeric part of autonumber (counters only)
<$pagenum>	Page number

So, the default TOC definition inserts the text of the paragraph, followed by the page number.

You'll probably need to modify this setup for your chapter titles. For example, you probably want to include your chapter numbers in the table of contents. To do this, you need to add the chapter number into the definition. Let's assume that the autonumber definition for your chapter_title paragraph tag looks like this:

```
H:Chapter <n+>
```

H: is the series label, which ties all the chapter_title formats together across chapters. "Chapter" is just typed-in text, and <n+> is the counter, which displays an Arabic number and increments the counter by one each time it's used. (Therefore, every time you use the chapter_title tag, your chapter number will increase by one.)

For more information about autonumbering, see Chapter 4. For autonumbering examples, see Chapter 22.

You could modify the reference page definition of chapter_titleTOC to look like this:

```
<$paranum> <$paratext> <$pagenum>
```

The result would be:

Chapter 1 Introduction 1

That is, the autonumber (Chapter 1), followed by the paragraph's text (Introduction), followed by the page number (1). You could also write it like this:

```
Chapter <$paranumonly> <$paratext> <$pagenum>
```

This definition has the exact same result has the previous one, but instead of pulling the word *Chapter* from the autonumbering definition, you add it in the reference page definition. The output on the body pages is identical.

Instead of using building blocks to retrieve the chapter number from the files, you could instead set up the chapter_titleTOC format to use an autonumber. This creates the autonumber in the TOC file instead of retrieving it from the chapter files. I don't recommend this approach, because it introduces another numbering series. I prefer to pull the numbers from the chapter files, because this lets me use the table of contents to check my chapter numbering. If you use an autonumbered . . . TOC paragraph, the numbering in the TOC file has no relationship to the numbering in the chapter file. This could mask problems in the chapter numbering.

Character tags

The overall appearance of each entry is determined by its paragraph tag (see the next section for more information). But if you want to insert additional character-level formatting into the table of contents definition, you can do so. For example, you could specify that the paragraph text should be italicized, like this:

```
Chapter <$paranumonly> <Emphasis><$paratext><Default Para
          Font> <$pagenum>
```

(I'm assuming here that the Emphasis character tag creates italics.)

The <Emphasis> tag is applied to all the text following the tag — until you reach the <Default Para Font> tag, which restores the default paragraph formatting. So, if you want to italicize everything except the page number, your entry would look like this:

```
<Emphasis> Chapter <$paranumonly><$paratext><Default Para
          Font> <$pagenum>
```

In this case, Emphasis character tag is applied from the beginning of the entry to just before the page number.

Things to remember about the TOC specification

Here are a few things to keep in mind when working with the TOC specification:

- ✔ You can only gather up information in the "current" paragraph. That is, unlike cross-references, you can't set up a reference to the chapter title in the heading 2 paragraph by using <$paratext[chapter title]>. It just won't work.

- ✔ If you need to put information from two paragraphs on the same line in your generated TOC, you need to use a run-in head for the first style on the line. (See Chapter 4 for details on run-in heads.)

- ✔ Character formatting in the chapter files (for example, an italicized word in a heading) isn't preserved when you generate the table of contents.

- ✔ Keep in mind that the codes can be much longer or much shorter than the text that replaces them. As a result, it can be difficult to see how a particular formatting option will work. I recommend that you look at your body pages when you're modifying the paragraph tags.

- ✔ Don't forget to regenerate after you change the TOC specification!

Understanding paragraph tags

You work with the paragraph tags in your table of contents file just like any other paragraph tags. For example, you can change the Heading2TOC paragraph tag through the Paragraph Designer, and when you regenerate the file, those changes are retained. See Chapter 4 for details about changing paragraph tags.

For each paragraph tag that you include in your document, you'll have a corresponding paragraph tag with TOC appended. For example, Heading1 generates Heading1TOC paragraphs, sidebar generates sidebarTOC paragraphs, and so on.

Your paragraph tags and information in your TOC specification for that paragraph tag need to match. For example, if you have a tab in the reference page flow, you need to make sure that your paragraph tag contains a corresponding tab stop (see "Setting Up ....Tabs" for more information).

Adding Introductory Information

At the beginning of your table of contents, you might need to insert some information that is not generated (perhaps a title like, "Table of Contents"). You can insert any text you want into the table of contents, but you must put it before the first generated paragraph. As long as the text is in front of the generated material, the inserted material is saved when you regenerate.

Setting Up ....Tabs

If you want to separate the page number from the content information with a tab, you need to do two things. First, you have to insert the tab into the TOC specification lines. Second, you have to format the corresponding paragraph tags so that they include a tab.

For example, you want an entry that looks like this:

Chapter 1: Introduction 4

To accomplish this, you need to modify the TOC specification to include a tab, as shown in Figure 18-2. Don't worry if the tab just sits there. It'll work after you put a tab stop in the corresponding paragraph tag.

Figure 18-2:
This refer-
ence page
definition
includes a
tab.

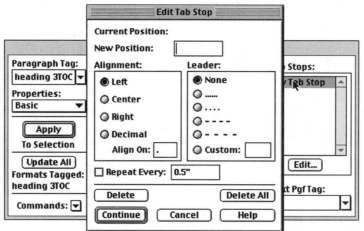

< $paranumonly > < $paratext > $pagenum >¶

Next, you need to set up the paragraph tag. Assume that you're working with the chap_titleTOC paragraph tag. You'll need to insert a tab stop in this paragraph tag. Display the Paragraph Designer (select Ctrl+M, Command+M, or Esc o p d) and in the Basic properties, double-click the New Tab Stop entry in the Tabs section. This displays the Tab dialog box (see Figure 18-3).

Figure 18-3:
Double-click
the words
New Tab
Stop in the
Paragraph
Designer
(where the
arrow is) to
create a
new tab in
the Edit Tab
Stop dialog
box.

The tab position needs to be on the right side of your column. The exact setting depends on your column width, but start with 5.5 inches. Make sure you set this tab to be a right tab, and set the leader to be lots of little dots (.......). Click Continue to set up this tab and return to the Paragraph Designer.

WAIT! You're not done yet! Don't close the Paragraph Designer just yet. First, click Update All. Now, you're finished. Well, almost finished. You still need to generate your table of contents so that FrameMaker rescans the reference pages and inserts the new tab.

No book file required

You can create a table of contents for a single file instead of an entire book. To do so, open the file and select Generate/Book. Select Table of Contents and click Generate. This creates a *file-level* table of contents.

Controlling Line Breaks in the Table of Contents

The generated file feature in FrameMaker lets you create tables of contents (and other generated files) quickly and easily. You may, however, have some trouble with line breaks in your table of contents. Usually, the line breaks you need in the table of contents are different from the line breaks needed in the chapter file. But how do you set up the files to create different line breaks?

The simplest and most labor-intensive way to do this is to tweak the table of contents after you generate it to correct any bad line breaks. This method is simple, but those changes are destroyed every time you regenerate the file, so wait until the last time you generate the table of contents before correcting the line breaks.

A more permanent solution is to put forced returns (Shift+Enter) into the headings in your chapter file. Those forced returns are included when you generate the file. Unfortunately, this method rarely works, because the line length in your chapter file is usually different from the line length in your table of contents file.

This brings me to the last option: hard spaces. If you are having trouble with line breaks in your table of contents file, you can insert hard spaces in your chapter file to "glue" the last few words of the heading together. These hard spaces don't have any visible effect in the chapter file but will provide a better line break in the generated table of contents file.

Chapter 19

Indexing Your Masterpiece

· ·

In This Chapter

▶ Making a game plan

▶ Creating index entries

▶ Formatting indexes

· ·

*T*he indexing feature handles the tedious process of alphabetizing and concatenating (that means *combining* for those of us who speak normal English) index entries, although you do have to tell FrameMaker what index entries you want. You create an index by putting index information in markers. By placing a marker on a particular page, you instruct FrameMaker to print the text in your index entry, along with the page number of the marker, in the index.

Indexing Strategy

Before you begin inserting index markers, think about what you need to accomplish with your index. Here are some general recommendations:

✔ Your index is probably the *first* part of the book that a reader will investigate, so take the time to provide a complete index.

✔ Index terms only where they are defined or where a detailed discussion of that term occurs. Don't index every occurrence of a term (or you'll wind up with an extremely long, but not very useful, index that will annoy your readers.)

✔ If you have more than two or three entries for a term, create subentries and provide informative subheadings to help readers figure out which one they want.

✔ Index actions and compound terms "both ways." For example, index *baking cake* and *cake, baking*. And don't forget *chocolate mousse* and *mousse, chocolate*.

✔ Remember that your readers don't necessarily understand your jargon. Provide *see* references so that if they look up *semisweet* they are redirected to *bittersweet.*

✔ Use ranges to indicate a lengthy discussion of a topic (for example, 45–50).

Some excellent indexing books are available, including these two:

✔ *The Art of Indexing,* by Larry S. Bonura (John Wiley & Sons)

✔ *Indexing Books,* by Nancy C. Mulvany, (University of Chicago Press)

If you plan to spend a lot of time indexing, I highly recommend that you consult an indexing book.

And Now the Main Event . . . Index Entries

And now, on to the main event: creating an index. To create an index in FrameMaker, you insert index markers on various pages in your FrameMaker file(s). You add a generated index file to your book (or generate an index from a single file). You regenerate, and FrameMaker scans all the index markers, arranges them in alphabetical order, and combines all matching entries into a single line.

Where to begin? Find a page for which you need an index entry and follow these steps:

1. **Select Special⇨Marker to display the Marker dialog box (see Figure 19-1).**

   Make sure that the marker type is Index.

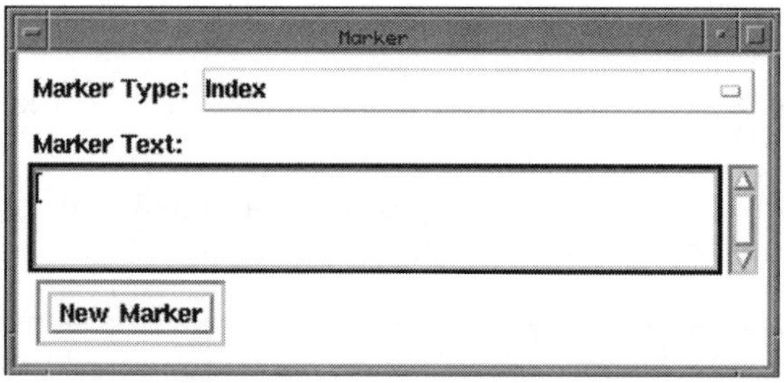

Figure 19-1:
Use the
Marker
dialog box
to build your
index
entries

Marker
Marker Type: **Index**
Marker Text:
[
New Marker

2. **Type the text you want shown in the index into the Marker Text box. Click the New Marker button to save the marker.**

The simplest index marker is a marker with no text at all. A blank marker picks up the first word to the right of the marker and uses that as the marker text.

If you select text in your document and then select Special⇨Marker, the selected text automatically appears in the Marker dialog box.

If you forget to click New Marker (or Edit Marker if you're changing an existing marker), your changes will be lost. When in doubt, click it just in case.

Creating subordinate entries

A *subordinate entry* is an entry that is sorted underneath another entry. Figure 19-2 shows an example.

Figure 19-2:
The mousse and rabbit entries are subordinate to their main topic — chocolate.

```
c
chocolate
              mousse 36
              rabbit 44
```

To create the information in Figure 19-2, you need two index entries. (Follow the instructions in the section above to add these entries.) The entry on page 36 looks like this:

```
chocolate:mousse
```

The entry on page 44 looks like this:

```
chocolate:rabbit
```

Notice the colon. It separates the primary entry (chocolate) from the secondary entry (mousse or rabbit).

Stacking entries in a single marker

Each index marker can include up to 255 characters (counting spaces). You can put more than one index entry into a single marker. For example, if you want entries in your index for "French silk pie" and "pie, French silk" you could insert a single marker that looks like this:

```
French silk pie;pie, French silk
```

The semicolon separates two independent entries.

If you plan to translate your documents from English to other languages, be careful about how long you make your marker text. Relative to other languages (such as German and French), English text is relatively compact. So, if your marker text is close to the limit in English, the translated German version might exceed the 255-character limit. You don't want that. (If the marker is too long, any text past the 255-character limit is ignored. And you don't get any error messages to warn you that it's happened. The excess text just doesn't appear in your index. The only clue is that you may spot a term in the index that cuts off in the middle of a word.)

Creating a "see" reference

Your index occasionally requires references to other entries in the index. These *see* references don't point to a page in the book; instead, they direct the reader to another index entry. This is much more efficient that repeating the information in two places in the index (especially if the entry is an important one with lots of subordinate entries).

Figure 19-3 shows an example.

Figure 19-3:
If readers look under cocoa, the reference directs them to entries under chocolate.

C
cocoa, *see* chocolate

This reference looks a little different from your regular index entry. The word *see* is italicized, and the page number is missing.

Here is the marker text that created that index entry:

```
cocoa, <Emphasis>see<Default Para Font> chocolate<$nopage>
```

Three codes in angle brackets create the formatting. Here's what they do:

- ✓ **<Emphasis>:** Inserts the Emphasis character tag (which is normally italic).
- ✓ **<Default Para Font>:** Turns off the Emphasis.
- ✓ **<$nopage>:** Suppresses the display of the page number for this index entry.

You have to type in all that formatting manually (the Marker dialog box doesn't have a list of building blocks that you can select), so if you need to create more than a few *see* references, I strongly recommend that you copy and paste.

Creating a "see also" reference

A *see also* reference is normally used when you think that the reader might be looking for a word related to the current index entry, but that isn't shown in the current entry. (You can't use a *see* reference because there are subordinate entries hanging around.) For example, take a look at Figure 19-4.

Figure 19-4:
A see also
reference
for some
misguided
souls.

```
C
chocolate
          see also carob
          mousse 36
          rabbit 44
```

The corresponding marker looks like this:

```
chocolate:<Emphasis>see also<Default Para
          Font>carob<$nopage>[chocolate:aaa]
```

Let's break down what's going on in there:

- ✓ **<Emphasis>:** Inserts the Emphasis character tag (which is normally italic).
- ✓ **<Default Para Font>:** Turns off the Emphasis.
- ✓ **<$nopage>:** Suppresses the display of the page number for this index entry.
- ✓ **[chocolate:aaa]:** Changes the placement of the *see also* entry. Without this entry, *see also* would be alphabetized under S, and thus come after the rabbit entry.

Indexing quick reference

Your index marker syntax includes a few special commands. They are

Command	Result
;	Separates the marker text into individual index entries.
:	Creates subordinate entries.
<$nopage>	Suppresses the page number in the index for this marker.
<$singlepage>	Cancels the <$nopage> command. Rarely needed.
<$startrange>	Marks the beginning of an index range.
<$endrange>	Marks the end of an index range.
<$autorange>	Used on the reference pages in the index flow. Collapses identical markers on consecutive pages into a range.
[ ] (square brackets)	Alphabetizes the preceding index entry as if it used the information in the brackets.
\ (backslash)	"Escapes out" the character that follows. Used to insert otherwise special characters into the index. (To insert a colon in an index entry, type in \:).
<character tag>	A character tag name, in angle brackets, results in that character tag being used in the index entry. Don't forget to end it with <Default Para Font>. The character tag you use must be defined in the index file.

Finally, Format That Index!

Now that you've created all the tags for your index, it's time to generate the index and refine its formatting. The index is a generated file so, like the table of contents, the reference pages include information about how to format the index information. And, like the table of contents, you have a number of paragraph tags to work with. (But unlike the table of contents, the names of these paragraph tags in the index are consistent from one book to another.)

Before you go any further, make sure that you read the section on setting up and generating an index file in Chapter 17. You should also peruse Chapter 15, which discusses the concept of reference pages.

Reference pages

The reference pages let you control the sort order and setup of your index. Go to the reference pages (select View⇨Reference Pages) and find the index

---

Help me, IXGen!

If you're getting the idea that creating an index can be a tedious endeavor, you're right. If you're using FrameMaker on a Windows or UNIX platform, considering adding IXGen to your list of tools. IXGen is a FrameMaker add-on that makes index editing much easier and faster. See Appendix C for more details.

---

specification. This is a text frame with a flow tag of IX. Figure 19-5 shows an example.

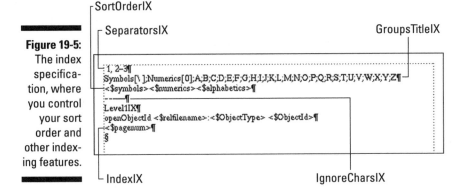

Figure 19-5:
The index specification, where you control your sort order and other indexing features.

The index specification contains several paragraphs. The paragraph tag for each paragraph determines what its purpose is. The tags are

- ✔ **IgnoreCharsIX:** Lists characters that are ignored when the index is sorted. To add additional characters to be ignored, put them on this line.

- ✔ **SeparatorsIX:** Sets the separators used between the index entry and the first page number, between page numbers (when you have more than one page number in a single entry), and between numbers in a range. The default setting is for a space before the first page number, a comma and a space between page numbers, and an en dash between numbers in a range. You can change these settings, but you must use 1, 2, and 3 as your sample numbers.

- ✔ **SortOrderIX:** Sets the overall sort order. You can replace the building blocks with a specific sort order; refer to the FrameMaker online help for details.

- ✔ **GroupTitlesIX:** Lists the titles used for each section of the index.
- ✔ **IndexIX:** Sets the format of the page numbers.

Paragraph tags

To make the index look the way you want it, you need to format some of the paragraphs used in the generated index. The following paragraph tags are used to format your index entries:

- ✔ **GroupTitlesIX:** Formats the section headers (A, B, C, and so on).
- ✔ **Level1IX:** Formats the primary entries.
- ✔ **Level2IX:** Formats the secondary entries.
- ✔ **Level3IX:** Formats the tertiary entries.

If you need additional index levels, you can add Level4IX, Level5IX, and so on.

To format one of these paragraph tags, just open it in the Paragraph Designer in the index file and make the changes. (For details on the Paragraph Designer, see Chapter 4.)

Character tags

To use character tags in an index entry, you must embed the character tag command in the index entry. You must also be sure that the character tag you embed is actually available in the index! (To check for it, just display the Character Catalog in the index file. See Chapter 5 for details.)

For details on embedding character tags in index markers, see "And Now the Main Event . . . Index Entries" earlier in this chapter.

Part V
The Part of Tens

The 5th Wave   By Rich Tennant

"WELL, SHOOT! THIS EGGPLANT CHART IS JUST AS CONFUSING AS THE BUTTERNUT SQUASH CHART AND THE GOURD CHART. CAN'T YOU JUST MAKE A PIE CHART LIKE EVERYONE ELSE?"

In this part . . .

This part is full of those little information tidbits that save you untold hours of time. It includes a chapter full of little problems that are easy to solve — if someone provides the secret decoder ring. Well, consider this your decoder ring. After that, you'll look at some ideas on how to set up good templates and how to use autonumbering in ways you probably haven't thought of. One chapter lists important building blocks.

Chapter 20

Ten Things I Wish Someone Had Told Me

· ·

In This Chapter

▶ Try invisible tables for formatting

▶ Use MIF for power search and replace

▶ You need to clean up tables imported from Word

▶ You just can't change some things

▶ Fonts AWOL?

▶ Use cross-references, tables of contents entries, and index entries as jumps

▶ Find and change more than just text

▶ Make global changes

▶ Import a template from the current document to eliminate overrides

▶ Don't despair: Framers are there

· ·

*T*his is the chapter that I wish someone had given me. It's full of those interesting and useful tips and tricks that I learned the hard way — after I pulled all my hair out trying those other, less efficient ways.

Invisible Tables Are Useful For Formatting

Most of my templates contain a table tag called invisible. It's a table with no lines and no shading. I use it to create multicolumn lists. For example, if I have 15 relatively short bullet items, they look much better in three columns of five items each than they will as a single, lonely column wandering down the page.

Plus, with an invisible table tag, this is very fast.

If you plan to convert your file to a structured format (such as HTML), consider the implications of using a table to express nontable data. You're taking advantage of the table function for formatting purposes, and this may or may not fly with the style police in your company. (But then, you probably *are* the style police.)

Use MIF for Power Search and Replace

FrameMaker files are normally binary, but a text format is available. Maker Interchange Format (MIF) is very handy for automating tasks that would be horribly tedious through the interface. For example, in FrameMaker 5.5.6, an obscure bug — ahem, "unexpected functionality" — introduces lots of color definitions into your document even though you didn't ask for them. Cleaning out these colors is extremely labor-intensive through the FrameMaker interface, because you have to delete them one at a time. But if you save the file to MIF, you can strip them in one fell swoop. (For details about how MIF works, check out the MIF Reference included in the FrameMaker online manuals, by selecting Help➪Online Manuals.)

Crime and Punishment: If You Import a Table From Word, You Have to Clean It Up

So, you imported a file from you-know-where. You apply the appropriate FrameMaker table tag to your table and . . . what?! It's not cleaned up. The problem here is that the table formatting information from Word is imported as custom overrides to the table formatting. So, even applying the table tag won't help you because you still have overrides. To correct this problem, you need to select the entire table (press Ctrl in Windows, Option on the Mac, or Meta on UNIX and triple-click) and then strip the custom formatting. To do this, select Table➪Custom Ruling and Shading to display the Custom Ruling and Shading dialog box (see Figure 20-1). Set every setting to From Table, make sure all the check boxes are checked, click Apply, and ta-da! You bought yourself a clean table.

Another problem you'll see is that your table heading row is not translated as a heading row. It becomes a regular row at the beginning of your table. To correct this, add a heading row (select Table➪Add Rows and Columns), and then copy and paste the information into the heading row.

Figure 20-1:
Word makes cleaning up your tables extra difficult.

Instead of using the Custom Ruling and Shading dialog box, you can also convert the table to text and then convert it back to a table using the table tag you want. This has an additional advantage in that you can set up your heading rows properly (they're not converted from Word's heading rows).

Some Things You Just Can't Change

Many things in FrameMaker are configurable . . . but a few are not. Here are a couple of items that are extra annoying.

Default location of backup files

If you create backup files when you save (select File➪Preferences to turn this on or off), the backup files are *always* saved in the same directory as the working files. You can't change it.

Default left/right master pages for new pages

If you're creating new pages in a document (whether by adding text or by using the dreaded Special➪Add Disconnected Page), the new page always will use one of the default master pages, either Left or Right (depending on whether the page is even or odd). You cannot set up FrameMaker to automatically assign a custom master page to new page. Sorry.

What to Do About AWOL Fonts?

Before you open a file that contains fonts that you don't have installed on your system, make sure that you first turn on Remember Missing Fonts in your Preferences (by selecting File⇨Preferences). This ensures that the font settings are preserved until you get the right fonts (or go back to your Mac where all the good fonts are).

If you want to get rid of the missing fonts once and for all, turn off the missing fonts preference, open the file, and save it. This strips the fonts that aren't available and replaces them with default fonts (usually Times or Times New Roman).

Think twice before you do this. Once you've set FrameMaker *not* to remember fonts, you can't easily get them back. (Unless, of course, you have a template with all the right font settings.)

Jump Around with Cross-References, Table of Contents Entries, and Index Entries

You can use several items in your document as hyperlinks. For example, on a Windows machine, hold down the Ctrl and Alt keys and click a cross-reference. You'll jump to the source for that cross-reference. On a Macintosh, you use Ctrl+Option+click. On a UNIX machine, things get a little sticky. You can't use this trick unless you first make your file view-only (Esc Shift+f l k). Then, just click the cross-reference. To make your file editable, press Esc Shift+f l k again.

Find/Change More Than Just Text

Sometime when you have a few spare minutes, check out the Find/Change dialog box (see Figure 20-2). To display it, select Edit⇨Find/Change.

The basic search and replace features are there, but you can also search for lots of different items, such as unresolved cross-references, anchored frames, tables, and more.

Figure 20-2:
The
Find/Change
dialog box
offers lots
and lots of
different
search
options.

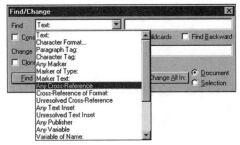

You also have a couple of interesting replacement options. The most powerful (and least known) one is By Pasting (see Figure 20-3).

Figure 20-3:
Replace By
Pasting
means that
you can put
items on the
clipboard
and use
them as
your
replacement
items.

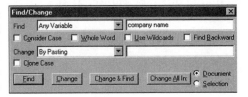

Imagine, for example, that you need to find a text string and replace it with a variable. You had typed in the name of a product, and now you want to use a variable for the product name instead. (If you're wondering why on earth this would be useful, count your blessings. You obviously haven't worked in an environment where product names change every week!)

First you create the variable. Call it product name and put the product name *du jour* in as the definition. Today's product name might be WidgetMaster. Insert the variable somewhere in your document. Now, click the variable (once) to select it, and select Edit➪Copy. This puts the variable on the clipboard. In the Find/Change dialog box (select Edit➪Find/Change), type in the product name text (WidgetMaster) in the Find field. In the Replace drop-down list, select By Pasting. Click Change All if you're feeling confident, or click Find to locate the next match and Change (or Change and Find) to replace that text with the variable.

Tomorrow, when Marketing changes the product's name from WidgetMaster to ObjectLord, you can just redefine your variable. (See Chapter 10 for the scoop on changing variable definitions.)

Think Locally, Change Globally in the Paragraph Designer

If you're cleaning up renegade formats from a document, FrameMaker provides an efficient way to replace one paragraph tag with another. For example, you might have a document whose body text tag is called Body. But you still have a few renegade Normal tags lurking. To correct this, follow these steps:

1. **Click in a Body paragraph. (This isn't mandatory, but it saves some steps.)**

2. **In the Commands drop-down list, select Global Update Options to display the corresponding dialog box (see Figure 20-4).**

Figure 20-4:
The Global Update Options dialog box is handy for getting rid of unwanted paragraph tags.

3. **Select All Properties in the upper half of the dialog box.**

4. **In the lower half, select All Tagged and then either type in or select the tag you want to replace (Normal) in the field.**

5. **Click Update and confirm that you want to replace all Normal tags with Body tags.**

   FrameMaker changes all Normal tags to Body tags and uses the Body tag formatting on these new Body paragraphs. The Normal tag is also removed from your paragraph catalog.

Use this technique immediately after converting a file from one of those "other" formats to save lots of cleanup time.

Import Template from Current Document to Eliminate Overrides

You're probably tired of hearing about how to import formats from one document to another. But have you considered importing formats from your *current* document instead of from an outside template? Probably not. If you have a document that contains formatting overrides, but whose underlying tag catalogs are still clean, you can use an import from the current document to easily clean out the overrides.

1. **Open the document and select File⇨Import⇨Formats to display the Import Formats dialog box (see Figure 20-5).**

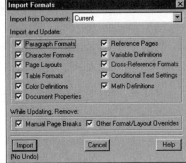

Figure 20-5: Selecting Current as your document might be a little unorthodox, but it's a great clean-up tactic.

Leave the default (Current) in the Import From drop-down list. Then check every available check box, including the two to remove manual page breaks and other formatting overrides.

2. **Click Import. This cleans up your tags.**

This technique can't help you if someone has actually redefined tags in the catalogs. It can only fix overrides. For the former problem, I recommend sending hate mail.

Don't Despair: Framers Are There

The framers e-mail list is an invaluable resource for FrameMaker questions. See Appendix B for information on how to subscribe to it.

Chapter 21

(Almost) Ten Template Questions

This chapter covers some common questions I get from FrameMaker users.

How Many Tags Should Be in a Template?

This highly subjective question has no definite answer. Your template should have as many tags as it needs — and no more. The real question is whether you create a tag for every possible contingency or whether you occasionally allow overrides (gasp!). For most simple book-length documents, 20 to 30 paragraph tags are usually enough. But your books may be complicated and need more. One framer I knew used the screen as a guideline. If the paragraph catalog could not fit on the screen without scrolling, it was deemed "too long." Of course, you could get around this by using a large monitor!

Who Should Own the Template?

In many organizations, one person is the designated template owner. That person is the only one authorized to make changes to the template. If you're not the template owner, you must humbly submit a change request if you need a new tag in the template.

This approach makes sense in a large writing environment because it's the only way to maintain and keep the template up to date. If each writer has the authority to add custom tags, the template will quickly turn into a collection of templates, where each writer uses a slightly different version.

In my company, we designate a template owner for each project. This person is different for different projects, but each project has an officially designated person who owns the template. That person makes changes as necessary and distributes updated templates to the people working on that project.

I recommend that you assign only experienced FrameMaker users as template owners. Often, a change in the template can have a ripple effect across your documents, and an experienced user will anticipate these changes.

If you're just starting to use FrameMaker, consider hiring somebody to create your template for you. A FrameMaker expert can quickly design a template that's customized for your requirements. As you learn more about FrameMaker, you can take over the maintenance of the template.

What Supporting Material Should I Include with the Template?

If you're designing a template that will be used by many people, it's a good idea to provide information about the template's styles. (Follow your own advice and document your work!) In the official template file, write a brief explanation of the various catalogs in the document. Explain when and how to use each one. The people using the template will appreciate the information and spend less time trying to figure it out on their own; you'll spend less time answering questions about the template; and if you leave for another job, you won't leave your colleagues in the lurch.

Should I Use Conditional Text?

If the overlap between two related documents is significant (more than 40 percent), consider using conditional text to maintain both documents in a single file. (See Chapter 16 for details about conditional text.)

You might also use conditional text for "temporary" information, such as queries to reviewers and notes to yourself.

Conditional text can be a very useful tool; just start out slowly. It's easy to get carried away and create a huge, unmanageable list of conditions, so keep it simple until you're comfortable and be cautious about adding new tags.

How Do I Create a Template for Multiple Languages?

If your template if going to be used for more than one language, here are some pointers to make the template multilingual.

Handling page breaks

Compared to other languages, English is relatively compact. That means that a page of content in English might become more than a page after translation. Because of this text expansion, custom page breaks (set with paragraph overrides) from your original English text will probably not work in the translated version.

Consider setting up the main sections of your document to start the top of a page by default. This certainly won't eliminate custom page breaks, but it will minimize them.

From a design perspective, setting up a particular heading level to start at the top of a page may not be ideal, and the time saved is small if you're translating just one book to just one language. But if you have lots of documentation (thousands of pages) and you're translating to several languages, the savings in copyfitting time will be substantial.

Tight spacing in tables

If your tables are tightly packed with information and provide little white space, then during translation you have no room for expansion. The result? After translation, someone has to go through and check every table for squished text. A better solution is to leave enough room in the table to accommodate text expansion.

Expanding callouts

Callouts are another issue where text expansion is critical. If callouts barely fit in your English version, with no room for possible expansion, you're going to have a problem after translation. Leave enough space around your graphics to accommodate longer callouts.

An unfriendly building block

After translation, you'll probably need to adjust some of your template formats. For example, a cross-reference format like "see page <$pagenum>" will need to be changed for each language ("siehe Seite <$pagenum>"). But some building blocks will cause significant problems. For example, the <$paratag> building block displays the name of the referenced paragraph tag. If you have a paragraph tag named "Chapter" and use this in your template to avoid having to type in the word Chapter, you're going to have a big problem. Once you translated your file to German, the cross-reference needs to be "Kapitel 18," not "Chapter 18." But because the word "Chapter" is coded in as <$paratag[Chapter]>, you'll have to change the paragraph tag name! After you change the paragraph tag name, you still have to modify the cross-reference format to pick up the new paragraph tag name. This is way too much work. Instead, just type in the word "Chapter" and when appropriate, replace it with Kapitel.

How Do I Restart Page Numbering Within a File?

You don't. It's not possible. If you need to restart page numbering, use multiple files and combine them in a book file.

Can I Automatically Put the Name of a Chapter in the Header?

Instead of typing the chapter or section title onto your master page, create an appropriate running header/footer variable. The variable is updated automatically when the chapter title changes, which saves you maintenance time.

What Is a Good Naming Convention for Tags?

I recommend that you use all lowercase for your tags because the default FrameMaker tags all start with a capital letter. So, if your names are lowercase, you can immediately tell the two apart. (If you import files from Word, you'll also see tags with initial capitals.)

Where Can I Get Templates?

Adobe provides several Template Packs on their Web site. You might also check out www.frameusers.com. And, of course, you can seek out the help of professional template designers (like myself). (See Appendix B for a list of Web sites and other resources where you could ask for help.)

Chapter 22

(Nearly) Ten Autonumbering Examples

• •

In This Chapter

▶ Setting up bulleted paragraphs

▶ Adding repeated text

▶ Using autonumbering for steps

▶ Creating steps within steps

▶ Trying another way to create steps

▶ Numbering headings

▶ Adding figures and tables to the mix

▶ Putting it all together now

• •

*A*utonumbering is one of the most powerful features in FrameMaker. But before I get too far into a discussion of autonumbering, it's important to recognize this: *Despite the name, autonumbering is not just for numbers.* Autonumbering lets you set up a paragraph tag with automatic numbering (thus the "auto-numbering"), but it's also useful for bullets, dingbats to end a paragraph, and text that's standard at the beginning of a paragraph (for instance, **NOTE:**).

You cannot delete autonumbers from paragraphs by backspacing over them. If you try it, FrameMaker just skips over the autonumber. If you want to get rid of an autonumber, you'll need to apply a different (non-autonumbered) paragraph tag or change the paragraph tag definition to remove the auto-number.

You do all of this work in the Paragraph Designer. If you haven't already read Chapter 4, now would be a good time to do so.

Bullet Ballet

If you need to set up bulleted paragraphs, you need autonumbering. To make a bulleted paragraph work properly, you'll also change some of the indents and tab settings on the Basic properties (select Format⇨Paragraphs⇨ Paragraph Designer).

The autonumbering for a bulleted paragraph is shown in Figure 22-1.

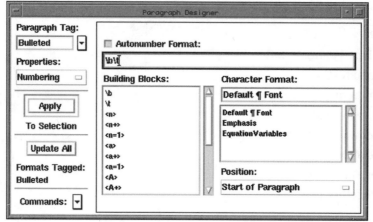

Figure 22-1: The Auto-numbering tab. The \b means "bullet." The \t means "tab."

On the Macintosh, you can type in a bullet directly into the autonumbering definition by pressing Option+8. The bullet appears as a bullet, not as a \b (see Figure 22-2). However, \b also works on the Mac.

Figure 22-2: On the Mac, you can create an actual bullet instead of using \b.

So, your autonumbering for this paragraph is a bullet followed by a tab. Now, in a bulleted paragraph you usually want your bullet to be slightly indented, and then the bullet text indented from the bullet, as shown in Figure 22-3.

Figure 22-3:
A well-
behaved
bulleted
paragraph
should have
a hanging
indent.

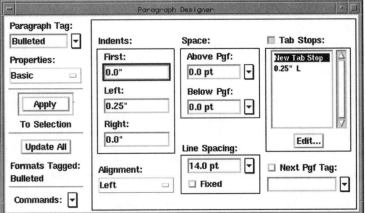

- Do your homework.
- Clean up your room.
- Don't forget to walk the dog.

To format the paragraph this way, you need to set indents and tabs. The First Indent setting controls the left indent on the first line of the paragraph. The Left Indent setting controls the left indent of all other lines. (The Right Indent controls the indentation of all lines on the right, but you don't need that here.)

Figure 22-4 shows sample indent settings.

Figure 22-4:
The First
Indent
positions
the bullet;
the Left
Indent
positions
text on all
the other
lines.

You still need one other item to make your bullets behave: a tab.

By default, your FrameMaker paragraphs don't have any tabs set. As a result, the tab embedded in the autonumber has no effect.

The Autonumbering properties contain a tab after the bullet. That tab needs to align with the other indented paragraphs, so that tab's setting should be the same as the Left Indent setting. In Figure 22-4, I've already set up the tab where it needs to be.

Red Alert! (And Now That I Have Your Attention...)

Autonumbering is very useful for repeated text that begins certain paragraphs. For example, you may need to put notes in your text (see Figure 22-5):

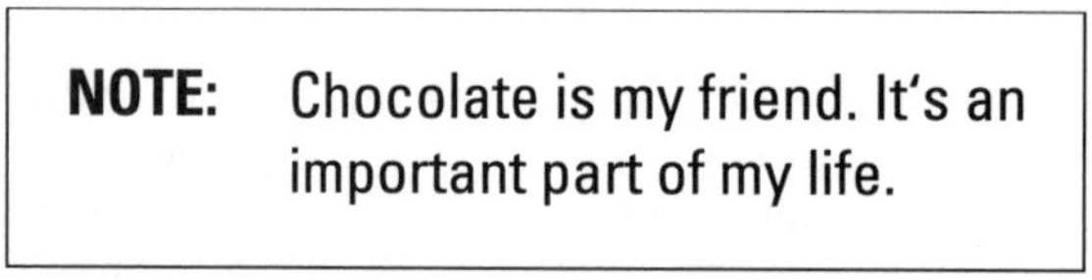

Figure 22-5:
A typical
note.

> **NOTE:**   Chocolate is my friend. It's an important part of my life.

You could type in the word *NOTE:* every time you need a note, and make it boldface, but why not let FrameMaker do the work? Create a Note paragraph tag with autonumbering for the note. To make the autonumber boldface, select a character format in the Character Format list on the Numbering tab.

Every time you need a note paragraph, just apply the Note tag. FrameMaker will automatically add *NOTE:* to the beginning of the paragraph and make it bold for you.

You can see where the words came from, but how do you make the *NOTE:* text bold? The boldface is applied because I selected a character tag in the Character Format area. The character tag that you select on the Autonumbering tab is applied to the autonumbering text only, not to the rest of the paragraph. This gives you the ability to make your autonumbered text (or numbers, but I'll get to those) look different from the rest of the paragraph.

And the whole thing is automatic. I love automatic.

Baby Steps

It's time to talk about actual numbers in autonumbering. (And you thought I'd never get there.) If you want to set up a series of steps in your document, you need to set up autonumbering.

With steps, you need to resolve a couple of new issues. First, you need to automate your incrementing, so you need to set up the <n+> building block. Next, you need a way to reset a new list to 1; this requires the <n=1> building block. So, to begin with, you need two paragraph tags:

Step1   Used to begin a list

Step2+   Used to continue a list

You use the Step1 format whenever you need to start a list. Figure 22-6 shows Step1's autonumbering.

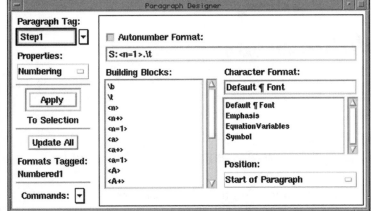

Figure 22-6: The autonumber for Step1 begins the list at the number 1.

And you need to increment your autonumbering with Step2+, as shown in Figure 22-7.

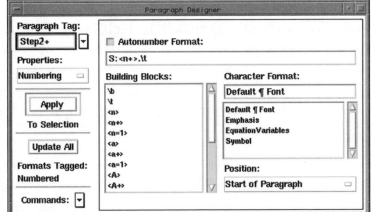

Figure 22-7: The autonumber for Step2+ continues the numbering.

Notice that each of these formats contains some additional code that you haven't seen before. Each of the autonumbering steps contains "S:" at the beginning of the autonumbering string. This is called a *series label*. It tells FrameMaker that the numbering in the Step1 format and the numbering in the Step2+ format are related.

Why didn't the bullets and notes have series labels? They don't need series labels because their values don't change (they're not dependent on the previous tag) and because they are using only one paragraph tag. FrameMaker assumes that the numbering in a single paragraph tag is in the same series.

The S: is important because it distinguishes Step1 and Step2+ from all the other series in this document.

Steps Within Steps

What if you need two sets of step lists? Perhaps your document looks something like Figure 22-8.

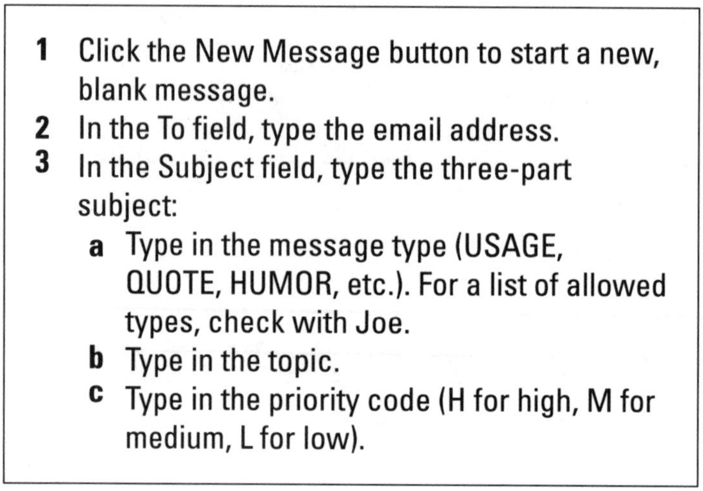

1 Click the New Message button to start a new, blank message.

2 In the To field, type the email address.

3 In the Subject field, type the three-part subject:

   a Type in the message type (USAGE, QUOTE, HUMOR, etc.). For a list of allowed types, check with Joe.

   b Type in the topic.

   c Type in the priority code (H for high, M for medium, L for low).

Figure 22-8: This document includes a first-level and second-level list of steps.

You need four paragraph tags for this case, two for the first-level list and two for the second-level list. The autonumbering would look like this:

Tag	Autonumbering Code
Step1	S:<n=1>
Step2+	S:<n+>

Tag	Autonumbering Code
Step a	T:<a=1>
Step b+	T:<a+>

A Totally Different Step Technique

Perhaps you're appalled by the inefficiency of using two step tags for a single list type. You do have another alternative. Instead of using a "single-purpose" Step1 tag to reset your numbered list, you can use a heading to reset the numbered list.

This approach works only for a document where you don't have multiple step lists within a single section. Or, put another way, you must always have a heading before each step list so that the list is reset.

The autonumbering setup would look like this:

Tag	Autonumbering Code
Step	S:<n+>
Heading	S:

Here, the Step tag just keeps increasing, but the Heading tag also belongs in that autonumbering series, and because it skips the counter, the counter is reset to zero (the Heading tag gets the number 0). So, for example, the result would look something like this:

Tag	Result
Heading	0 (but not displayed)
Step	1
Step	2
Step	3
Step	4
Heading	0 (but not displayed)
Step	1
Step	2

You could add to the fun by tying in your second-level step tag, as well. Just set it up so that it's reset by the Heading or Step tag:

Tag	Autonumbering Code
Step	S:<n+>
StepAB	S:< ><n+>
Heading	S:

The empty counter < > (with that all-important space inside) suppresses the display of the first counter but doesn't change its value.

Quick and Easy Numbered Headings

If you're required to use numbered headings, you may have spent untold hours wrestling with that "other program" to get them to work. In FrameMaker, it takes a few minutes — and the numbers will maintain themselves when you add or delete headings.

You'll need to tie together the four headings with a series label. They'll look like this:

Tag	Autonumbering Code	Result
1Head	H:<n+>	1, 2, 3
2Head	H:<n>.<n+>	1.1, 1.2, 1.3
3Head	H:<n>.<n>.<n+>	1.1.1, 1.1.2, 1.1.3
4Head	H:<n>.<n>.<n>.<n+>	1.1.1.1, 1.1.1.2, 1.1.1.3

That's it! Try it for yourself.

This setup works because the skipped counters are reset to zero. So, for example, the 3Head format doesn't have the fourth counter, which resets that counter to zero.

Provided that you always keep your headings in order (that is, you can't have a 2Head followed immediately by a 4Head), this numbering will work perfectly and maintain itself even when you move sections around.

Mix It Up: Adding Figures and Tables

Chapter-specific figure and table numbers (that is, 1-1, 1-2, 1-3, and so on) give your readers a useful cue that helps them figure out what part of the book they are in.

Numbering by chapter is fine for printed books, but is probably not the ideal choice for books that you deliver via Adobe Acrobat (PDF) files. The PDF file itself contains a page numbering scheme in the status bar, and if possible, it's a good idea to make your book page numbers match the PDF page numbers. But unfortunately, the PDF file starts on page 1 and counts all the way through the file. So, numbering by chapter and especially numbering front matter with roman numerals will cause confusion for your readers. See Chapter 14 for more on PDF.

If you're numbering figures and tables, you want the numbering to look like this:

Figure   1-1, 1-2, 1-3, . . ., 2-1, 2-2, 2-3, . . .

Table   1-1, 1-2, 1-3, . . ., 2-1, 2-2, 2-3, . . .

The figure and table numbering series share the same chapter number, but other than that, they need to be independent. So how do you tie together the figure with the chapter number and the table with the chapter number without interference?

Your first attempt might look like this:

Tag	Autonumbering Code	Result
Chapter	C:<n+>	1, 2, 3
Figure	C:<n>-<n+>	1-1, 1-2, 1-3, . . ., 2-1, 2-2, 2-3, . . .
Table	C:<n>-<n+>	1-1, 1-2, 1-3, . . ., 2-1, 2-2, 2-3, . . .

Looks good, right? But look at what happens when you have figures and tables together:

Tag	Result
Chapter	1
Figure	1-1
Figure	1-2

(continued)

Tag	Result
Table	1-3
Table	1-4
Figure	1-5
Chapter	2
Table	2-1
Figure	2-2

The figures and tables are using the same numbering sequence! Probably not what you had in mind.

To prevent the figures and tables from interfering with one another, you'll need to set up separate counters for the figures and the tables. The correct numbering sequence would look like this:

Tag	Autonumbering Code
Chapter	C:<n+>
Figure	C:<n>-<n+>< >
Table	C:<n>-< ><n+>

Now, the first counter belongs to the chapter number (which is as it should be). The second counter is used and displayed by the Figure tab, and suppressed but not changed by the Table tag. The third counter is used and displayed by the Table tag and suppressed but not changed by the Figure tab.

In other words, you've set up two counters that are incremented independently of each other. The result for the same sequence of paragraphs as shown above is much more useful:

Tag	Result
Chapter	1
Figure	1-1
Figure	1-2
Table	1-1
Table	1-2
Figure	1-3

Tag	Result
Chapter	2
Table	2-1
Figure	2-1

All Together Now: Chapters, Figures, Tables, and Headings

In the real world, you're going to need headings, figures, and tables in a single document — not separated into nice little antiseptic examples. So let's put it all together.

This is how the final product would look:

Tag	Result
1Head	1, 2, 3
2Head	1.1, 1.2, 1.3, . . ., 2.1, 2.2, 2.3, . . .
3Head	1.1.1, 1.1.2, 1.1.3, . . ., 1.2.1, 1.2.2, 1.2.3, . . .
4Head	1.1.1.1, 1.1.1.2, 1.1.1.3, . . ., 1.1.2.1, 1.1.2.2, 1.1.2.3, . . .
Figure	1-1, 1-2, 1-3, . . ., 2-1, 2-2, 2-3, . . .
Table	1-1, 1-2, 1-3, . . ., 2-1, 2-2, 2-3, . . .

To accomplish this, you'll need the following autonumbering codes:

Tag	Autonumbering Code	Result
1Head	H:<n+>	1, 2, 3
2Head	H:<n>< >< >.<n+>	1.1, 1.2, 1.3
3Head	H:<n>< >< >.<n>.<n+>	1.1.1, 1.1.2, 1.1.3
4Head	H:<n>< >< >.<n>.<n>.<n+>	1.1.1.1, 1.1.1.2, 1.1.1.3
Figure	H:<n>-<n+>< >< >< >< >	1-1, 1-2, 1-3
Table	H:<n>-< ><n+>< >< >< >	1-1, 1-2, 1-3

The 1Head format contains only the chapter number, which resets every other counter to zero.

The second-, third-, and fourth-level headings need to be at the end of the sequence of counters, because this allows you to use the "missing counter" technique to reset subheadings to zero. For example, the 2Head tag resets the third- and fourth-level heading counters to zero.

Chapter 23

Ten Building Blocks
You Should Know

● ●

In This Chapter

▶ Showing the content of a referenced paragraph with <$paratext>

▶ Displaying the autonumber and numeric counter with <$paranum> and <$paranumonly>

▶ Showing the page number with <$pagenum>

▶ Collating automatically with <$autorange>

▶ Creating ranges manually with <$startrange> and <$endrange>

▶ Setting numeric counters in your paragraph autonumbering with <n> building blocks

▶ Making capitalized alphabetical counters with the <A> building blocks

▶ Creating lowercase alphabetical counters with the <a> building blocks

▶ Setting numeric counters with the <R> building blocks

▶ Setting numeric counters with the <r> building blocks

▶ Using the building blocks quick reference

● ●

*B*uilding blocks are small chunks of code. They perform a function (for example, <$year> prints the current year). Many of them are used in more than one FrameMaker feature, so it's useful to take a look at them. I've highlighted some of the more commonly used building blocks and provided a quick reference to all building blocks at the end of this chapter.

<$paratext>

The <$paratext> building block displays the content of the referenced paragraph. In reference pages, you'll see <$paratext> used to set up the definitions for tables of contents and other generated files. In cross-reference formats, <$paratext> is used to insert the text of the source paragraph. In system variables (such as running headers and footers), you use <$paratext> and specify the paragraph that you want to pick up (for example, <$paratext[heading 1]>.

<$paranum>, <$paranumonly>

The <$paranum> building block displays the autonumber of the referenced paragraph. The <$paranumonly> building block displays just the numeric (counter) portion of the referenced paragraph. You'll see these building blocks used in the same places as the <$paratext> building block — in reference pages, cross-reference formats, and system variables.

An autonumber can contain both text and numbers. For example, you might use *NOTE:* as an autonumber.

<$pagenum>

The <$pagenum> building blocks display the page number of the referenced item. Although you can redefine the Page Number system variable to include prefixes (such as 3-1, 3-2, 3-3, 3-4), the <$pagenum> building block will only pick up the "basic" page number (1, 2, 3, 4 in the example above). Techniques for including the page number prefix vary. For generated files, you need to specify the prefixes in the chapter files at the book level. (To do so, open the book file, select the appropriate chapter in the list, then select File⇨Set Up File, and type the chapter prefix into the Prefix field.) For cross-references and system variables, you can instead pick up the chapter prefix from the paragraph that includes the chapter autonumber. For example, if your chapter number is stored in an autonumbered paragraph called ChapterTitle, then you would display the multipart page number like this:

```
<$paranumonly[ChapterTitle]>-<$pagenum>
```

<$autorange>

The <$autorange> building block is probably the most obscure of the bunch, but it's a very cool feature. If you insert <$autorange> in the index flow definition, FrameMaker will automatically collate your index entries into ranges. You must put identical entries on consecutive pages, and FrameMaker does the rest. For example, imagine that you discuss the topic of "fierce killer rabbit" from pages 45 to 49. You could use range markers (see the next section), but here's how to do it with <$autorange>.

1. **First, put an index entry on pages 45, 46, 47, 48, and 49. Each index entry needs the same text:**

```
fierce killer rabbit
```

2. **Go to the index file's reference pages, and insert the <$autorange> building block before the IndexIX paragraph.**

   (By default, it contains just <$pagenum>.) The resulting IndexIX paragraph should look like this:

   ```
   <$autorange><$pagenum>
   ```

3. **After you regenerate the index, you'll see an index entry like this:**

   fierce killer rabbit 45-49

<$startrange>, <$endrange>

If you want more control over ranges than is provided by the <$autorange> building block, you can use <$startrange> and <$endrange> instead to create ranges manually. To create the same "fierce killer rabbit" entry as shown in the section above, you would need two index entries. On page 45, the index marker text would be:

```
fierce killer rabbit<$startrange>
```

On page 49, the marker text would be:

```
fierce killer rabbit<$endrange>
```

The text preceding the <$startrange> and <$endrange> building blocks must match exactly; otherwise, FrameMaker can't resolve the ranges properly. If ranges don't resolve, you'll see double question marks in the generated index, like this:

```
fierce killer rabbit 45-??
```

The <$autorange> building block has the advantage that you don't have to worry about matching up starting and ending index markers. But with <$autorange>, you have to make sure that every page that you want to include in a range contains a marker with the appropriate text.

Which is better? You'll have to decide, based on the number of ranges in your document and how those ranges go across pages, whether the automatic range generation (<$autorange>) or manual range creation (<$startrange> and <$endrange>) is a better choice.

<n+>, <n>, <n=1>

The <n> building blocks let you set numeric counters in your paragraph autonumbering. The result of any <n> building block is a single number (like 5, 7, or 27).

Counter	Result
<n+>	Increases the value of the counter by 1 and displays it.
<n>	Doesn't change the value of the counter and displays it.
<n=1>	Sets the value of the counter to 1 and displays 1.
<n=57>	Sets the value of the counter to 57 and displays 57.

<A+>, <A>, <A=1>

The <A> building blocks let you set capitalized alphabetical counters in your paragraph autonumbering. The result of any <A> building block is a letter (like A, B, or R).

Counter	Result
<A+>	Increases the value of the counter by 1 and displays the letter than corresponds to the number (for example, 1 equals A, 2 equals B, 3 equals C, and so on).
<A>	Doesn't change the value of the counter and displays the letter that corresponds to the number.
<A=1>	Sets the value of the counter to 1 and displays A.
<A=5>	Sets the value of the counter to 5 and displays E (the fifth letter in the alphabet).

<a+>, <a>, <a=1>

The <a> building blocks let you set lowercase alphabetical counters in your paragraph autonumbering. The result of any <a> building block is a letter (like a, c, or g).

Counter	Result
<a+>	Increases the value of the counter by 1 and displays the letter that corresponds to the number (for example, 1 equals a, 2 equals b, 3 equals c, and so on).
<a>	Doesn't change the value of the counter and displays the letter that corresponds to the number.
<a=1>	Sets the value of the counter to 1 and displays a.
<a=7>	Sets the value of the counter to 7 and displays g (the seventh letter in the alphabet).

<R+>, <R>, <R=1>

The <R> building blocks let you set numeric counters in your paragraph autonumbering. The result of any <R> building block is an uppercase Roman numeral (such as II, IV, or IX).

Counter	Result
<R+>	Increases the value of the counter by 1 and displays it as a Roman numeral.
<R>	Doesn't change the value of the counter and displays it as a Roman numeral.
<R=1>	Sets the value of the counter to 1 and displays I.
<R=19>	Sets the value of the counter to 19 and displays XIX.

<r+>, <r>, <r=1>

The <r> building blocks let you set numeric counters in your paragraph autonumbering. The result of any <r> building block is a lowercase Roman numeral (such as iii, vii, or xxiii).

Counter	Result
\<r+\>	Increases the value of the counter by 1 and displays it as a lowercase Roman numeral.
\<r\>	Doesn't change the value of the counter and displays it as a lowercase Roman numeral.
\<r=1\>	Sets the value of the counter to 1 and displays i.
\<r=42\>	Sets the value of the counter to 42 and displays xlii.

Building Blocks Quick Reference

Table 23-1 summarizes the building blocks presented in this chapter.

Table 23-1	Building Blocks Quick Reference						
Building Block	**Displays**	**Auto-number**	**Cross-ref**	**HTML Flow**	**Index Marker**	**Text Flow**	**Variable**
< >	Keeps value of first counter, undisplayed	✔					
<=0>	Resets value to zero, undisplayed	✔					
<A+>	Uppercase alphabetic numbering, value increased by 1	✔					
<A>	Uppercase alphabetic numbering, value unchanged	✔					
<A=1>	Uppercase alphabetic numbering, value set to 1	✔					
<R+>	Uppercase roman numeral numbering, value increased by 1	✔					
<R>	Uppercase roman numeral numbering, value unchanged	✔					
<R=1>	Uppercase roman numeral numbering, value set to 1	✔					
<a+>	Lowercase alphabetic numbering, value increased by 1	✔					
<a>	Lowercase alphabetic numbering, value unchanged	✔					
<a=1>	Lowercase alphabetic numbering, value set to 1	✔					
<n+>	Numeric numbering, value increased by 1	✔					
<n>	Numeric numbering, value unchanged	✔					
<n=1>	Numeric numbering, value set to 1	✔					

(continued)

Table 23-1 (continued)

Building Block	Displays	Auto-number	Cross-ref	HTML Flow	Index Marker	Text Flow	Variable
<r+>	Lowercase roman numeral numbering, value increased by 1	✓					
<r>	Lowercase roman numeral numbering, value unchanged	✓					
<r=1>	Lowercase roman numeral numbering, value set to 1	✓					
$alphabetics>	Sort order for alphabetic entries					✓	✓
$AMPM>	Uppercase morning or evening designation (AM)		✓				✓
$ampm>	Lowercase morning or evening designation (am)		✓				✓
$autorange>	Automatic page ranges					✓	✓
<$condtag[condtag]>Condition tag							
$curpagenum>	Page number (used only on Master Page)					✓	✓
$dayname>	Name of the day (Monday)		✓				✓
$daynum01>	Number of the day with leading 0 where needed (01)		✓				✓
$daynum>	Number of the day (1)		✓				✓
$defaulttitle>	Text of the first document heading					✓	✓
$endrange>	End of a page range				✓		
$filename>	Name of the file		✓				✓
$fullfilename>	Name of the path and file (platform-dependent)		✓				✓
$hour01>	Hours with leading 0 (01)		✓				✓
$hour24>	Hours in 0-24 military format (13)		✓				✓

Building Block	Displays	Auto-number	Cross-ref	HTML Flow	Index Marker	Text Flow	Variable
`<$hour>`	Hours (1)		✓				✓
`<$lastpagenum>`	Last page number in document		✓				✓
`<$marker1>`	Header/Footer $1 marker text						✓
`<$marker2>`	Header/Footer $2 marker text						✓
`<$minute00>`	Minutes with leading 0 where needed (01)		✓				✓
`<$minute>`	Minutes (1)		✓				✓
`<$monthname>`	Name of the month (January)		✓				✓
`<$monthnum01>`	Number of the month with leading 0 where needed (01)		✓				✓
`<$monthnum>`	Number of the month (1)		✓				✓
`<$nextsubdoc>`	URL of the next document					✓	
`<$nopage>`	Suppresses the page number				✓		
`<$numerics>`	Sort order for numeric entries					✓	
`<$pagenum>`	Page number		✓			✓	✓
`<$paranum[tag]>`	Paragraph's autonumber, including text (Chapter 1)		✓	✓		✓	✓
`<$paranumonly[tag]>`	Paragraph's autonumber, excluding text (1)		✓	✓		✓	✓
`<$paratag[tag]>`	Paragraph's tag name (Chapter)		✓	✓		✓	✓
`<$paratext[+,tag]>`	Text of last paragraph on page matching the tag		✓	✓		✓	✓
`<$paratext[tag]>`	Text of first paragraph on page matching the tag		✓	✓		✓	✓

(continued)

Table 23-1 *(continued)*

Building Block	Displays	Auto-number	Cross-ref	HTML Flow	Index Marker	Text Flow	Variable
<$parentdoc>	URL of the first document					✓	✓
<$prevsubdoc>	URL of the previous document					✓	✓
<$relfilename>	Name of the path and file, starting from the current file's directory					✓	✓
<$second00>	Seconds with leading 0 where needed (01)		✓				✓
<$second>	Seconds (1)		✓				✓
<$shortdayname>	Name of the day (Mon)		✓				✓
<$shortmonthname>	Name of the month (Jan)		✓				✓
<$shortyear>	Year (97)		✓				✓
<$singlepage>	Designates single page number after <$nopage>				✓		
<$startrange>	Beginning of page range				✓		
<$symbols>	Sort order for symbolic entries					✓	
<$tblsheetcount>	Total number of table sheets						✓
<$tblsheetnum>	Number of current table sheet						✓
<$variable[varname]>	Text of the variable					✓	
<$year>	Year (1997)		✓				✓

Part VI
Appendixes

The 5th Wave   By Rich Tennant

WANDA HAD THE DISTINCT FEELING HER HUSBAND'S NEW
SOFTWARE PROGRAM WAS ABOUT TO BECOME INTERACTIVE.

In this part . . .

Keyboard shortcuts are useful, but let's face it; they're about as interesting as watching paint dry. I've included a detailed here list, along with a description of all the goodies you'll find on the companion CD, and a list of online resources where you can get more information about FrameMaker.

Appendix A
Keyboard Shortcuts

● ●

*I*f you're a fan of keyboard shortcuts, you're in luck! FrameMaker offers a shortcut for just about every action you could imagine. In this appendix, I've first listed some of the more commonly used keyboard shortcuts and then provided a list by menu item.

For even more shortcuts, refer to the *FrameMaker Quick Reference* and FrameMaker's online help (select Help⇨Keyboard Shortcuts). Some of the lesser-used commands, like equations, aren't described here.

FrameMaker offers platform-specific keyboard shortcuts (like Ctrl+o to open a file on a Windows machine and Command+o to open a file on a Macintosh), but those shortcuts aren't available for all commands. A more comprehensive set of keyboard shortcuts is available that works across all platforms (Mac, PC, and UNIX). The tables that follow list these keyboard shortcuts in the All column.

If you use FrameMaker on multiple platforms (or think you might need to do so in the future), consider learning the generic keyboard shortcuts. Because these shortcuts are the same across platforms, you can learn a single set of shortcuts and use them on any platform. This is much more efficient than learning three sets! And remember, the UNIX platform always uses the generic shortcuts.

Here are some general guidelines for keyboard shortcuts:

- ✔ When using keyboard shortcuts, make sure that Caps Lock is off.
- ✔ Unless otherwise noted, the document window must be the active window.
- ✔ Some menu commands have no keyboard shortcut; those are not listed.

Reading the Shortcut Commands

Many of FrameMaker's keyboard shortcuts involve pressing several keys in sequence, instead of all together. Here's how they are listed in this appendix:

Command	Meaning	Example	Description
+	Press the keys together.	Ctrl+s	Press and hold the Ctrl key, then press the letter *S*.
<space>	Press the keys in sequence.	Esc f s	Press and release the Esc key, then press and release the *f* key, and then press and release the *s* key.
		Esc Shift+f l k	Press and release the Esc key, then press and hold the Shift key, press the letter *f*, release the Shift and *f* keys, then press and release the *l* key, then press and release the *k* key.

Document Basics

Here are some of the most commonly used shortcuts. A detailed list by menu follows later in this appendix.

Opening, saving, and closing files

You can also select the Open All, Save All, and Close All menu selections by selecting Shift, selecting the File menu, and then selecting the "All" option you want.

Command	All	PC	Mac
Open a document or book	Esc f o	Ctrl+o	Command+o
Open all files in an active book window	Esc f Shift+o		
Save a document or book	Esc f s	Ctrl+s	Command+s
Save all open files	Esc f Shift+s		
Close a document or book	Esc f c, Esc f q	Ctrl+w	Command+w
Close all open files	Esc f Shift+c, Esc f Shift+q		

Getting help

Command	All	PC	Mac
Display online Help	Esc f h	F1	
Activate context-sensitive Help pointer		Shift+F1	Command+?
Display Help on keyboard shortcuts	Esc ? k		

Canceling and undoing commands

Some FrameMaker commands cannot be cancelled or undone. FrameMaker usually (but not always) warns you before you perform an action that cannot be undone.

Command	All	PC	Mac
Cancel last command	Esc		Ctrl+c
Undo last command	Esc e u	Ctrl+z	Command+z

Navigating through documents

Command	All	PC	Mac
Go to the first page	Esc p f	Alt+PgUp	Command+PgUp
Go to the last page	Esc p l (lowercase L)	Alt+PgDn	Command+PgDn
Go to the previous page	Esc p p	PgUp	Option+PgUp
Go to the next page	Esc p n	PgDn	Option+PgDn
Display Go to Page dialog box	Esc v p	Ctrl+g	Ctrl+g

Working with windows

Command	All	PC	Mac
Close the active window	Esc w c	Ctrl+F4	Command+w
Refresh a document window	Esc w r (lowercase L)	Ctrl+l (lowercase L)	Ctrl+l
Minimize the document window	Esc w c		

Document zoom

Command	All	PC	Mac
Zoom in one setting	Esc z i		
Zoom out one setting	Esc z o		
Fit page in window	Esc z p		
Fit window to page	Esc z w		
Zoom to 100%	Esc z z		

Editing Text

If you thought that your only option for selecting text was to click and drag, you're in for a surprise.

Understanding the basics

Command	All	PC	Mac
Transpose characters		Ctrl+F9	Ctrl+t
Cut	Esc e x	Ctrl+x	Command+x, F2
Copy	Esc e c	Ctrl+c	Command+c, F3
Paste	Esc e p	Ctrl+v	Command+v, F4

Moving the insertion point

Command	All	PC	Mac
Next character	Right arrow		Ctrl+f
Previous character	Left arrow		Ctrl+b
Beginning of a word		Ctrl+left arrow	Option+left arrow
End of a word		Ctrl+right arrow	Option+right arrow
Beginning of next word	Esc b w		Command+right arrow
Beginning of a line		Home	Ctrl+a
End of a line		End	Ctrl+e
Previous line	Up arrow		Ctrl+p
Next line	Down arrow		Ctrl+n
Beginning of a sentence		Ctrl+Home	Ctrl+Command +left arrow
End of a sentence		Ctrl+End	Ctrl+Command +right arrow
Beginning of the next sentence	Esc b s		
Beginning of a paragraph		Ctrl+up arrow	Command+up arrow
End of the current paragraph		Ctrl+down arrow	Option+down arrow
Beginning of the next paragraph	Esc b p		Command+down arrow
Top of a column		Ctrl+PgUp	Control+Option+ left arrow
Bottom of a column		Ctrl+PgDn	Control+Option+ right arrow
Beginning of a flow		Alt+Shift+PgUp	Command+Home
End of a flow		Alt+Shift+PgDn	Command+End
Start of first visible flow		Ctrl+Shift+i	Option+Tab

Selecting text

In this section, several commands have special functions when they are repeated. For example, if you want to select a sentence and then the next sentence, press Esc h s Esc h s. Each time you repeat Esc h s, you'll select another sentence.

To Select...	All	PC	Mac
A range		Click at beginning of text, then Shift+ click at the end	
Next character	Esc h c, Shift+ right arrow		
Previous character	Esc Shift+h Shift+c, Shift+left arrow		
A word	Double-click word		
A word, then next words	Double-click word then drag		
Current word, then next	Esc h w	Ctrl+Shift+right arrow	Command+Shift+ right arrow
Current word, then previous	Esc Shift+h Shift+w	Ctrl+Shift+left arrow	Command+Shift+ left arrow
Current sentence, then next	Esc h s	Ctrl+Shift+End	
Current sentence, then previous	Esc Shift+h Shift+s	Ctrl+Shift+Home	
Current line, then next	Esc h l (lowercase L)	Shift+End	
Current line, then previous	Esc Shift+h Shift+l (lowercase L)	Shift+Home	
A paragraph	Triple-click paragraph		
A paragraph, then next	Triple-click paragraph then drag		
Current paragraph, then next	Esc h p	Ctrl+Shift+ down arrow	Command+Shift+ down arrow

To Select . . .	*All*	*PC*	*Mac*
Current para-graph, then previous	Esc Shift+h Shift+p	Ctrl+Shift+up arrow arrow	Command+Shift+up
To top of column	Esc h t	Shift+PgUp	
To bottom of column	Esc h m	Shift+PgDn	
To beginning of flow	Esc h g	Ctrl+Shift+PgUp	Command+ Shift+Home
To end of flow	Esc h n	Ctrl+Shift+PgDn	Command+ Shift+End
All text around insertion point with same character format	Esc h Shift+f	Ctrl+Shift+f	

Deleting text

To Delete a . . .	*All*	*PC*	*Mac*
Previous character		Backspace	Ctrl+h
Next character		Delete	Ctrl+d
Backward to end of previous word	Esc k b	Ctrl+Backspace	
Backward to the start of a line		Shift+Backspace	Ctrl+u
Backward to the end of previous sentence	Esc k a		
Forward to the end of a word	Esc k f	Ctrl+Delete	
Forward to the end of a line		Ctrl+Shift+Delete	Ctrl+k
Forward to the end of a sentence		Ctrl+Option+k	
Forward to the start of the next sentence	Esc k s		

Changing capitalization

For other text formatting, such as bold and underline, see the shortcuts for the Format menu (in the menu reference later in this chapter).

You Want to ...	All	PC	Mac
Make all uppercase		Alt+Ctrl+u	Ctrl+Option+u
Make all lowercase		Alt+Ctrl+l (lowercase L)	Ctrl+Option+l (lowercase L)
Initial caps		Alt+Ctrl+c	Ctrl+Option+c
Small caps	Esc c m	Ctrl+e	Command+Shift+a

Inserting special characters

For a complete list of special characters, consult FrameMaker's online Help (from the Help menu, select Online Manuals⇨FrameMaker Character Sets) or the *FrameMaker Quick Reference Guide*.

Character	All	PC	Mac
Bullet (•)	Ctrl+q Shift+5		Option+8
Ellipsis (...)	Ctrl+q Shift+i		
Em dash (—)	Ctrl+q Shift+q		
En dash (–)	Ctrl+q Shift+p		
Hyphen, discretionary	Ctrl+-(minus)		Command+- (minus)
Hyphen, non-breaking	Esc - (minus) h		
Hyphen, suppress	Esc n s		
Registered trademark (®)	Ctrl+q Shift+9		
Space, non-breaking	Ctrl+space bar		Option+space bar
Trademark (™)	Ctrl+q Shift+8		

Using Tables

For tables, you have a somewhat overwhelming collection of shortcuts. In some cases, the item you select depends on where you click. If you want to select a row, make sure that you click near the border between two cells in the same row. If you want to select a column, click near the border between two cells in the same column.

Selecting in tables

To Select a . . .	All	PC	Mac
A cell		Ctrl+click cell	Option+click cell
A row		Ctrl+double-click column (vertical) border in the row	Option+double-click column (vertical) border in the row
A column		Ctrl+double-click row (horizontal) border in the row	Option+double-click row (horizontal) border in the row
All text in current cell	Esc t h a		
Current cell, then next	Esc t h e		
Current row, then next	Esc t h r		
Current column, then next	Esc t h c		
Body cells in current column, then next	Esc t h b		
Current table	Esc t h t	Ctrl+triple-click cell	Option+triple-click cell

Typing a tab character in a cell

When you're inside a table, pressing the Tab key moves you to the next cell in the table. But what if you want to insert a tab character inside the cell? You'll need this handy shortcut.

Command	All	PC	Mac
Type a tab character	Esc Tab		

Variables, Markers, and Condition Tags

Command	All	PC	Mac
Insert a variable (by typing the first characters of its name until FrameMaker recognizes it and then pressing Enter/Return)	Esc q v	Ctrl+0 (zero)	Control+0 (zero)
Insert a marker (The marker is the current default marker type.)	Esc m k		Command+Option+k
Apply a condition tag (by typing the first characters of the tag until FrameMaker recognizes it and then pressing Enter/Return)	Esc q Shift+c	Ctrl+4	Ctrl+4
Remove a condition tag (by typing the first characters of the tag until FrameMaker recognizes it and then pressing Enter/Return)	Esc q Shift+d	Ctrl+5	Ctrl+5
Make text unconditional	Esc q Shift+u	Ctrl+6	Ctrl+6

Working with Graphics

You have shortcuts for many of the options on the Graphics tools and for the Graphics menu as well.

Choosing tools

Tool	All	PC	Mac
Display Tool Palette	Esc 1 (one) w		Command+3
Keep a tool active after use	Shift+click tool		
Arc	Esc 1 (one) a		
Graphic Frame	Esc 1 (one) m		
Freehand	Esc 1 (one) f		
Last tool selected	Esc 1 1 (both ones)		
Line	Esc 1 (one) l (lowercase L)		
Object Selection	Esc 1 (one) o		
Oval	Esc 1 (one) e		
Polygon	Esc 1 (one) p g		
Polyline	Esc 1 (one) p l (lowercase L)		
Rectangle	Esc 1 (one) r		
Rounded Rectangle	Esc 1 (one) Shift+r		
Smart Selection	Esc 1 (one) s		
Text Frame	Esc 1 (one) t f		
Text Line	Esc 1 (one) t l (lowercase L)		

Manipulating and moving drawing objects

Command	All	PC	Mac
Move object horizontally or vertically	Shift and drag object		
Maintain object's proportions while resizing	Shift and drag a corner handle		
Display selected object's properties	Esc g o		

(continued)

Command	All	PC	Mac
Display reshape handle and control points for selected object (line, polyline, polygon, freehand curve)	Esc g r	Ctrl+r	Command+Shift+Option+r
Run text around the contour of selected graphic	Esc g w		
Run text around the bounding box of selected graphic	Esc g Shift+w		
Turn text runaround off for selected graphic	Esc g q		
Quick-copy selected object		Alt+drag object	Ctrl+drag object
Turn display of graphics off or on	Esc v v		
Open a referenced graphic file in the application that created it			Option+double-click graphic
Move object one point		Alt+arrow key	Option+arrow key
Move object six points		Alt+Shift+arrow key	Shift+Option+arrow key

Aligning objects

Command	All	PC	Mac
Align along tops	Esc j t	Ctrl+F1	Command+Option+up arrow
Align along top/bottom centers	Esc j m	Ctrl+F2	
Align along bottoms	Esc j b	Ctrl+F3	Command+Option+down arrow
Align along left sides	Esc j l (lowercase L)		Command+Option+left arrow
Align along left/right centers	Esc j c		Command+Shift+c
Align along right sides	Esc j r		Command+Option+right arrow

Rotating objects and pages

Command	All	PC	Mac
Rotate object 90° clockwise	Esc g + (plus)		
Rotate object 90° counter clockwise	Esc g – (minus)		
Display Rotate Selected Object dialog box (to rotate object precisely)	Esc g t		Command+Shift +Option+o
Rotate again	Esc g x		
Return object to unrotated orientation (0°)	Esc g 0 (zero)		
Return object from unrotated orientation to previous orientation	Esc g 1 (one)		
Rotate an object arbitrarily		Alt and drag a corner or reshape handle	Command and drag a corner or reshape handle
Constrain rotation to 45° increments		Alt+Shift and drag a corner or reshape handle	Command+Shift and drag a corner or reshape handle
Rotate a page clockwise	Esc p Shift+o		
Rotate a page counterclockwise	Esc p o		
Unrotate a page	Esc p Shift+u		

Menu Commands

If you prefer to look up your commands by their menu location, check out this section.

File menu

The items marked (book only) are available only if your active document is a book file.

Menu Item	All	PC	Mac
New	Esc f n	Ctrl+n	Command+n
Open	Esc f o	Ctrl+o	Command+o
Open All Files in Book (book only)	Esc f Shift+o		
Close	Esc f c, Esc f o	Ctrl+w	Command+w
Close All Open Files	Esc f Shift+c, Esc f Shift+q		
Close All Files in Book (book only)	Esc f Shift+c		
Save	Esc f s	Ctrl+s	Command+s
Save All Open Files	Esc f Shift+s		
Save All Files in Book (book only)	Esc f Shift+s		
Save As	Esc f a		
Revert to Saved	Esc f r		
Import⇨File	Esc f i f		Command+i
Import⇨Formats	Esc f i o		Command+ Option+o
Import⇨Object	Esc f i b		
Print	Esc f p	Ctrl+p	Command+p
Print Setup		Ctrl+Shift+p	
Add File (book only)	Esc f f		
Set Up File (book only)	Esc f d		
Generate/Update (book only)	Esc f g		Command+u
Generate/Book	Esc f g		Command+u
Utilities⇨Compare Documents	Esc f t c		
Utilities⇨Compare Books (book only)	Esc f t c		
Utilities⇨Document Reports	Esc f t r		

Menu Item	All	PC	Mac
Preferences	Esc f Shift+p		
Exit			Command+q

Edit menu (Document window)

Menu Item	All	PC	Mac
Undo/Redo	Esc e u	Ctrl+z, Alt+Backspace	Command+z
Cut	Esc e x	Ctrl+x	Command+x
Copy	Esc e c	Ctrl+c	Command+c
Paste	Esc e p	Ctrl+v	Command+v
Clear	Esc e b		
Copy Special⇨ Paragraph Format	Esc e y p		Command+Option+c
Copy Special⇨ Character Format	Esc e y c		Command+Option+x
Copy Special⇨ Conditional Text Setting	Esc e y d		Command+Option+z
Copy Special⇨ Table Column Width	Esc e y w		
Select All	Esc e a	Ctrl+a	Command+a
Find/Change	Esc e f	Ctrl+f	Command+f
Find Next	Esc e Shift+f	Ctrl+Shift+f	Command+g
Spelling Checker	Esc e s		Command+l (lower-case L)
Thesaurus	Esc e t		Command+Shift+t
Suppress Automatic Reference Updating (book only)	Esc e Shift+s		

Format menu

Menu Item	All	PC	Mac
Style⇨Plain	Esc c p	F2	Command+Shift+p, Shift+F9
Style⇨Bold	Esc c b m	F4, Ctrl+b, Ctrl+Shift+b	Command+Shift+b, F10
Style⇨Italics	Esc c i	F5, Ctrl+i	Command+Shift+i, F11
Style⇨Underline	Esc c u	Ctrl+u, Ctrl+Shift+u	Command+Shift+u, F12
Style⇨Double Underline	Esc c d		Ctrl+Command+ Shift+u
Style⇨Overline	Esc c o		Option+Shift+o, Option+F12
Style⇨Strikethrough	Esc c s		Command+Shift+m Shift+F12
Style⇨Change Bar	Esc c h	Ctrl+Shift+h	Command+Shift+y
Style⇨Superscript	Esc c + (plus)		Command+ Shift++ (plus sign)
Style⇨Subscript	Esc c - (minus)		Command+Shift+- (minus sign)
Style⇨Small Caps	Esc c m	Ctrl+e	Command+Shift+a
Characters⇨Designer	Esc o c d	Ctrl+d	Command+d, Shift+F14
Characters⇨Catalog	Esc o c c		Command+2, Shift+F13
Characters⇨Default Paragraph Font	Esc o c p		Command+Shift+ space bar, F9
Paragraphs⇨Designer	Esc o p d	Ctrl+m	Command+m, F14
Paragraphs⇨Catalog	Esc o p c		Command+1 (one), F13
Page Layout⇨Column Layout	Esc o c l (lowercase L)		Command+Option+ l (lowercase L)
Page Layout⇨Line Layout	Esc o l l (both lowercase Ls)		
Page Layout⇨ Page Size	Esc o p s		

Menu Item	All	PC	Mac
Page Layout⇨ Master Page Usage	Esc o m u		
Page Layout⇨ New Master Page	Esc o m p		
Page Layout⇨Update Column Layout	Esc o u p		
Customize Layout⇨ Customize Text Frame	Esc o c f		Option+F14
Customize Layout⇨ Connect Text Frames	Esc Shift+c Shift+c		
Customize Layout⇨ Disconnect Previous	Esc Shift+c Shift+p		
Customize Layout⇨ Disconnect Next	Esc Shift+c Shift+n		
Customize Layout⇨ Disconnect Both	Esc Shift+c Shift+b		
Customize Layout⇨ Split Text Frame	Esc Shift+c Shift+s		
Customize Layout⇨ Rotate Page Clockwise	Esc p Shift+o		
Customize Layout⇨ Rotate Page Counterclockwise	Esc p o		
Customize Layout⇨ Unrotate Page	Esc p Shift+u		
Customize Layout⇨ Combined Fonts	Esc o c o		
Document⇨Numbering	Esc o d n		
Document⇨ Change Bars	Esc o b		
Document⇨ Footnote Properties	Esc o f		
Document⇨Text Options	Esc o t o		Command+F14

(continued)

Menu Item	All	PC	Mac
Document⇨Rubi Properties	Esc o r		
Headers & Footers⇨ Insert Page #	Esc o h p		
Headers & Footers⇨ Insert Page Count	Esc o h c		
Headers & Footers⇨ Insert Current Date	Esc o h d		
Headers & Footers⇨ Insert Other	Esc o h o		
QuickAccess Bar	Esc v q		Command+8
Formatting Bar	Esc v Shift+f		
Borders	Esc v b		Command+Option+h
Text Symbols	Esc v t		Command+y
Rulers	Esc v r		Command+Option+u
Grid Lines	Esc v g		Command+Option+i
Options	Esc v o		
Go to Page	Esc v p	Ctrl+g	Command+t
Body Pages	Esc v Shift+b		Command+Option+b
Master Pages	Esc v Shift+m		Command+Option+m
Reference Pages	Esc v Shift+r		Command+Option+r
Color⇨Views	Esc v c v		
Color⇨Definitions	Esc v c d		
Menus⇨Quick	Esc v m q		
Menus⇨Complete	Esc v m c		

Special menu

Menu Item	All	PC	Mac
Page Break	Esc s p b		
Anchored Frame	Esc s a		Command+h

Menu Item	All	PC	Mac
Footnote	Esc s f		Command+e
Cross-Reference	Esc s c		Command+k
Variable	Esc s v		Command+b
Hypertext	Esc s h		
Marker	Esc s m		Command+j
Equations	Esc s e		Command+4, Option+F13
Conditional Text	Esc s Shift+c		Command+5
Rubi	Esc s r		
Add Disconnected Pages	Esc s p a		Command+Option+a
Delete Pages	Esc s p d		Command+Option+d

Graphics menu

Menu Item	All	PC	Mac
Tools	Esc g Shift+T Esc 1 (one)	w	
Group	Esc g g		Command+Shift+Option+g
Ungroup	Esc g u		Command+Shift+Option+u
Bring to Front	Esc g f		Command+Shift+Option++ (plus)
Send to Back	Esc g b		Command+Shift+Option+- (minus)
Align	Esc g a		Command+Shift+Option+a
Distribute	Esc g d		Command+Shift+Option+d
Reshape	Esc g r		Command+Shift+Option+r
Smooth	Esc g s		Command+Shift+Option+m
Unsmooth	Esc g m		Ctrl+Command+Shift+Option+m
Flip Up/Down	Esc g v		Command+Shift+Option+v
Flip Left/Right	Esc g h		Command+Shift+Option+h
Rotate	Esc g t		Command+Shift+Option+o
Scale	Esc g z		Command+Shift+Option+s

(continued)

Menu Item	All	PC	Mac
Set # Sides	Esc g n		Command+Shift+Option+n
Join	Esc g j		Command+Shift+Option+j
Object Properties	Esc g o		Command+Shift+Option+p
Pick Up Properties	Esc g Shift+o		
Runaround PropertiesOverprint	Esc g Shift+r Esc g e		Command+Shift+Option+w Command+Shift+Option+b
Gravity	Esc g y		Command+Shift+Option+y
Snap	Esc g p		Command+Shift+Option+l (lowercase L)

Table menu

Menu Item	All	PC	Mac
Insert Table	Esc t i		Command+Shift+Option+t
Table Designer	Esc t d	Ctrl+t	Command+Option+t
Row Format	Esc t r		
Custom Ruling & Shading	Esc t x		
Add Rows or Columns	Esc t a		
Resize Columns	Esc t z		Command+Option+s
Straddle/Unstraddle	Esc t l (lowercase L)		
Convert to Table/Convert to Paragraphs	Esc t v		

Window menu

Menu Item	All	PC	Mac
Cascade		Shift+F4	
Tile		Shift+F5	
Refresh		Ctrl+l (lowercase L)	

Appendix B
Online Resources

• •

A huge number of online resources are available. I've listed a few of the most popular ones for FrameMaker users here.

Web sites

The World Wide Web is great for technical support, frequently asked questions, collections of links, and much more! Some of these Web sites even support discussion groups.

www.adobe.com

Adobe Systems makes FrameMaker and Acrobat software. Their Web site contains product information, support information, and more. (And let's not forget those all-important PostScript printer drivers!)

www.wellengaged.com/engaged/ adobe.cgi?c=FrameMaker

Adobe sponsors a FrameMaker User to User Forum at this site. You'll need to set up an account (it's free) to access the forum. You can also link to these forums from Adobe's Web site.

www.scriptorium.com

My company, Scriptorium Publishing, offers FrameMaker template design, training, and consulting. Our Web site contains lots of useful white papers and a collection of links to other FrameMaker resources. And of course, we have lots of sales propaganda for our training and consulting services.

www.frameusers.com

An unofficial FrameMaker resource site. It contains information about FrameMaker service providers, add-on software, and more.

If you're looking for FrameMaker plug-ins, trainers, utilities, and the like, you can't go wrong with this site. It's somewhat graphics-intensive, but it's worth it.

www.frame-user.de (German)

Another unofficial FrameMaker resource site. If you speak German, this is the site for you. Even if you don't speak any German, check it out. The Web site creator designed the site to look like a FrameMaker document; it's quite a unique look for a Web site!

www.stc.org

The Society for Technical Communication (STC) is a professional association for technical writers and other technical communicators. The STC Web site includes information about the organization, its conference, and links to various local chapters. Chapters are mostly in the United States, but there are also several in other parts of the world.

www.pdfzone.com

A Web site with resources for Adobe Acrobat users. It includes tips and tricks, resources, and more.

www.wwpusers.com

An unofficial Web site for WebWorks Publisher users, sponsored by Scriptorium Publishing. The site includes frequently asked questions, template samples, code snippets, lists of trainers, and more.

www.hwg.org

The HTML Writers Guild Web site. It includes a wealth of resources for HTML creators, including HTML specifications, Web site validators, and other goodies.

www.raycomm.com/techwhirl/index.html

This Web site is the companion to the techwr-l (tech writers') mailing list described in the next section. It includes resources, books, lists of contract technical writers, archives of the technical writers lists, and more.

www.prc.dk/user-friendly-manuals/ufm/maillist.htm

Peter Ring's Web site is a list of lists (of mailing lists for technical communicators, that is). Check it out for tons of lists that I didn't have room for here.

Mailing Lists

Web sites are great, but for immediate gratification, you can't beat mailing lists. You send out a question, and within hours (and sometimes minutes) your mailbox overflows with responses from all over the world.

Before you post your question, check the archives and hang out for a few days to get the feel of the list. This will help you avoid the dreaded newbie label.

framers@frameusers.com

`framers@frameusers.com` is a mailing list for FrameMaker users. The framers list has been around for at least five years; its membership includes both new FrameMaker users and experts. Some individuals have been on the list for five years or more. List traffic is heavy, but generally fairly well focused on issues related to FrameMaker.

To subscribe, send e-mail to `majordomo@frameusers.com`. In the body of the message, type **subscribe framers**.

framers@omsys.com

Similar to the framers list based at frameusers.com. Many topics are posted to both lists. This framers list tends to be more focused on power user issues than the other. Right now, the `framers@omsys.com` list has less traffic than `framers@frameusers.com`.

To subscribe, send e-mail to `majordomo@omsys.com`.

In the body of the message, type **subscribe framers**.

Frame-talk list (German)

This is a German-language mailing list for FrameMaker users. Similar to the framers list, but the traffic is lighter (and the discussion is in German!).

To subscribe, send e-mail to `frame-on@list.globalworks.de`.

Publisher

Quadralay Corporation sponsors a mailing list for WebWorks Publisher. Traffic is light to moderate, and discussions are usually highly focused on WebWorks Publisher-specific topics.

To subscribe, visit Quadralay's Web site at `www.quadralay.com/pic/listwiz.asp`. You'll need to register with the Web site to register for the list.

techwr-l

Techwr-l is a mailing list for technical writers. It is managed by Eric Ray (author of _HTML for Dummies_ and many other fine titles). Traffic on the techwr-l list is extremely heavy, and discussion often veers away from technical writing topics to other matters. But if you have the energy to sort through 100 or so daily postings, you'll find a lot of useful information on this list.

To subscribe, send e-mail to `listserv@listserv.okstate.edu`. In the body of the message, type **subscribe techwr-l** _**YourFirstName YourLastName**_.

Adobe Acrobat lists

PDFZone sponsors several PDF lists, including a beginner list, an advanced list, and a list for developers. Get details about the different lists at `www.pdfzone.com/resources/lists.html#pdf`.

winhelp-l

A mailing list for Windows online help developers. To subscribe, send e-mail to listserv@admin.humberc.on.ca. In the body of the message, type **subscribe winhlp-l** *YourFirstName YourLastName*.

Newsgroups

Before the content explosion on the World Wide Web (yes, I realize that this was only about four years ago), newsgroups played an important role in disseminating information. Today, Web sites full of resources and e-mail lists have really taken the place of newsgroups. And unfortunately, participating in some newsgroups can expose you to some rather unsavory characters. However, some useful newsgroups are out there still. Here are some relevant ones:

comp.text.frame	A newsgroup for FrameMaker users
comp.text.pdf	A newsgroup for Adobe Acrobat (PDF) users
comp.text.sgml	A newsgroup for Standard Generalized Markup Language (SGML) users

Appendix C

About the CD

• •

*T*he CD included with this book includes a demo version of FrameMaker, along with a bunch of interesting add-on software that extends FrameMaker's functionality in different ways. For example, I've included software that provides macro editing, conversion to HTML and WinHelp formats, and more.

On the CD-ROM:

- FrameMaker 5.5.6, the star of this book!
- Filtrix, a collection of filters to convert to and from FrameMaker format
- FrameScript, which lets you write scripts (like macros) for FrameMaker
- QuicKeys, which adds macros to your FrameMaker arsenal
- S-Tagger, which saves all the FrameMaker features when you export into Microsoft Word
- WebWorks Publisher, which converts FrameMaker files to HTML, Windows online help, HTML Help, and several other formats

System Requirements

Make sure that your computer meets the minimum system requirements listed below. If your computer doesn't match up to most of these requirements, you may have problems using the contents of the CD. The CD includes Windows, and Mac, software; system requirements for each are listed separately.

Windows

For a Windows machine, the system requirements are

- A PC with a Pentium 120MHz or faster processor.
- Microsoft Windows 95, 98, or NT.

- At least 32MB of RAM, 64MB is recommended.
- At least 400MB of hard drive space available to install all the software from this CD. (You need less space if you don't install every program.)
- A CD-ROM drive — double-speed (2x) or faster.
- A sound card.
- A monitor capable of displaying at least 256 colors or grayscale.
- Internet access. (You will need access to the World Wide Web to get temporary license keys for some of the software.)

Macintosh

For a Macintosh, the system requirements are

- A Mac OS computer with a PowerPC processor.
- Mac OS system software 7.5 or later.
- At least 32MB of RAM, 64MB is recommended.
- At least 400MB of hard drive space available to install all the software from this CD. (You need less space if you don't install every program.)
- A CD-ROM drive — double-speed (2x) or faster.
- A monitor capable of displaying at least 256 colors or grayscale.
- Internet access. (You will need access to the World Wide Web to get temporary license keys for some of the software.)

If you need more information on the basics, check out *PCs For Dummies,* 6th Edition, by Dan Gookin; *Macs For Dummies,* 6th Edition, by David Pogue; or *Windows 98 For Dummies* or *Windows 95 For Dummies,* by Andy Rathbone; (all published by IDG Books Worldwide, Inc.).

Using the CD with Microsoft Windows

To install the items from the CD to your hard drive, follow these steps:

1. **Insert the CD into your computer's CD-ROM drive.**
2. **Click Start⇨Run.**

3. **In the dialog box that appears, type** D:\SETUP.EXE.

   Replace *D* with the proper drive letter if your CD-ROM drive uses a different letter. (If you don't know the letter, see how your CD-ROM drive is listed under My Computer in Windows 95/98/NT or File Manager in Windows 3.1.)

4. **Click OK.**

   A license agreement window appears.

5. **Read through the license agreement, nod your head, and then click the Accept button if you want to use the CD — after you click Accept, you'll never be bothered by the License Agreement window again.**

   The CD interface Welcome screen appears. The interface is a little program that shows you what's on the CD and coordinates installing the programs and running the demos. The interface basically enables you to click a button or two to make things happen.

6. **Click anywhere on the Welcome screen to enter the interface.**

   Now you are getting to the action. This next screen lists categories for the software on the CD.

7. **To view the items within a category, just click the category's name.**

   A list of programs in the category appears.

8. **For more information about a program, click the program's name.**

   Be sure to read the information that appears. Sometimes a program has its own system requirements or requires you to do a few tricks on your computer before you can install or run the program, and this screen tells you what you might need to do, if necessary.

9. **If you don't want to install the program, click the Go Back button to return to the previous screen.**

   You can always return to the previous screen by clicking the Go Back button. This feature allows you to browse the different categories and products and decide what you want to install.

10. **To install a program, click the appropriate Install button.**

    The CD interface drops to the background while the CD installs the program you chose.

11. **To install other items, repeat Steps 7 through 10.**

12. **When you've finished installing programs, click the Quit button to close the interface.**

    You can eject the CD now. Carefully place it back in the plastic jacket of the book for safekeeping.

Using the CD with Mac OS

To install the items from the CD to your hard drive, follow these steps:

1. **Insert the CD into your computer's CD-ROM drive.**

   In a moment, an icon representing the CD you just inserted appears on your Mac desktop. Chances are, the icon looks like a CD-ROM.

2. **Double-click the CD icon to show the CD's contents.**

3. **Double-click the Read Me First icon.**

   The Read Me First text file contains information about the CD's programs and any last-minute instructions you may need in order to correctly install them.

4. **To install most programs, just drag the program's folder from the CD window and drop it on your hard drive icon.**

5. **Other programs come with installer programs — with these, you simply open the program's folder on the CD, and then double-click the icon with the words "Install" or "Installer."**

   Sometimes the installers are actually self-extracting archives, which just means that the program files have been bundled up into an archive, and this self extractor unbundles the files and places them on your hard drive. This kind of program is often called an .sea. Double click anything with .sea in the title, and it will run just like an installer.

   After you have installed the programs you want, you can eject the CD. Carefully place it back in the plastic jacket of the book for safekeeping.

What You'll Find

Here's a summary of the software on this CD arranged by category. If you use Windows, the CD interface helps you install software easily. (If you have no idea what I'm talking about when I say "CD interface," flip back a page or two to find the section, "Using the CD with Microsoft Windows.")

If you use a Mac OS computer, you can take advantage of the easy Mac interface to quickly install the programs.

If you're using UNIX, well, then you're on your own. You're tough. You can handle it.

FrameMaker 5.5.6

For Windows 95, 98, & NT and Mac. Tryout version.

The FrameMaker software provided on the CD is fully functional — except that you can't save or print. FrameMaker, in case you missed the first 330 pages of this book, is a high-end package for producing technical content, such as dissertations, technical manuals, and more.

If you are using a Mac, you need to e-mail Adobe at `framemaker-demo@adobe.com` in order to receive a serial number.

Installing the FrameMaker tryout for Windows

In order to bring you both versions of this great software to try (Windows and Mac), I am including a special version of the software that requires a few extra steps to install.

When you click on the Install button in the interface, a little batch file will start up (don't worry about it, if you don't know what that means) that will ask you a series of questions regarding the installation:

1. **The first thing it does is start the FrameMaker installation. This happens automatically, so just sit back and enjoy the ride. Follow the instructions in this installer like you usually would.**

2. **Once the installer is finished, you will see a black and white window on your desktop, with a single question on it: Do you want to install Adobe Acrobat Reader (Y/N)? Answer Y for Yes and N for No. The file will wait until you give an answer.**

3. **There are several more components to go through, each time you can select Y or N. I recommend that you install all components, but if you have trouble fitting everything on your hard drive, you might decide to omit a couple. If you find that your computer has problems running the FrameMaker tryout, you can always go back and install the component you left off before.**

4. **Once you're done, you can close the black and white window to return to the interface.**

Filtrix

For Windows 95, and 98. Demo version.

Filtrix, version 3.5.4, is a collection of filters that convert FrameMaker files to other formats (and other formats to FrameMaker). The options include FrameMaker to ASCII, DCA/RFT, HTML, Interleaf, Word, WordPerfect, and many others. If you are trying to get from another format to FrameMaker, Filtrix supports ASCII, DCA/RFT, DisplayWrite, HTML, Interleaf, Word, MultiMate, WordPerfect, WordStar, XyWrite, and several others that I don't have room for here!

For more information about Filtrix (including a comprehensive list of their supported formats), visit Blueberry Software on the Web at `www.blueberry.com`.

FrameScript

For Windows 95, 98, & NT 4.0. Trial version.

Late-breaking news: FrameScript is being ported to the Macintosh! The new software didn't make it onto the CD, but if you're interested, go to the FrameScript Web site (the address is at the end of this section).

FrameScript, version 1.23, is a scripting language that works inside FrameMaker. You can write scripts and create menu choices for them inside FrameMaker. This lets you automate many tasks inside FrameMaker. The functionality provided by FrameScript is also available using the FrameMaker Developer's Kit, but FrameScript is much easier to use.

For more information about FrameScript, see `www.framescript.com`.

QuicKeys

For Windows 95, 98, & NT 4.0 and Macintosh.

QuicKeys is a powerful macro editor. You can use it to automate those annoying repetitive tasks you need to do in FrameMaker. (You aren't restricted to FrameMaker; QuicKeys works with all your applications.)

For more information about QuicKeys, check out `www.quickeys.com`.

S-Tagger

For *Windows 95, 98, and NT 4.0. Trial version.*

If you thought the battle to get FrameMaker for you was hard, wait until you take on your first translation project. Many translation companies accept FrameMaker files, and they should be your first choice. But if your translator insists on using Microsoft Word, then S-Tagger is a critical tool for you. S-Tagger exports FrameMaker files into Microsoft Word format, but it preserves all the FrameMaker features (such as variables, cross-references, index markers) in special tags. The translator can then edit the Word file (and ignore the special tags). Once the translation is complete, you run the Word file back through S-Tagger to restore your FrameMaker file — with translated content.

For more information about S-Tagger, see www.trados.com.

WebWorks Publisher 2000

For Windows 95, 98, and NT 4.0. Trial version.

WebWorks Publisher 2000, version 5.0, lets you convert FrameMaker files into online formats, including HTML, WinHelp, HTML Help, and others. If you need to deliver information developed in FrameMaker in multiple online formats, WebWorks Publisher is the way to go. It lets you map FrameMaker template information (such as paragraph tags, character tags, conditions, and others) to produce the output that you want. You can also selectively exclude information from the output.

To run the trial version (which is fully functional for 30 days), you will need a license key, which is available at www.quadralay.com/publisher/try.asp.

For more information about WebWorks Publisher, see www.quadralay.com.

If You've Got Problems (Of the CD Kind)

I tried my best to compile programs that work on most computers with the minimum system requirements. Alas, your computer may differ, and some programs may not work properly for some reason.

The two likeliest problems are that you don't have enough memory (RAM) for the programs you want to use, or you have other programs running that are affecting installation or running of a program. If you get error messages like Not enough memory or Setup cannot continue, try one or more of these methods and then try using the software again:

- ✔ **Turn off any anti-virus software that you have on your computer:** Installers sometimes mimic virus activity and may make your computer incorrectly believe that it is being infected by a virus.

- ✔ **Close all running programs:** The more programs you're running, the less memory is available to other programs. Installers also typically update files and programs; if you keep other programs running, installation may not work properly.

✔ **In Windows, close the CD interface and run demos or installations directly from Windows Explorer:** The interface itself can tie up system memory, or even conflict with certain kinds of interactive demos. Use Windows Explorer to browse the files on the CD and launch installers or demos.

✔ **Have your local computer store add more RAM to your computer:** This is, admittedly, a drastic and somewhat expensive step. However, if you have a Windows 95 PC or a Mac OS computer with a PowerPC chip, adding more memory can really help the speed of your computer and enable more programs to run at the same time.

If you still have trouble installing the items from the CD, please call the IDG Books Worldwide Customer Service phone number: 800-762-2974 (outside the U.S.: 317-572-3342).

Index

Notes

IDG Books Worldwide, Inc.,
End-User License Agreement

READ THIS. You should carefully read these terms and conditions before opening the software packet(s) included with this book ("Book"). This is a license agreement ("Agreement") between you and IDG Books Worldwide, Inc. ("IDGB"). By opening the accompanying software packet(s), you acknowledge that you have read and accept the following terms and conditions. If you do not agree and do not want to be bound by such terms and conditions, promptly return the Book and the unopened software packet(s) to the place you obtained them for a full refund.

1. **License Grant.** IDGB grants to you (either an individual or entity) a nonexclusive license to use one copy of the enclosed software program(s) (collectively, the "Software") solely for your own personal or business purposes on a single computer (whether a standard computer or a workstation component of a multiuser network). The Software is in use on a computer when it is loaded into temporary memory (RAM) or installed into permanent memory (hard disk, CD-ROM, or other storage device). IDGB reserves all rights not expressly granted herein.

2. **Ownership.** IDGB is the owner of all right, title, and interest, including copyright, in and to the compilation of the Software recorded on the disk(s) or CD-ROM ("Software Media"). Copyright to the individual programs recorded on the Software Media is owned by the author or other authorized copyright owner of each program. Ownership of the Software and all proprietary rights relating thereto remain with IDGB and its licensers.

3. **Restrictions on Use and Transfer.**

   (a) You may only (i) make one copy of the Software for backup or archival purposes, or (ii) transfer the Software to a single hard disk, provided that you keep the original for backup or archival purposes. You may not (i) rent or lease the Software, (ii) copy or reproduce the Software through a LAN or other network system or through any computer subscriber system or bulletin-board system, or (iii) modify, adapt, or create derivative works based on the Software.

   (b) You may not reverse engineer, decompile, or disassemble the Software. You may transfer the Software and user documentation on a permanent basis, provided that the transferee agrees to accept the terms and conditions of this Agreement and you retain no copies. If the Software is an update or has been updated, any transfer must include the most recent update and all prior versions.

4. **Restrictions on Use of Individual Programs.** You must follow the individual requirements and restrictions detailed for each individual program in the "About the CD" section of this Book. These limitations are also contained in the individual license agreements recorded on the Software Media. These limitations may include a requirement that after using the program for a specified period of time, the user must pay a registration fee or discontinue use. By opening the Software packet(s), you will be agreeing to abide by the licenses and restrictions for these individual programs that are detailed in the "About the CD" section and on the Software Media. None of the material on this Software Media or listed in this Book may ever be redistributed, in original or modified form, for commercial purposes.

5. **Limited Warranty.**

   (a) IDGB warrants that the Software and Software Media are free from defects in materials and workmanship under normal use for a period of sixty (60) days from the date of purchase of this Book. If IDGB receives notification within the warranty period of defects in materials or workmanship, IDGB will replace the defective Software Media.

   (b) **IDGB AND THE AUTHOR OF THE BOOK DISCLAIM ALL OTHER WARRANTIES, EXPRESS OR IMPLIED, INCLUDING WITHOUT LIMITATION IMPLIED WARRANTIES OF MERCHANTABILITY AND FITNESS FOR A PARTICULAR PURPOSE, WITH RESPECT TO THE SOFTWARE, THE PROGRAMS, THE SOURCE CODE CONTAINED THEREIN, AND/OR THE TECHNIQUES DESCRIBED IN THIS BOOK. IDGB DOES NOT WARRANT THAT THE FUNCTIONS CONTAINED IN THE SOFTWARE WILL MEET YOUR REQUIREMENTS OR THAT THE OPERATION OF THE SOFTWARE WILL BE ERROR FREE.**

   (c) This limited warranty gives you specific legal rights, and you may have other rights that vary from jurisdiction to jurisdiction.

6. **Remedies.**

   (a) IDGB's entire liability and your exclusive remedy for defects in materials and workmanship shall be limited to replacement of the Software Media, which may be returned to IDGB with a copy of your receipt at the following address: Software Media Fulfillment Department, Attn.: *FrameMaker 5.5.6 For Dummies*, IDG Books Worldwide, Inc., 10475 Crosspoint Blvd., Ste. 100, Indianapolis, IN 46256, or call 800-762-2974. Please allow three to four weeks for delivery. This Limited Warranty is void if failure of the Software Media has resulted from accident, abuse, or misapplication. Any replacement Software Media will be warranted for the remainder of the original warranty period or thirty (30) days, whichever is longer.

   (b) In no event shall IDGB or the author be liable for any damages whatsoever (including without limitation damages for loss of business profits, business interruption, loss of business information, or any other pecuniary loss) arising from the use of or inability to use the Book or the Software, even if IDGB has been advised of the possibility of such damages.

   (c) Because some jurisdictions do not allow the exclusion or limitation of liability for consequential or incidental damages, the above limitation or exclusion may not apply to you.

7. **U.S. Government Restricted Rights.** Use, duplication, or disclosure of the Software by the U.S. Government is subject to restrictions stated in paragraph (c)(1)(ii) of the Rights in Technical Data and Computer Software clause of DFARS 252.227-7013, and in subparagraphs (a) through (d) of the Commercial Computer–Restricted Rights clause at FAR 52.227-19, and in similar clauses in the NASA FAR supplement, when applicable.

8. **General.** This Agreement constitutes the entire understanding of the parties and revokes and supersedes all prior agreements, oral or written, between them and may not be modified or amended except in a writing signed by both parties hereto that specifically refers to this Agreement. This Agreement shall take precedence over any other documents that may be in conflict herewith. If any one or more provisions contained in this Agreement are held by any court or tribunal to be invalid, illegal, or otherwise unenforceable, each and every other provision shall remain in full force and effect.

Installation Instructions

The *FrameMaker 5.5.6 For Dummies* CD-ROM contains software you can use to enhance your use of FrameMaker. The installation instructions for the PC, Mac, and UNIX platforms are too long to summarize here. For step-by-step installation instructions, please turn to Appendix C at the end of this book.

Discover Dummies Online!

The Dummies Web Site is your fun and friendly online resource for the latest information about *For Dummies*® books and your favorite topics. The Web site is the place to communicate with us, exchange ideas with other *For Dummies* readers, chat with authors, and have fun!

Ten Fun and Useful Things You Can Do at www.dummies.com

1. Win free *For Dummies* books and more!
2. Register your book and be entered in a prize drawing.
3. Meet your favorite authors through the IDG Books Worldwide Author Chat Series.
4. Exchange helpful information with other *For Dummies* readers.
5. Discover other great *For Dummies* books you must have!
6. Purchase Dummieswear® exclusively from our Web site.
7. Buy *For Dummies* books online.
8. Talk to us. Make comments, ask questions, get answers!
9. Download free software.
10. Find additional useful resources from authors.

Link directly to these ten fun and useful things at
http://www.dummies.com/10useful

For other technology titles from IDG Books Worldwide, go to
www.idgbooks.com

Not on the Web yet? It's easy to get started with Dummies 101®: The Internet For Windows® 98 or The Internet For Dummies® at local retailers everywhere.

Find other *For Dummies* books on these topics:
Business • Career • Databases • Food & Beverage • Games • Gardening • Graphics • Hardware
Health & Fitness • Internet and the World Wide Web • Networking • Office Suites
Operating Systems • Personal Finance • Pets • Programming • Recreation • Sports
Spreadsheets • Teacher Resources • Test Prep • Word Processing

IDG BOOKS WORLDWIDE
BOOK REGISTRATION

Register This Book and Win!

We want to hear from you!

Visit **http://my2cents.dummies.com** to register this book and tell us how you liked it!

✔ Get entered in our monthly prize giveaway.

✔ Give us feedback about this book — tell us what you like best, what you like least, or maybe what you'd like to ask the author and us to change!

✔ Let us know any other *For Dummies*® topics that interest you.

Your feedback helps us determine what books to publish, tells us what coverage to add as we revise our books, and lets us know whether we're meeting your needs as a *For Dummies* reader. You're our most valuable resource, and what you have to say is important to us!

Not on the Web yet? It's easy to get started with *Dummies 101®: The Internet For Windows® 98* or *The Internet For Dummies®* at local retailers everywhere.

Or let us know what you think by sending us a letter at the following address:

For Dummies Book Registration
Dummies Press
10475 Crosspoint Blvd.
Indianapolis, IN 46256

BESTSELLING BOOK SERIES